Key Events on September 11th, 2001

7:59 am   Flight **11**; takes off from Boston.

8:01 am   Flight **93**; ready to take off from New Jersey.

8:10 am   Flight **77**; takes off from Washington DC.

8:14 am   Flight **175**; takes off from Boston.

8:24 am   Flight **11**; A controller hears hijackers over the plane's radio: "We have some planes. Just stay quiet and you will be OK. We are returning to the airport. Nobody move."

8:42 am   Flight **93**; takes off, after waiting 40 minutes.

8:46 am   Flight 11; crashes into the North Tower.

8:57 am   Flight **77**; plane vanishes from radar near Ohio and turns around towards Pentagon.

9:03 am   Flight 175; crashes into the South Tower.

9:20 am   Flight **93**; one of Tom Burnett's calls to his wife; he tells her of the hijacking.

9:29 am   Flight **93**; one of Jeremy Glick's calls to his wife; he learns about WTC attack.

9:40 am   Flight 77; crashes into Pentagon after being in the air for 1½ hours, half of it while hijacked.

9:45 am   Flight **93**; Todd Beamer talks to a telephone operator.

9:49 am   FAA stops all flights in nation; they finally realize something is wrong.

9:50 am   Flight **93**; Sandra Bradshaw calls husband.

9:58 am   Flight **93**; Beamer lays phone down to fight hijackers, and CeeCee Lyles calls husband. All phone calls end about this time.

9:59 am   South Tower collapses.

10:04 am   Flight **93**; local airport reports it is flying low and erratic, but no phone calls come from plane.

10:06 am   Flight 93; crashes in Pennsylvania; in the air for 1¼ hours, half of it while hijacked.

10:29 am   North Tower collapses.

3:00 PM   Photos of Building 7 show a few small fires on two floors.

4:10 PM   Somebody reports Building 7 on fire.

5:20 PM   Building 7 collapses.

As the towers collapsed, dust shot out of some windows many floors below the area that was collapsing.

ISBN: 1-931947-05-8

Printed in the USA, 4th printing.
Endpoint Software
Goleta   CA

Contents

View of North Tower and Building 7 from the top of the South Tower.

About the Photos

Front cover aerial photo of rubble by James R. Tourtellotte.

Front cover photo before the attack and the above photo by Mirko Balke

Rear cover photo of Pentagon engine by FEMA.

Rear cover drawing of unicorns courtesy of Bollyn Books, from an upcoming ABC book for children.

The Internet is full of unidentified photos, and some are in this book. They are marked as **unknown.** If you know the source of any of the photos, please contact me. Also, if you have photos that would serve as replacements, please let me know.

PainfulQuestions@aol.com

The Various Investigations

1

> *"I wish I had more time to inspect steel structure and save more pieces before the steel was recycled."*
>
> Professor Astaneh-Asl of Berkeley, at the Committee on Science hearing, March 6, 2002

An analogy:

Imagine clean-up crews arriving immediately after a murder. When detectives arrive the most important bullets have been sold to recyclers; the dead body has been buried; and most of the blood has been washed away.

Also imagine that the cleanup crews have more authority than the detectives, so the detectives must ask permission to take photos and retain evidence.

The Science Committee of the House of Representatives held a meeting March 6, 2002 to discuss the investigation of the World Trade Center collapse. Their report concluded that the investigation was "hampered." One problem was that clean-up crews arrived the same day and immediately began disposing of the rubble. The result was:

> *Some of the critical pieces of steel ... were gone before the first [investigator] ever reached the site.*

When investigators finally arrived at the site they discovered they were subservient to the clean-up crews:

> *...the lack of authority of investigators to impound pieces of steel for examination before they were recycled led to the loss of important pieces of evidence...*

Why was the investigation given such a low priority? Or should that question be phrased: Why was the *disposal of rubble* given *first* priority? Were New York residents simply too shocked by the attack and too concerned about finding survivors to care about saving the rubble for scientists?

According to an article on December 25, 2001, the *New York Times* asked city officials about the destruction of the rubble:

> *Officials in the mayor's office declined to reply to written and oral requests for comment over a three-day period about who decided to recycle the steel and the concern that the decision might be handicapping the investigation.*

Their silence provides support for one of Congressman Boehlert's accusations:

> *I must say that the current investigation ... seems to be shrouded in excessive secrecy.*

"No one is in charge"

With thousands of missing people, and with statistics showing that many would die within 24 hours, rescuers were under a lot of pressure on September 11th to find survivors quickly. Neither the emotionally charged rescuers nor the families of the missing people had time to carefully document the rubble. Rather, rescuers tore through the rubble as soon as the dust had settled, and they worked throughout the night. There were so many rescuers and they worked so fast that by the next morning Mayor Rudy Giuliani announced that they had disposed of 120 dump trucks of rubble.

Building 4 of the World Trade Center

Destroying rubble was understandable during the first few days of the rescue. However, some portions of the rubble were smoking because of the high temperatures, and those piles of hot rubble should have been left alone. The only sensible place to look for survivors was in the cool areas. Consequently, all of the hot piles of rubble should have been untouched when the investigators arrived.

By the seventh day it was extremely unlikely that people were still alive in the rubble. After one month looking for survivors was ridiculous. However, the frantic destruction of rubble continued month after month, regardless of the possibility of finding survivors. Furthermore, Building 7 had been evacuated many hours before it collapsed, so there was no reason to look in *that* pile of rubble.

By April of 2002 virtually all of the rubble had been removed. It appears as if these cleanup crews were so incapable of thinking that after having received orders to search for survivors, they continued to do so even when it made no sense. They also searched areas where nobody could possibly be found. Who was supervising this situation?

Perhaps the words of Congressman Boehlert in the report of the Committee on Science are more accurate than we want to believe:

> *...there are no clear lines of authority ....*
>
> *No one is in charge...*

Was the New York City government simply incapable of dealing with such an unusual and extreme disaster?

Bush and Cheney want to "limit" the investigation

On January 25, 2002 vice-president Cheney called Senator Daschle on the phone and asked him to "limit the scope and the overall review of what happened." Cheney did not bother to explain his intentions to the American people, but we have Daschle's remark to CNN reporters:

> *The vice president expressed the concern that a review of what happened on September 11 would take resources and personnel away from the effort in the war on terrorism,*

Daschle was not convinced that there was a shortage of resources or personnel, so four days later President Bush had a private meeting with him and asked him again to limit the investigation.

Was the Bush administration correct that investigating the September 11th attack would hamper the war on terrorism? Consider that the investigation of the September 11th attack is actually two, separate studies:

1) The technical investigation.
   An analysis of the rubble by scientists to determine the cause of the collapses would *not* interfere with an investigation of terrorism.

"... there are no clear lines of authority .... No one is in charge..."

"I must say that the current investigation — some would argue that 'review' is the more appropriate word — seems to be shrouded in excessive secrecy."

"...valuable evidence has been lost irretrievably, and blueprints were unavailable for months."

Congressman Boehlert, Chairman, Committee on Science, from the hearing on March 6, 2002

"...we are staffing the [investigation] with part-time engineers and scientists on a shoestring budget."

"The building performance assessment currently being conducted of the World Trade Center collapse is just that: an assessment, not an investigation."

"In addition, the [group of investigators] studying the collapse has apparently been hampered in accessing building construction documents."

Professor Corbett, John Jay College of Criminal Justice, at the Committee on Science hearing, March 6, 2002

"Do you realize how serious this is? This man wants training on a 747. A 747 fully loaded with fuel could be used as a weapon!"

A Minneapolis flight instructor complaining to the FBI about the suspicious request of Zacarias Moussaoui.

Imagine if you were to find this in the *LA Times*:

Correction, Sept 12, 2001.

A September 11th article reported that Osama bin Laden was responsible for the 9/11 attack. However, Osama **flatly denied the accusation**.

The *Times* has since learned that the accusation was based on a British newspaper report, not reputable sources. The *Times* regrets the mistake. Osama is innocent.

2) The analysis of the terrorists.
   This would be an analysis of where the terrorists lived, how they financed their operation, where they learned to fly, and how they took four airplanes off course without the FAA or military doing anything about it. The FBI and CIA would be involved in this analysis. Since the FBI and CIA also investigate terrorism, Bush could claim that there were not enough agents to carry on regular business *and* investigate the September 11th attack.

An FBI agent sent a memo about suspicious foreigners to both FBI headquarters and to a New York FBI unit that was looking for Osama bin Laden. As the *New York Times* explained it:

> *An F.B.I. agent in Phoenix told counterterrorism officials at the bureau's headquarters last July that he had detected an alarming pattern of Arab men with possible ties to terrorism taking aviation-related training, and urged a nationwide review of the trend.*

No action was taken by the FBI. Were Bush and Cheney trying to protect the FBI, FAA, CIA, military, and/or the Bush administration from accusations of incompetence?

Did the CIA interfere with the investigation?

On September 20th the *Los Angeles Times* reported that Israel had warned the FBI and CIA a month before the attack that terrorists were slipping into America to conduct "a major assault." The next day the *Times* printed a brief correction that claimed the accusation was false. The "proof" that the original report was false was explained as:

> *...the CIA flatly denied the story, and FBI officials said they knew of no such advisory.*

This situation is as silly as a court dismissing charges against a person on the grounds that he "flatly denied" the accusations.

The *Times* also offered this statement as proof that the original report was false:

> *The Times has since learned that the [accusation] was based on a British newspaper report, not on independent information.*

Apparently British newspapers cannot be trusted. Does that mean we can trust American newspapers? If so, an American newspaper reported that a flight instructor in Minneapolis phoned the FBI to complain that a possible terrorist wanted to learn how to fly a commercial jet. I suppose the FBI would flatly deny that report, but perhaps the FBI and CIA are simply trying to suppress the evidence they dislike.

Perhaps US government officials wanted to stop the investigation because they feared investigators would conclude that there were so many warnings and clues that even a troop of Girl Scouts would have been able to stop the terrorists.

Building 5 of the World Trade Center

Who made the suspicious investments?

On September 18, 2001 the Chicago Board Options Exchange announced that they were investigating the possibility that terrorists had profited from the attack. Officials said there was an unusually high volume of suspicious activity in which investors were betting that the price of United Airlines and American Airlines stock would drop. These suspicious trades occurred on each of the three business days prior to the September 11th attack, implying that some people learned of the attack a few days before it occurred. The Securities and Exchange Commission also began an investigation of these trades. (Incidently, nobody is denying that these investments took place.)

The *San Francisco Chronicle* reported that 2.5 million dollars in profits were never collected by the investors. Were the investors afraid of getting caught if they asked for their profit?

Nearly a year has passed since the attack, and we are still waiting for the results of the SEC investigation. Who were those investors? Were they friends and family members of the terrorists or Osama bin Laden? Did the investors disguise themselves so well that one year is not enough time to identify them? If so, why didn't they collect their 2.5 million dollars in profit?

There may be a sensible explanation for the investments and the inability to identify the investors, but the silence surrounding this issue is suspicious and fueling accusations. For example, some people accuse CIA officials as being the investors. If those accusations are correct, those officials decided to take advantage of the attack rather than try to prevent the attack.

Is Caspian oil affecting our government?

The earth's oil supplies are dwindling, and no large pools have been discovered for years. The world's last remaining source of oil is in the Caspian Sea area. Since no nation has yet shown an interest in developing alternatives to oil, all nations will need access to that Caspian oil as the Mideast oil wells run dry during the next few decades. The Caspian Sea could soon become the world's most important piece of land.

If the Russians get control of Caspian oil, they could create economic hardship for other nations beyond anything OPEC could get away with. Not surprisingly, American and British oil companies have been trying for years to put oil pipelines to the Caspian sea through Afghanistan. Unfortunately, the Taliban had refused to agree to any of the proposals, perhaps because they were waiting for a higher fee.

Oil could be one possible reason that some people allowed this terrorist act to take place. Perhaps the CIA, the Bush family, or British government officials wanted to let the attack occur so they could accuse the Taliban of allowing Osama to operate terrorist camps in Afghanistan, then use that as an excuse to destroy the Taliban.

The September 11th attack was devastating, but perhaps the CIA did not expect such damage. Perhaps they expected the planes to merely punch a small hole in the side of the towers, as an airplane did to the Empire State Building in 1945 when it crashed into it. Or perhaps the CIA assumed the military would intercept the airplanes. Or perhaps they were under the impression that only one or two planes would be hijacked.

"The potential prize in oil and gas riches in the Caspian sea, valued up to $4 trillion, would give Russia both wealth and strategic dominance."

"Central Asian resources may revert back to the control of Russia or to a Russian led alliance. This would be a nightmare situation."

"We had all better wake up to the dangers..."

From an article in 1999 by Mortimer Zuckerman, the editor of U.S. News and World Report. He advocated getting control of the Caspian oil before the Russians get it.

How many people in the U.S. Government would be tempted to take advantage of a terrorist attack to justify going after Caspian oil? Would any members of the British government be tempted to let the attack occur?

Does OPEC frighten you? How would you feel with Russia in control of the world's last remaining oil supplies?

"[the oil companies]...cannot begin construction [of a pipeline] until an internationally recognized Afghanistan government is in place."

From the testimony of John Maresca, VP of Unocal Corporation at the House Committee On International Relations, February 1998. He is an example of people in the oil business who wanted the Taliban out of power. Would these people be tempted to allow the attack to take place?

Compare the investigation of Clinton to that of the 9/11 attack:

Ken Starr spent 40 million tax dollars investigating Clinton's sexual activities. By comparison, there was so little money for the 9-11 investigation that some scientists volunteered to work for free on weekends.

Perhaps half the population did not want to investigate Clinton's sexual activities, but Republicans pushed for an investigation anyway. By comparison, most people want an investigation of the 9-11 attacks, but Bush has pushed to "limit" the investigation.

Most people tolerate lies and secrecy in regards to sex, but Republicans demanded Clinton be honest about his sexual activities anyway. By comparison, most people do not consider lies or secrecy acceptable in terrorist attacks, fires, or building collapses, but our government is secretive and interfering with the investigation anyway.

The FBI laboratory analyzed the stains in Monica Lewinsky's dress. By comparison, NIST does not want to analyze the remains of Building 7.

Courtesy of The CoStar Group, Inc.

Building 6 of the World Trade Center

When the CIA saw how destructive the attack was, they may have panicked and put pressure on the government to suppress all investigations. Perhaps the unclaimed 2.5 million dollars in investment profits belongs to American citizens who became so upset over the incident that they wished they had never invested.

Unless we investigate, we learn nothing

Most people blame the collapse of the two towers on _fire_, not the _airplane crashes_. Building 7 collapsed also, and since it was not hit by an airplane its collapse has been blamed on fire. How did fire cause three, steel-framed buildings to collapse? No fire had ever caused a steel building to crumble, but on that day a fire did to three buildings what no fire had done before. Are there other office buildings, apartment buildings, or shopping malls that could also collapse from a fire? How should we design future buildings to resist fires?

NIST is one of the government agencies that investigated the collapse of the towers. However, Dr. Bement, the director of NIST, did not seem interested in investigating Building 7. As he explained to the Committee on Science:

> ...[NIST] would possibly consider examining WTC Building 7, which collapsed later in the day.

Notice that Bement did not say he would _possibly investigate_; rather, he said he would _possibly_ **consider** investigating.

Furthermore, Bement made this remark at a meeting in March of 2002. This was nearly six months after the building had collapsed, and most of the rubble had already been removed. How many more months would have to pass before he would "possibly consider" investigating? Was he waiting for _all_ rubble to be removed so he could avoid dealing with the issue? Or was he simply following President Bush's suggestion to "limit" the investigation?

If another agency had conducted a thorough investigation of Building 7, or if the rubble had been saved until more personnel and resources were available, then Dr. Bement's lack of interest would be understandable. However, no agency thoroughly investigated any of the buildings that collapsed and, more importantly, no agency made an attempt to save the rubble.

Unless we figure out how fire caused these buildings to collapse, we will never know how to determine if a building is susceptible to collapsing from a fire. An investigation would also help us determine whether our building codes need revision. Unfortunately, the rubble was never properly analyzed. Rather, within hours of the collapse the crews began hauling the large pieces of steel to scrap yards and dumping the rest into landfills. Not only was this destruction of rubble irresponsible but, according to the editor-in-chief of _Fire Engineering_ magazine, it was an illegal destruction of _evidence_:

> I have combed through our national standard for fire investigation, NFPA 921, but nowhere in it does one find an exemption allowing the destruction of evidence for buildings over 10 stories tall.

There are two main reasons that we have laws demanding preservation of evidence. First, a proper analysis takes more than a few glances of the evidence by one person; it may require days or months of inspections and experiments, and individuals at different laboratories may be needed. Second, unless the evidence is preserved, we cannot perform further analyses if we have doubts about the original analysis, or if other questions arise in the future. So why did our government violate our laws? Furthermore, why are they allowed to get away with violating our laws? Why are they allowed to interfere with the investigation? Why are so few people in Congress complaining about these violations? Compare this tolerance of law-breaking with the frequent public condemnation of Clinton for violating our laws in regards to Monica Lewinsky.

By January, 2002 the editor-in-chief of *Fire Engineering* magazine reached his limit of tolerance. He published an article that month accusing the investigation of being *"a half baked farce."* He also demanded: *"The destruction and removal of evidence must stop immediately."* In support, other firemen wrote an article in which they pleaded with readers to send e-mails to our government to hold a real investigation.

Unfortunately, everybody who complained about the pathetic investigation or the destruction of evidence was ignored (or worse; some were insulted as "unpatriotic" or "conspiracy nuts"). By April, 2002 virtually all of the rubble had been destroyed. Now, with no evidence, determining how the fires caused those buildings to collapse is impossible.

When terrorists attack, the US government acts suspiciously

The American government responded to the terrorist acts by violating our laws and conducting a pathetic investigation. This atrocious behavior opened America up to accusations of corruption, incompetence, paranoia, stupidity, and conspiracies. One accusation came from the government itself. In the report from the March 6, 2002 hearing at the Committee On Science:

> *The building owners, designers and insurers, prevented independent researchers from gaining access and delayed the [investigators] in gaining access to pertinent building documents largely because of liability concerns.*

Should we accuse the Committee On Science of being a group of "conspiracy nuts"? Before you answer that question, let's look at a previous FEMA investigation.

FEMA investigates Meridian Plaza fire in 1991

On February 23, 1991 a fire started on the 22nd floor of a 38 story office building at One Meridian Plaza in Philadelphia, Pennsylvania. Although the fire was initially small, it spread to eight floors of the building, burned for 19 hours, and caused the deaths of three firefighters. FEMA investigated the fire and produced a detailed report of explanations, recommendations, and photos. They determined that

---

Should we demand that Bush follow the law, as millions of people demanded of Clinton during the Clinton / Lewinsky investigation? Here are a few of the remarks from back then:

"We elect a President to enforce these laws."

From Sen. Michael DeWine's impeachment of Clinton statement, February 12, 1999

"The President cannot be judged on a different standard than anyone else simply because he is the President."

Statement of Rep. Cass Ballenger on Impeaching Clinton, December 18, 1998

"We are a nation of laws...."

Millions of people made that remark.

"...the Office of Independent Counsel (OIC) hereby submits substantial and credible information that President Clinton obstructed justice..."

From the report produced by Ken Starr, in the section "Grounds for Impeachment"

On April 24, 2002, Federal Reserve Bank of New York estimated the cleaning and rebuilding to cost up to $29 *billion*.

If $29 billion is not serious enough for a full investigation, at what price point is a full investigation granted?

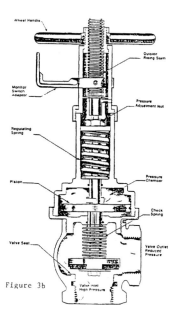

Figure 3b

This is one of several drawings of pressure valves in the report FEMA produced about the fire at One Meridian Plaza in 1991. This report was so detailed that it explained how these valves work and how to use them properly.

Obviously, in 1991 FEMA was capable of producing serious reports. Why couldn't they do the same with the World Trade Center?

the fire started in a pile of rags that contained linseed oil, and that negligence allowed it to spread. Improperly maintained smoke detectors and improperly set pressure valves on water lines were cited as examples of negligence. The fire was finally extinguished when it reached a floor where the sprinkler system functioned properly. The report on the Meridian Plaza fire provides two interesting points:

- First, the report proves that in 1991 FEMA was capable of properly investigating fires. Therefore, their pathetic investigation of the World Trade Center is either a deliberate refusal to investigate, or changes in our government have resulted in FEMA becoming an incompetent or ineffective organization.

- Second, the report estimated $4 billion in civil damage claims as a result of the fire. Now consider the financial ramifications if three deaths and the destruction of eight floors of a building result in $4 billion in damage claims in 1991. How many billions are likely in 2001 when fires at the World Trade Center kill thousands, destroy the entire complex, damage the underground subway beneath the complex, and damage neighboring buildings?

On December 13, 2001 the *New York Times* reported that the fireproofing materials in the World Trade Center had been in need of repairs for years, and that government officials insisted those accusations were simply exaggerations of salesmen who were trying to sell fireproofing material. While it is true that salesmen sometimes push the truth to sell their product, those reports of faulty insulation would be tempting to use as justification for a court case. Were landlords and insurance companies worried about thousands of lawsuits?

The Committee On Science accuses landlords and insurance companies of "interfering" with the investigation, but those people may have done more than merely "interfere." They may have pushed government officials into destroying the rubble. Additionally, city officials may have been worried about potential lawsuits. All of these people may have pressured Bush and Cheney into requesting a limit to the investigation.

The FEMA report on the World Trade Center Collapse

FEMA published their report in May, 2002. The title is *World Trade Center Building Performance Study*. It is report #403. The report contains a lot of interesting information about the buildings, but it does *not* explain their collapse. For example, on why the towers collapsed:

With the information and time available, the sequence of events leading to the collapse of each tower could not be definitively determined.

In that sentence they imply that they are innocent investigators who simply did not have enough information. They neglect to explain that the reason there is so little information is because the rubble was *destroyed* and the investigators were "hampered."

The courtyard. Building 5 is on the left, Building 4 along the right.

On why Building 7 collapsed the report mentions:

The specifics of the fires in WTC 7 and how they caused the building to collapse remain unknown at this time. ...Further research, investigation, and analyses are needed to resolve this issue.

Again they imply they are innocent investigators who need to do further research. However, by the time they published the report (May 2002), all of the rubble had been destroyed. Therefore, it was impossible for them to do further research. If FEMA had truly been interested in researching Building 7, they would have done the research *before* the rubble was destroyed, or they would have put aside some of the rubble for a later analysis.

One of the excuses FEMA gives for their inability to explain the collapse is that the collapse was a unique event:

As with any first-time event, difficulties were encountered at the beginning of the relationship between the volunteer engineering community and the local government agencies.

Many disasters can be referred to as a "first-time event." Rarely does an earthquake, fire, hurricane, tornado, airplane accident, chemical spill, or train derailment happen exactly like a previous disaster. FEMA is simply making excuses for their lousy investigation.

Furthermore, why were they using a "volunteer engineering community" to investigate the collapse? At a meeting on 24 October 2001, Edward DePaola announced that SEAoNY was looking for volunteers "to help collect data." Why were they looking for volunteers near the end of October rather than in September? More amazing, why didn't anybody ask the US Government for money to hire scientists and engineers to work *full time*? Is it possible that the management at FEMA, SEAoNY, NIST, and other agencies truly believed that 200,000 tons of rubble could be properly investigated with volunteers on a tiny budget?

I doubt that *anybody* in management could be as naive as the people in control of the WTC investigation make themselves appear. I think these agencies either had no intention of investigating, or they were under pressure to "limit" the investigation. The FEMA report even supports the accusation that the investigators were hampered:

Also, because there was no identification system in place for the first few days, it took up to 3 hours for SEAoNY volunteers to get to the command center from the outer perimeter of the site, a distance of less than six blocks.

The area around the World Trade Center was blocked off to keep out the public, and checkpoints were set up at several entrances. The people who were destroying the rubble quickly passed through the checkpoints, but the investigators were often delayed for hours. Why would the lack of an "identification system" cause *only the investigators* to be delayed? Why wouldn't all people be delayed equally? And why would the delays be so long?

"Some of the engineers are volunteering their time, and others are being paid. The Federal Emergency Management Agency is financing the effort, which will cost about $600,000"

"...[the engineers] communicate mostly by phone as they continue to hold their regular jobs"

Compare their budget to the $40 million spent by Ken Starr during his investigation of Clinton's sexual activities. Starr had full time help, not weekend volunteers.

From an Associated Press article in January, 2002 describing engineers who were inspecting the rubble.

"These pieces were accidentally processed in salvage yard operations before being documented."

A remark from the May 2002 FEMA report on the WTC.

Some investigators wandered through the scrap yards in the hope of finding steel beams that would help explain the collapse. They marked the beams they wanted for the investigation with paint. However some of those beams were "accidently" destroyed.

Since our government cannot properly investigate the collapse of three buildings, can we trust them to deal with our economy, city planning, health care, or education?

A view of Building 7 from the top of the North Tower.

Building 7 of the World Trade Center

Why so many dead firemen?

The airplanes caused the towers to shake a bit upon impact, but after a few seconds the towers settled down and appeared to have survived. From a structural perspective, there were no signs that the towers were unstable; i.e., no noises from the building; no cracks developing, and no pieces falling off.

As a result of the stable appearance, hundreds of firemen ran into the towers without fear, just as they had run into other steel buildings on fire. Their thoughts were to extinguish the fires and help people get out of the buildings, not whether the buildings would crumble. A short time later, without warning, the towers crumbled.

In addition to the firemen, several photographers were injured, and at least one died. Were these photographers foolish to get so close to the towers? No. As with the firemen, the photographers had no reason to worry about the structural stability of the towers. Neither the photographers nor the firemen were fools; rather, they were victims of the world's most bizarre building collapses. How could such a strange event not justify a serious investigation?

Building 7: diesel fuel, high voltage, and spies

Photos of Building 7 show an apparently conventional office building, but inside was a giant cavity that took up most of the first five floors. Two of the city's electrical substations were inside the cavity, with a total of ten giant transformers, each 35 feet tall and 40 feet wide. The transformer inputs were 13,800 volts. The reason this strange situation came about is that the substations were already on the land. Due to the lack of vacant land in Manhattan, Building 7 was designed to sit on top of the substations and completely enclose them.

To make the structure stranger (and more dangerous), the tenants of the building installed tanks of diesel fuel to power emergency generators in case the electric power to the city was cut off. American Express had a 275 gallon tank for their backup generator; Mayor Giuliani had a 6,000-gallon tank to supply three 500 kW generators for his Emergency Command Center; the investment firm Salomon Smith Barney had two 6,000 gallon tanks for their nine 1.725 MW generators, and the landlord installed two 12,000 gallon tanks for two 900 kW generators. If the FEMA report is correct, the building had the capacity to hold 42,000 gallons of diesel fuel, and the generators had a total capacity of about 20 megawatts of electricity. Not surprisingly, the New York fire department complained more than once that the situation was risky.

The diesel tank and generator used by American Express were so small that they were placed together on the 8th floor. However, the other tanks and generators were gigantic, so they were separated from each other. The large tanks were near the ground floor, except for the Mayor's 6,000 gallon tank, which was on the 2nd floor. The generators were on the 5th, 7th, and 9th floors. Pumps and pipelines carried the fuel from the large tanks up to small tanks that fed the generators. As you can imagine, if any of those pipelines were to leak, fuel could drip down as many as nine floors, and out into the street.

Is the electric power supply in New York City so unreliable that office buildings truly need this much backup power capacity?

Apparently so; the FEMA report implies that Building 7 was a "normal" office building:

> *An array of fuels typically associated with offices was distributed throughout much of the building.*

Do you know of any "typical" office buildings that have several pipelines to carry 42,000 gallons of diesel fuel to 15 or more generators with a combined capacity of 20 megawatts? Was something going on in Building 7 that nobody wants to admit to?

Building 7 belongs in an industrial zone where people are casting metal objects or firing pottery. Why did the city allow such a hazardous situation in a public office building? Perhaps Mayor Giuliani, Salomon Smith Barney, and the landlord wanted the rubble destroyed to prevent investigators from blaming the collapse of Building 7 on their giant fuel tanks and network of pipelines.

Part of the secrecy with Building 7 may be due to the CIA, Department of Defense, and Secret Service, all of which had offices in that building. The FEMA report claims that two 12,000 gallon tanks of diesel fuel belonged to the landlord, but the landlord does not show up as a tenant in the building, so it appears as if the landlord provided the fuel to his tenants. The FEMA report mentions that both the Mayor and the Secret Service took fuel from the landlord's 12,000 gallon tanks, but the landlord may have supplied fuel and backup generators for some of his other tenants, also, such as the CIA and Department of Defense. Perhaps all the people involved with these diesel tanks pushed for the destruction of the rubble so that nobody would accuse them of being the reason the building collapsed. This would also prevent lawsuits against the CIA and other agencies.

The US Government is creating suspicion, not respect

Almost everyone in the world was sympathetic towards the USA on September 11th. Unfortunately, during the ensuing months, the strange response from the US Government has caused some of that sympathy to be replaced with suspicion and anger.

No sensible reason exists to limit the investigation of the World Trade Center collapse or to depend on volunteers to investigate; America has enough money and manpower to do the job properly. Secrecy about Building 7 cannot be justified, either; our government should not hide irresponsible and/or illegal behavior of landlords, the CIA, or the mayor of New York City. Additionally, there is no sensible explanation for why the Securities and Exchange Commission cannot identify the suspicious investors of airline options.

The behavior of the US government leads me to conclude that some government officials are hiding something. I doubt that President Bush is so naive that he truly believes America has a shortage of investigators; certainly he has some other reason to interfere with the investigation. I also suspect that FEMA officials knew that destroying the rubble was both illegal and irresponsible; that FEMA deliberately allowed our laws to be violated. Something is going on, and it is not likely to be legal.

How much is 42,000 gallons of diesel?

It would provide about 330,000 kilowatt hours of electricity. I use 100 to 300 kilowatt hours per month, so it would provide electricity for me for at least 90 years.

How many decades could Building 7 provide *you* with electricity?

You probably heard about Zacarias Moussaoui, the 9-11 terrorist, asking to learn how to fly a plane, but not take off or land a plane.

The *American Free Press* reported on 3 June 2002 that the *New York Times* had a small article in which Norman Mineta, the Transportation Secretary, testified to the Senate Commerce Committee that Moussaoui never made such a statement.

Who is telling the truth?

...some individuals are put at risk for the benefit of the greater good.

From The Final Report of the Advisory Committee on Human Radiation Experiments, by the Department of Energy, 1994.

The DOE is justifying the secret experiments the US government conducted on American citizens.

A more honest remark would have been:

While it was immoral for Nazis to use people in medical experiments, it is righteous for Americans to do so.

Some government officials and private citizens advocate allowing the FBI to torture suspects.

These Americans are responding to a terrorist attack by advocating we get rid of some of the freedoms that America was created to provide.

"Our forefathers' act of civil disobedience created America."

Rick Stanley, in his statement January 9, 2002, encourages citizens to do *"...your very own personal act of civil disobedience, to make our country better."*

Stanley is one of many people who suggests resisting the attempts by the government to get dictatorial control of the nation.

The hotel (Building 3) at left, rear. The North tower is in the center, and the South Tower is at the extreme left edge.

The US Government is creating anger

Judging by the number of accusations and complaints on the Internet, I am just one of thousands of people who suspect something is seriously wrong. Some of these people are angry, and some are encouraging rebellion.

> *"Each act of civil disobedience will create a better America"*

That quote from Rick Stanley's statement on January 9, 2002 reflects the attitude of many citizens. As of May 2002, Stanley was a Libertarian candidate for the US Senate in Colorado. Stanley and others complain about a variety of issues that revolve around the terrorist attack on September 11th, such as "The Patriot Act"; the proposal to allow the FBI to use torture; and the destruction of the World Trade Center rubble.

Thousands of citizens are angry with the government. Ignoring them on the grounds that they are "conspiracy nuts" or "wackos" does not solve any problems.

"Let them eat cake!"

We should learn from Marie Antoinette that a government should deal with angry citizens, not laugh at or ignore them. Unfortunately, the only people who understand this concept are successful managers in private companies. A successful manager would not ignore anger among employees; rather, the best managers observe the attitudes among employees. They strive to keep the employees happy and their morale high. Compare that to the American government officials who not only ignore discontent, they also have no concern about the morale of the citizens.

Conspiracies

The September 11th attack is a serious problem that our government should acknowledge and deal with. The Internet, some books, and a few paper publications are full of accusations, calls for rebellion, and conspiracy theories. The angry and suspicious people are spreading anger and suspicion to other citizens. Ignoring these people is not the way to create a healthy nation.

In response to the charges of corruption and conspiracies, other citizens claim the nation is full of "conspiracy nuts" and idiots. However, these accusations only reinforce and divide the citizens. This fighting will hurt the morale of America, and that will hurt all of us.

The more shocking conspiracy theories claim that the rubble was destroyed to hide evidence that explosives were used to assist in the collapse of the buildings. An example of this type of conspiracy theory speculates that the CIA, Bush family, and others decided to fake the attack in an attempt to make the world angry at the Taliban, providing us with an excuse to destroy them so that we could try installing a government that would give us access to Caspian oil.

The US military action in Afghanistan is as suspicious as the superficial investigation of the World Trade Center collapse, thereby fueling conspiracy theories. Our government claimed that we bombed Afghanistan to search for Osama and his terrorist camps, but how do we locate Osama by flying high above the clouds and dropping bombs on people who had nothing to do with the September 11th attack? All we did with our bombs was kill innocent people and destroy some of the world's most primitive villages. The goal of US military appears to be the removal of the Taliban rather than locating Osama and his training camps.

After destroying the Taliban, the US military essentially gave Afghanistan to the Northern Alliance. There was no attempt to help the citizens of Afghanistan develop a sensible government. The suspicious aspect of our friendship with the Northern Alliance is that during the 1980's our government gave billions of dollars in weapons and other aid to Osama and his terrorists to help them defeat the Northern Alliance and the Russians. Osama was not a "terrorist" back then, however. Rather, when President Reagan welcomed some of Osama's Mujahadeen allies to the White House, he referred to them as, *"the moral equivalent of our founding fathers."*

The Russians supported the Northern Alliance then, and they still support them today. So why in 2002 did we give Afghanistan to the Northern Alliance? Are we trying to become their new best friend?

The Taliban, not Osama, has been the focus of the US military campaign. The US military never showed much interest in searching for Osama or his terrorist camps. Perhaps the US government believes the Northern Alliance will be so grateful to us that they will grant us access to Caspian oil.

Anger is spreading around the world

Americans are not the only people complaining about the US government. For example, in March of 2002 a Frenchman named Thierry Meyssan published the book *The Frightening Fraud* (or *The Appalling Deception*, depending on who translates it from French) in which he accused the US military of faking the crash of Flight 77 on September 11th. A remark by Thierry Meyssan in a recent interview could be an indication that the US government is creating enemies rather than impressing the world:

> *...since the U.S. has used [the 9-11 attack] as one of their arguments to launch an attack against Afghanistan and has asked the whole world to stand at its side in the war, this is no longer a purely American affair.*

Did Al-Qaeda really bring the US Military to its knees?

The US military refuses to release the video from the security cameras that recorded Flight 77 crashing into the Pentagon on September 11. We were practically forced to watch the airplanes hit the North and South Towers over and over and over again, so why not let us watch the video of the airplane hitting the Pentagon *just one time*?

The US military has the largest supply of advanced weapons on the planet, but they claim to be afraid of a few terrorists with primitive technology. The implication is that the terrorists might see something in that video that will allow them to hurt America. Are the people in control of the US military truly this foolish? Or, is *The Frightening Fraud* correct that the military faked the airplane crash?

Mirko Balke

View of a tower, from the ground.

"That's not what militaries do"

Remark by General Tommy Franks to a group of international reporters in April of 2002 when asked about the failure to find Osama bin Laden.

If our military is not searching for Osama, what are they doing in Afghanistan?

What *do* militaries do?

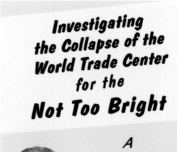

Investigating the Collapse of the World Trade Center for the **Not Too Bright**

A Reference for U.S. Government Officials

A book that should have been written

Facts from the CIA on Afghanistan (before the USA bombed it). The US military certainly studied these facts to prepare for the incredible danger they were facing:

The majority of the population continues to suffer from insufficient food…

the country suffers from enormous poverty, a crumbling infrastructure…

Population: 26,813,057
Telephones: 29,000
Internet Service Providers: 1
Military expenditures: $n/a
Literacy: 31.5%

the military does not exist on a national basis…

no functioning central government…

world's largest illicit opium producer…

narcotics trafficking is a major source of revenue.

Did high pressure punch holes in Building 6?

Photos shows a plume of dust rising upwards near Buildings 5 and 6 as each tower collapsed (Figure 1-1). This dust shot upwards so quickly that it passed the top of Building 7 (nearly 600 feet tall) within a few seconds. The collapse of the towers would have pushed dust into the underground shopping mall, parking lot, and passageways, increasing the air pressure underground. These plumes of smoke might be the result of the high pressure dust blowing open a hole in or near Buildings 5 and 6, and then shooting upwards. Building 6 (Figure 1-2) has two deep holes in it, and Building 5 has at least one mysterious hole. Were those holes blown open to release the high pressure?

Let's practice what we preach

Many people tell us that we either support the Bush administration 100% or we are a part of the Axis Of Evil. These people believe they are helping to unify America by making such remarks, but they are merely making themselves look like hypocrites. These people boast about our Freedom of Speech and our right to question our government, and at the same time they try to suppress both freedoms.

Furthermore, the attitude that obedience to President Bush will create a unified nation is as ridiculous as one of your friends announcing that the group of friends will become more unified if you obey him without question. Obedience does not create unity, nor does it create happier people. Rather, it sets up the people for abuse. Citizens need to take an active role in their nation, not become obedient soldiers.

Millions of Americans are appalled at the number of citizens who mindlessly followed Hitler and Saddam Hussein. Nevertheless, take note that Americans are behaving the same way if they refuse to look critically at their own government. The patriots who chant _"USA! USA! USA!"_, _"Support George Bush!"_, and _"You are either with us or against us!"_ should be chanting _"Think! Learn! Investigate!"_, _"Demand competent politicians!"_ and _"It is OK in the USA to question the government!"_

The courtyard of the World Trade Center

Figure 1-1   _The red arrow points to a large cloud near Building 5, 6, and 7 as the South Tower collapsed. This cloud shot upwards at very high speed._

The world improves when people discuss issues, not when patriots give blind obedience to their government. Blind obedience would be acceptable only if there were such a thing as a "perfect" government.

The US government's response to the September 11th attacks is worse than an embarrassment considering the anger it stimulated within America and internationally. Unless we deal with this issue we are no better than the people we criticize. We need to work together for beneficial causes, not fight with other. So let's stop promoting the idea that patriotism requires blind obedience to President Bush. Let's look closely at the attack and the collapse of the buildings.

There are a lot of mysterious aspects surrounding the events on September 11th. If the US government had cooperated with an investigation, sensible explanations for everything might have been discovered. However, the government's strange response to the attack is evidence that some people are trying to hide something. But hide what? And who wants to hide it?

This book will explain some of the mysterious aspects of the World Trade Center attack that are providing fuel for various conspiracy theories. Those of you who do not believe anything illegal occurred should look for explanations for these mysteries. The inability to properly explain the attack is simply more evidence that we are witnessing an incredible scam.

The September 11th attack devastated America. If two dozen terrorists with razors could orchestrate that attack, what would happen if 5,000 terrorists with advanced technology attacked us?

We should hope that 9-11 was a scam, and that thousands of people and many years of preparation were needed. The more difficult this scam was, the less likely it will be attempted a second time.

Figure 1-2   *The blue arrows point to two **deep** holes in Building 6. Did falling debris create those holes? Or were those holes blown open to release the high pressure in the basement?*

James R. Tourtellotte

When nobody knows anything, everybody is an expert

There are no scientific reports about what the airplane did to the structure of the towers because the rubble was destroyed before scientists had a chance to properly study it. We can only guess at whether the airplanes were shredded into pieces; whether large pieces penetrated deep into the tower; and how much damage was done to the structure of the towers. Also, there are no scientific reports on the effect the fire had on the structure. We can only guess at the temperature the steel beams reached; which of the beams reached a high temperature; and what effect those high temperatures had on the structure of the towers.

The only source of information about the collapse are photographs and television news reports. Unfortunately, those images show only the outside of the building. This incredible lack of information about the World Trade Center collapse creates an interesting situation: **there are no experts on the collapse.**

If FEMA had hired a group of scientists to analyze the collapse, those scientists would be the experts. In such a case, FEMA would have produced detailed reports and diagrams that showed which part of the steel structure was damaged by the airplanes; the temperature reached at various locations in the crash zones; and which part of the structures failed first. If anybody had questions about the collapse, those scientists would be the authorities.

Unfortunately, the FEMA report is mainly just structural information about the buildings; it does not explain why the towers collapsed. Their report also has a few brief speculations as to the possible temperatures in the fire zone and the damage caused by the airplane, but their guesses are no better than anybody else's. Their guesses are based on images from video and photographs, rather than scientific analyses of the rubble, but each of us is capable of looking at those same photographs and speculating on what they mean.

How can conspiracy theories be disproved?

The lack of serious information makes it easy to create conspiracy theories, and difficult to disprove them. Conspiracy theories cannot be disproved with material from the FEMA report, or with the reports of other experts, because nobody knows anything about the collapse. Disproving a conspiracy theory requires looking at the same photographs and news video that everybody else looks at, and then finding a more convincing speculation of what those photographs mean.

When everybody is blind...

Nobody can seriously claim to be an expert on the collapse of the World Trade Center simply because nobody had a chance to study the rubble. Everybody who has looked at the photographs and television news video knows as much about the collapse as the most knowledgeable scientists. Therefore, everybody who has viewed the photographs and video can claim to be an expert. I looked at the photos, for example; therefore, I am an expert. You will be an expert after you look at the photos in this book.

If you think my statements are an exaggeration, consider what some "official" experts are saying.

Charles Clifton, structural engineer

Clifton is a technical expert for the *Heavy Engineering Research Association* in New Zealand. One of his specialties is *"determining the behavior of steel framed buildings under the extreme events of severe earthquake or severe fire."* He wrote an analysis of the collapse of the towers that is referred to at hundreds of Internet sites, including universities that have the technical expertise to verify his analysis, such as the University of Illinois and the Institute for Structural Mechanics in Germany. This should qualify him as an "expert."

The first point I would like to make about his analysis is that he has a disclaimer that supports my previous remarks that nobody knows anything:

> *I don't have access to material / data from the wreckage of these buildings so I am not in a position to make detailed observations.*

He admits that his lack of information makes it impossible for him to truly explain the collapse, but he does not seem to realize that nobody else has any data, either. His remark would have been more accurate if he had written it this way:

> *Nobody has access to material / data from the wreckage of these buildings so nobody is in a position to explain the collapse.*

His theory is based on photographs and TV news. He described it this way:

> *On the basis of what I have seen and heard reported to date…*

A "real" analysis is not based on what was "reported." Normally, scientists do their own research and verify all facts rather than believe what they saw on television. A scientific report of the collapse would state: *"Our analysis of the steel beams in the rubble shows..."* rather than *"According to the Channel 4 Action Reporters..."*

Unfortunately, the rubble was destroyed, so every analysis of the collapse is actually just an analysis of photographs and CNN reports. This creates the bizarre situation in which scientists and engineers write highly technical reports and then support their theories with remarks about what they saw on television. In fact, Clifton actually quotes a television reporter:

> *Having done this calculation it is more easy to understand what our eyes showed us – namely the planes slicing through the perimeter frames "like a knife through butter" as one reporter has stated.*

If Clifton had been able to inspect the rubble he would have been able to create diagrams of the steel beams in the building that would identify the steel columns that broke or bent when the airplane hit them. He would also be able to show which of the floors and elevator shafts were damaged by the airplane, and how severe the damage was. Television reporters and magazines would reproduce his diagrams and quote passages from his report. However, since Clifton has no idea what happened when the plane entered the building, the situation was reversed; i.e., he quoted television reporters rather than reporters quoting him.

Clifton is an expert on severe fires in steel buildings. His experience with fires suggests to him that fire could not have caused the towers to collapse. His conclusion is that the *plane crash*, not the fire, was the main reason for the collapse:

> *This impact damage – not the severity of the fire – I contend is the principal cause of the ultimate collapse.*

Henry Koffman of USC

Many people believe the steel either melted or came close to melting. Henry Koffman, director of the Construction Engineering and Management Program at the University of Southern California, made such a remark in an interview:

> *The bottom line, in my opinion, is that intense heat from the jet fuel fires melted the steel infrastructure, which went past its yield strength and led to the collapse of the buildings...*

Professor Eagar of MIT

Thomas Eagar is a professor of Materials Engineering and Engineering Systems. The *Minerals, Metals & Materials Society* published his analysis that explains the fire could not possibly have been hot enough to melt steel. His main points were:

- Steel melts at 1500°C (2700°F).

- Jet fuel produces a maximum temperature of approximately 1000°C (1800°F) when mixed with air in *perfect* proportions.

- It is virtually impossible for an airplane crash to coincidentally mix the fuel and air in perfect proportions. Therefore, the temperature of the steel was certainly *significantly less* than the maximum of 1000°C.

People who claim the steel *melted* violate the laws of physics, and people who claim it reached temperatures *near 1000°C* violate the laws of statistics.

Professor Eagar did not discover something new about fire. Rather, it has been known for centuries that hydrocarbons cannot melt iron. Centuries ago it was discovered that charcoal produces a higher temperature than hydrocarbons, but even charcoal cannot melt iron unless the charcoal and iron are placed in a properly designed furnace. Also, air must be blasted on the charcoal to provide plenty of oxygen. This is where the expression "blast furnace" comes from.

Eagar points out that residential fires are usually in the 500°C to 650°C range. He does not speculate on the temperatures in World Trade Center fires, but he mentions that if the steel reached 650°C (1,200°F) it would have lost half its strength. However, he points out that the towers were designed to handle such high wind forces that even at half-strength the towers were strong enough to stand up. Eagar's conclusion is that the collapse was due to the combination of *thermal expansion* in the steel beams, which caused the beams to buckle, and a loss of strength from the high temperatures.

What temperature does Eagar believe is realistic for the fires in the tower? His written report did not give an estimate, although he hints at 650°C. In a television interview he gave estimates:

> *I think the World Trade Center fire was probably only 1,200°F or 1,300°F.*

The only problem with his estimate was that after three sentences he increased it:

> *The World Trade Center fire did melt some of the aluminum in the aircraft and hence it probably got to 1,300°F or 1,400°F.*

I suppose if he had continued to talk, after another few sentences the temperature would have climbed to 1500°F. Eagar was obviously making up temperature estimates right then and there, rather than reading from a report.

Eagar is one of the few experts who follow the laws of physics and statistics, but he has no idea why the buildings collapsed. Since nobody analyzed the rubble, nobody can say for certain if the fire had melted any aluminum, or if the steel structure reached temperatures as high as 1,400°F, or whether any beams buckled. Like everybody else, this professor has no data to support his theory or his temperature estimates.

Professor Bazant of Northwestern University

Professor Bazant published his theory in the *Journal of Engineering Mechanics.* He believes the fire was so hot that it caused the steel beams to bend and buckle. One of his remarks about the temperature:

> *...sustained temperatures apparently exceeding 800°C.*

Notice his phrase "apparently exceeding." Since he could not inspect the rubble, he has no idea what the actual temperature was. In his conclusions he puts the following remark in parentheses to prevent people from complaining about his 800°C (1470°F) estimate:

> *(though possibly well below 800°C)*

Bazant's theory requires the steel to reach very high temperatures, but in his conclusions he admits in parentheses that the steel may have been well below 800°C. However, if the steel was "well below" 800°C, his theory becomes invalid. In other words, the remark he put in parentheses should have been written like this:

> *(Though possibly well below 800°C, in which case please disregard my theory.)*

Bazant has no idea what was happening inside the towers; rather, he is merely speculating on the possible temperature.

Professor Connor of MIT

An article in the October, 2001 issue of *Scientific American* quotes Connor:

> *In my theory, the hot fire weakened the supporting joint connection...*

Since all joints and steel beams were sold as scrap or buried in landfills before anybody could analyze them, nobody knows what effect the fire had on those joints. For all we know the joints were weakened by the airplane crash, not the fire, which would mean Clifton was correct that the airplane crash was the most significant factor in the collapse. It is also possible that corrosion had weakened a lot of the joints years before the planes hit the building. Also, some of the bolts may not have been tightened properly, and some welds may have been defective. Those rusty and defective joints may have been the main reason the buildings collapsed; the airplane crash and fire may have only initiated the collapse.

Nobody knows nothing!

Some of the experts know more about fires or engineering than you and I, but they do not know what happened inside the towers after the airplanes crashed into them. The experts are looking at the same photographs and CNN video that you and I have seen. We are all experts on the collapse because nobody analyzed the rubble; we are all experts because we are equally ignorant about what happened that day.

The experts cannot even agree on whether the towers were designed properly. For example, the October, 2001 issue of *Scientific American* quotes Robert McNamara, president of the engineering firm McNamara and Salvia:

> *the World Trade Center was probably one of the more resistant tall building structures, ...nowadays, they just don't build them as tough as the World Trade Center.*

The FEMA reports also implies the towers were strong:

> *The floor framing system for the two towers was complex and substantially more redundant than typical bar joist floor systems.*

Other experts claim that *older buildings* were stronger than the "lightweight" and "economical" World Trade Center. Still other experts write articles that imply that the towers had an unusual "tube" design which was not as strong as the older, conventional designs.

Which of these experts is correct? Were the towers made of thin steel in order to save money? Or were the towers stronger than the older buildings? Was the "tube" design the reason the towers collapsed, or was it the reason the towers were "one of the more resistant" of buildings? Or are all of the experts merely making wild speculations?

Furthermore, why don't the experts have an explanation for the collapse of Building 7 if they know so much about fire and engineering?

Information is not easy to find

An article in *Science* magazine mentions that William Grosshandler, chief of the fire research division of Building and Fire Research Laboratory of NIST wants his lab to analyze the smoke plumes from the towers:

> *"But that sort of analysis requires high-quality video and still photos of the smoke plume, which have been hard to come by.*

Associated Press, Reuters, and other conventional news agencies will gladly provide photos, but locating photos and video taken by individuals is extremely difficult. Many citizens got together to give blood and raise money, but not many people want to help gather information for an investigation. To make the situation worse, a few newspapers have reported that the FBI confiscated video from some security cameras and individual citizens (this is discussed in the last chapter).

The difficulty in acquiring information has caused news reporters to provide inaccurate information. Two examples are from *USA Today* and *US News and World Report*.

US News and World Report

This magazine has an article that claims the temperature was beyond the maximum possible temperature of about 1800°F:

> *Weakened by the nearly 2,000-degree heat, the remaining columns buckle.*

> *The structural steel above and around the fire begins to expand and soften like heated plastic in the intense heat.*

Their report on the Internet had not been corrected as of June, 2002. They also claim that the top of the South Tower began its collapse by tipping and rotating. (Figure 2-1A).

However, I cannot see the top of the tower rotating when I look at videos or photographs. Their next diagram of the collapse (Figure 2-1B) could mislead readers into assuming the collapse started at the ground after the top stopped rotating. This drawing contradicts photos of the event.

Their drawing of the North Tower also implies it collapsed from the bottom. More amusing is the smoke ring around the middle of the tower; it reminds me of the rings on the planet Saturn (Figure 2-2). Some interesting ribbons and puffs of dust formed as the towers collapsed, but photos of the North Tower as it collapsed do not look anything like Figure 2-2 (take a quick glance at page 60).

USA Today

This newspaper posted an animated collapse at their Internet site. Rather than tilt and rotate, their animation shows the South Tower falling vertically (Figure 2-3). However, photos show the top tilted as it fell. They also claim the final pile of rubble was 6 or 7 stories tall. While the tips of some pieces of steel may have reached that high, the bulk of the rubble was low to the ground. There were even pits below ground level where basements collapsed. On September 23, the government agency *NOAA* flew an airplane over the World Trade Center to create a three-dimensional elevation map of the area, and their maps also show the piles of rubble very low to the ground.

Maps of the Pentagon are incorrect

Recently Steve Koeppel, a former Air Force pilot, pointed out to the Internet site *thepowerhour.com* that some maps show the airplane hitting the Pentagon at the wrong location. For example, a map by *Los Angeles Times* (Figure 2-4) shows the crash location at the southeast wall, but the true location is the *northwest* wall. Furthermore, according to military officials, the airplane hit the Pentagon at an angle rather than perpendicular, which means it was heading northeast when it hit, as shown in the corrected map (Figure 2-5).

A   **B**

Figure 2-1 *US News & World Report shows the South Tower tipping and rotating, and then collapsing from its bottom.*

Figure 2-2 *US News & World Report incorrectly imply the collapse of the North Tower started at the bottom.*

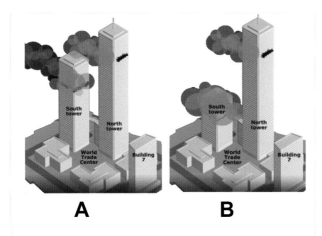

A   **B**

Figure 2-3   *USA Today incorrectly shows the top of the South Tower falling vertically. The top of the South Tower actually tipped towards Building 4. It was the **North** Tower that fell vertically.*

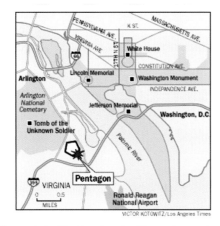

Figure 2-4   *The Los Angeles Times shows the plane hitting at the southeast wall*

Figure 2-5   *The correct location was the **northwest** wall. Also, the plane hit at an angle.*

US News and World Report shows the plane hitting the Pentagon while diving at a steep angle (Figure 2-6), but according to military officials it came in almost horizontal, and it was skimming the surface of the grass. It was so close to the ground that it knocked down a lamp post along the highway in front of the Pentagon. One *Washington Post* drawing is correct, but their closeup shows the plane hitting perpendicular to the building (Figure 2-7). The *ArmyTimes* also goofed (Figure 2-8. One of the few drawings that follows the official military explanation is from the group involved with Thierry Meyssan who wrote *The Frightening Fraud* (Figure 2-9).

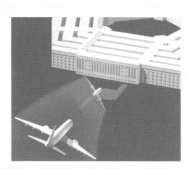

Figure 2-6

*The plane did **not** dive towards the Pentagon, as US News & World Report shows.*

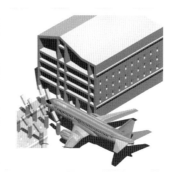

Figure 2-7

*The plane did **not** hit the Pentagon perpendicular, as one Washington Post drawing shows.*

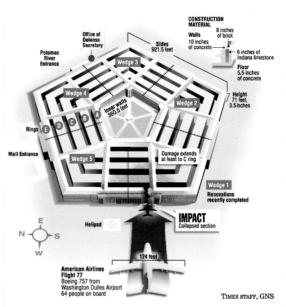

Figure 2-8   *The ArmyTimes incorrectly shows Flight 77 hitting perpendicular.*

The "9-11 Collages" should be removed

Thousands of people posted pages on the Internet in response to the 9-11 attack. Most are a random collection of photos, and most seem to be designed to stimulate anger towards terrorists. These pages remind me of children's collages.

These 9-11 collage pages are a nuisance because they contain highly compressed photos that can easily be misinterpreted, and they do not have links to the original, high resolution photos to allow verification of the images.[†] The three images in Figure 2-10 are examples. Somebody extracted those images from video, compressed to an extreme, and posted them on the Internet. A dark blob appears to travel across the sky (towards the right). Some people believe the blob is proof that the attack is a fraud and that the US military was involved. Their reasoning is:

- No commercial aircraft was flying at that location, so it must be a military aircraft.

- Since the military denies their aircraft were in the area at the time, the military must be involved with this attack.

Before you believe such a theory, note that other photographs show both TV news and police helicopters in the area, so the blob could be one of them. It is also possible that the blob in is just an "artifact" caused by the software that compressed the video. However, I suspect the person who posted the images deliberately created the blob to make fun of conspiracy theories or to fool people. (Some photos on the Internet have been obviously edited to deceive or amuse us, such as the photos that show the face of the devil in the smoke.)

Matt Drudge, the political commentator, was one of many people fooled by the images in Figure 2-10. Drudge wrote an article for his Internet site about the *"flying mystery object"* and included six frames of the video. While he had doubts about the validity of the video, the best policy is to ignore theories that are based on compressed images. Demand the original, high-resolution images. Also, take a look at other video and photos taken at the same time to ensure you are not viewing an edited photo.

Hopefully the photos and drawings in this book will clear up some of the confusion about what happened on September 11th. However, some people will probably scan pages from this book, compress them to such an extent that all details are lost, and then add the images to their collages without bothering to let readers know the source. This

defeats the purpose of the book, which is to *reduce* confusion by providing high quality images. Those of you with collages of photos should either explain where readers can find the original photos, or get rid of your collages.

Figure 2-9 *This 3-D simulation by the French group that wrote The Frightening Fraud shows the plane at the correct angle and distance above the ground.*

Figure 2-10 *Three frames of video that have been compressed to the point that all details have been lost.*

[†] The JPG compression technique causes a loss of detail as a side effect. The higher the level of compression, the greater the loss of detail. Unfortunately, most Internet images are compressed to an extreme to make them transmit faster.

The Location and Structure

Figure 3-1 is a section of a photo taken on June 30, 2000 by the IKONOS satellite. The towers were identical in appearance except for one feature, namely, there was a large antenna on top of the North Tower. The South Tower had an observation deck instead. Therefore, look for the antenna when you are wondering which tower is which.

Figure 3-1 *The World Trade Center from satellite, as of June 30, 2000*

The 47 Core Columns

At the center of the towers were 47 steel columns laid out in a slightly irregular, rectangular grid. These are often referred to as "core" columns. Figure 3-2 shows the location and orientation of these core columns, and the position of the airplanes when they hit the towers. The airplanes are the correct size in relation to the buildings, so if the airplanes seem small it is because the towers were so large. The entire airplane could fit inside a tower if the floors were tall enough and if there were no core columns or elevator shafts in the way.

The size and dimensions of the core columns varied at different elevations in the tower. At the base of the tower the walls of the core columns were 100mm (4 inches) thick, while at the very top of the tower the walls were only 6mm (¼ inch).

Figure 3-3 is a simplified diagram to show the arrangement of the exterior and core columns. Along the outside of the towers were steel columns every meter. There was a total of 236 of these exterior columns, although this diagram shows only 16. These columns were literally on the *exterior* of the tower. There was also a column at each of the four corners, making a total of 240 columns, but those four columns were inside the tower.

The gaps between the 47 core columns was used mainly for elevator shafts, stairways, utility rooms, and hallways.

By putting some of the columns in center of the tower and the others along the outside, there was an enormous amount of open space along the windows for people.

Figures 3-4 and 3-5 show some of the thicker core columns. Both photos can also make you wonder how the workers could claim they were looking for survivors. Nobody could be alive in those smoking piles of hot rubble.

It is also interesting to note that the rubble consists only of short steel beams and dust; no office furnishings, steel assemblies, or large pieces of the concrete floorings.

Figure 3-6 shows a core column, sliced into pieces and ready to sell as scrap metal. As is typical of photos of the rubble, there is no sign that the core columns buckled or bent. Rather, most columns appear to have broken at their joints. The columns were obviously very strong, but the joints appear to have been weak.

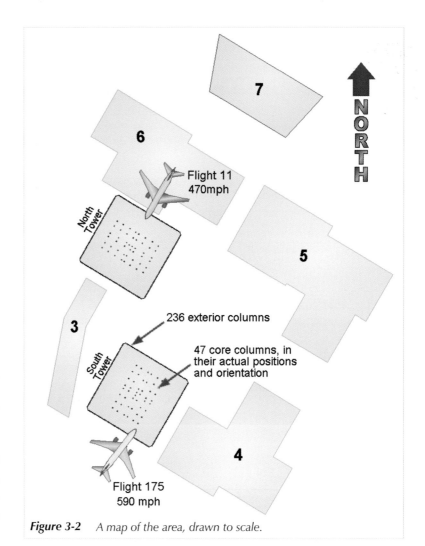

Figure 3-2   *A map of the area, drawn to scale.*

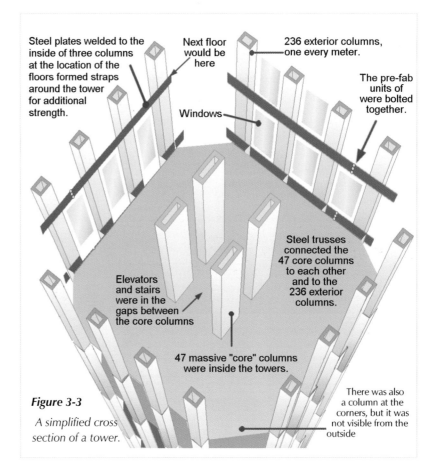

Figure 3-3

A simplified cross section of a tower.

** Unknown photo **

The large rectangular columns are **core** columns.

Figure 3-4   _The workers are cutting the steel with giant torches._

** Unknown photo **

Figure 3-5   _The core column in the center appears cut by a torch. The workers cut the steel_
so quickly that it is difficult to determine which damage was from them.

The 236 Exterior Columns

Figure 3-7 shows a cross-section of three of the exterior columns. Each column is a different thickness to show how the thickness varied from the bottom of the tower to the top. The steel was as thick as 100mm in the columns near the ground, but only 6mm at the top. A cross-section of one the most massive core columns is included in this figure to show its size and shape compared to the exterior columns. A core column with 100mm walls would be near the bottom of the tower.

Note that a fire inside the building would be in direct contact with only one of the four walls of these exterior columns; three walls were surrounded by the outside air. This made it difficult for a fire to raise the temperature of the exterior columns by a significant amount.

Three steel plates were welded to three columns while they were on the ground, creating a prefabricated unit (Figure 3-8). The units were hoisted into the tower and bolted together in a staggered manner (Figure 3-9). Supplemental welds were added to units near the bottom of the tower for additional strength. These plates formed straps around the tower.

Figure 3-10 shows two exterior columns that are still attached to the steel plates that formed straps around the tower. The thickness of the steel and the six bolt holes at the bottom of each column indicate that these were somewhere in the bottom half of the tower. Columns higher up in the tower were made of thinner steel and had only four bolt

holes on each column. Figure 3-11 shows the bolts that held the prefab units together.

Some people believe the towers collapsed because they were weak, but the steel in these towers was very thick and strong. The strength of the steel structure enabled the towers to survive the initial crash of the airplanes. The towers shook briefly, and then settled down.

Figure 3-6   Core columns, sliced and ready to sell as scrap. This photo was taken at the WTC on October 3rd, 2001.

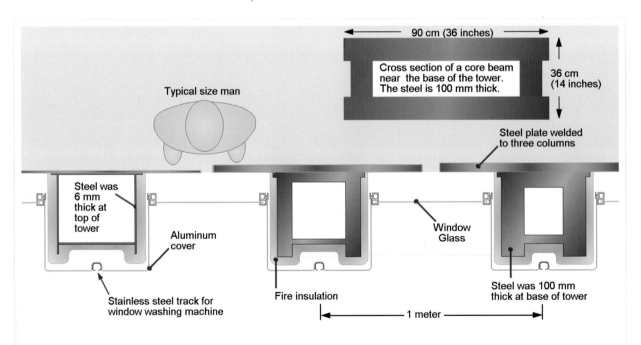

Figure 3-7   Cross section of exterior columns. The steel in each of these three columns is a different thickness to show how the columns varied from the bottom to the top of the tower. The thinnest column would be at the very top of the tower, and thickest would be at the ground. A cross section of the most massive core column is shows for a size comparison. A core column that thick would be at the bottom.

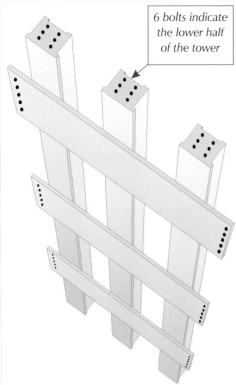

6 bolts indicate the lower half of the tower

Figure 3-8 *While still on the ground, three columns were welded to three steel plates, creating a prefabricated unit that was hoisted into the tower.*

The plates were at the location of the floors. Windows were placed in the gaps between the plates.

FEMA News Photo

Figure 3-10 *Two columns still attached to the three plates that made a pre-fab unit.*

The six bolt holes at the ends of the columns indicate that these were in the lower half of the tower. The units in the upper section had only four bolt holes.

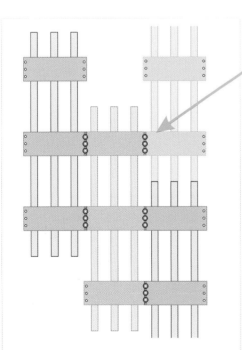

Figure 3-9 *The pre-fab units were staggered to increase strength.*

Bolts held the pre-fab units together

**Unknown **

Figure 3-11 *The bolts holding the pre-fab units together.*

The Floors were Grids of Steel

I have seen remarks on the Internet in which the floors are referred to as "slabs of concrete," as if the towers consisted of a stack of thin slabs of concrete connected to vertical beams in a precarious manner. Some people believe the towers collapsed after one slab fell down to the slab below, thereby starting a chain reaction. This has been called the "Pancake Theory" because the slabs of concrete pile on top of each other in a stack.

Concrete is used as a structural material in some bridges and buildings, but in the World Trade Center towers it was only a *flooring material*. The concrete was *not* holding the building together. Rather, the building was a 3-dimensional network of steel. Figure 3-12 is a view of two of the floors. The view is towards the windows, from a location near the core beams.

This diagram does not show all of the steel beams in the flooring. There was a similar set of trusses that ran perpendicular to the beams shown and connected to the columns on the other side of the tower. (The three purple lines along the right edge of the diagram show the direction and location of these criss-crossing trusses.) There were also diagonal braces at the ends of every truss to further stiffen them (two sets of these braces are shown as purple lines.)

Each floor was a network of steel beams, covered by corrugated steel deck, which in turn was filled with concrete. The trusses also held such items as heating and air-conditioning ducts, telephone lines, ceiling tiles, and electric power lines.

The concrete was 100mm (4 inches) thick, which gave it substantial strength, but to describe the floors as being "slabs of concrete" is as silly as describing the floors as "sheets of carpeting." The floors were **grids of steel**, or a **mesh** of steel. The concrete was just a filler to provide a flat and fireproof floor. Furthermore, these grids of steel were connected to the columns in a very sturdy manner.

The 47 core columns were also connected to each other by steel beams. The concrete in the floors in the core area was 125mm (5 inches) thick.

Trivia: the steel beams in the towers were so thick that American steel companies supposedly could not produce them. According to FEMA and other sources, nearly all the thick steel plate was produced in Japan.

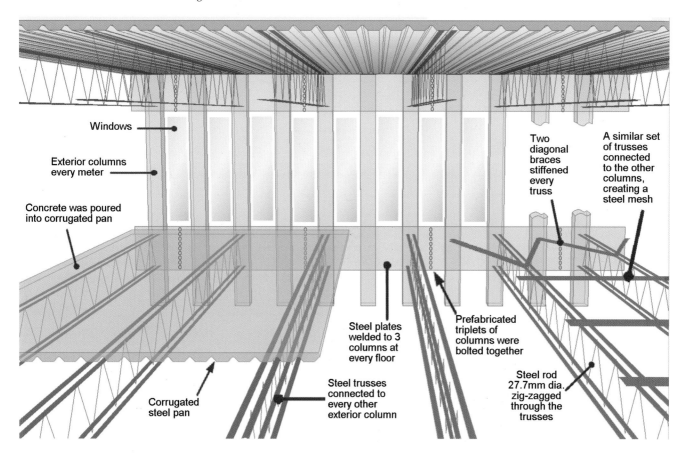

Figure 3-12 *This is a view of the flooring between the core and exterior columns. The view is from the core columns towards exterior columns.*

There were 56 exterior columns along each side of the tower. A truss connected to half of them, and diagonal braces connected the trusses to the other half. The trusses also connected to the 47 core columns. A similar set of trusses connected to the vertical steel columns created a steel mesh.

What Effect did the Fires Have? 4

The North Tower is hit first

Flight 11 crashed into the North Tower at 8:46 AM, hitting between floors 94 and 98. The hole created by the airplane (Figure 4-1) show that it broke through 45 of the exterior columns. The airplane was in the process of making a turn when it hit the tower, which is why the hole appears tilted.

FEMA's analysis of the hole shows that the fuselage and engines damaged three floors, but the wings did minimal damage to the structure of the tower. The last few feet at the tips of the wings did not even break through the exterior columns.

Was the airplane shredded?

Figure 4-2 shows that after the airplane broke through the exterior columns the fuselage was so large that it directly hit the edge of at least one floor. If the plane was slightly higher or lower than the diagram shows, or if the plane was tilted up or down, then the fuselage encountered two floors. The airplane is dimensionally accurate in these diagrams, and the objects and people inside the tower show the sizes of people and office furniture.

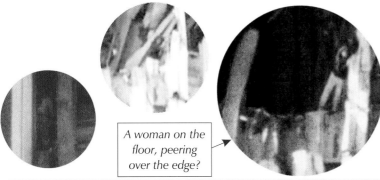

A woman on the floor, peering over the edge?

Figure 4-1   *The hole created by the airplane in the North Tower. The red arrows show people who were walking around in the area where 10,000 gallons of jet fuel were supposedly burning. The fire was not hot enough to kill people, but we are supposed to believe it was hot enough to cause the towers to disintegrate.*

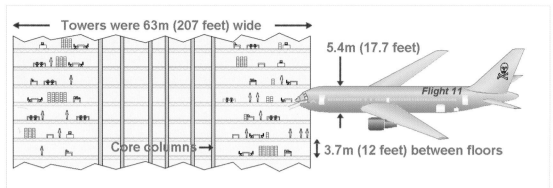

Figure 4-2   _The plane is horizontal (in the front to rear axis) in this diagram, but nobody knows its exact angle when it crashed. Normally an airplane is tilted slightly upward when flying._

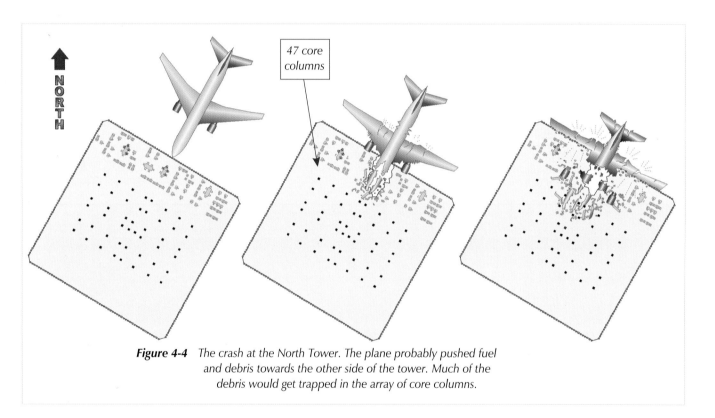

Figure 4-4   _The crash at the North Tower. The plane probably pushed fuel and debris towards the other side of the tower. Much of the debris would get trapped in the array of core columns._

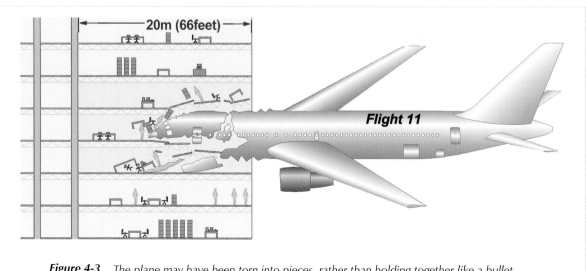

Figure 4-3   _The plane may have been torn into pieces, rather than holding together like a bullet._

The airplane was essentially a hollow aluminum bullet with a thin wall, and it was traveling at a low speed (low for a bullet). The floors were grids of steel, topped with a 100mm layer of concrete in a corrugated steel pan. The concrete was 125mm thick around the core columns. What happened when the airplane crashed into such large and sturdy floors? Was the plane sliced into a few large pieces? Or was it shredded into _thousands_ of pieces? Or did the airplane tear a hole in several floors and then come to rest inside the tower in almost one large piece, as bullets often remain in one piece?

Nobody will ever know what happened, but one of the landing wheel assemblies flew out the other side of the North Tower and ended up several streets away, with the rubber tire still clinging to the wheel. This shows that at least one piece of the airplane was torn off and passed though the maze of core columns, elevator shafts, and office furnishings. Since one piece tore off, we can assume other parts also tore off but never made it out the other side of the tower.

Figures 4-3 and 4-4 show my speculation in which the airplane was shredded into pieces in the North Tower, and Figure 4-5 shows the South Tower. I base my assumptions on other airplane crashes. Bullets are often recovered in one piece, but it is more common for airplanes to rip into pieces when they crash.

The plane swept flammable material to the core

The area between the core columns was mainly elevator shafts, with a few stairways, hallways, and maintenance rooms. Not much flammable material was in the core area.

However, the plane would act as a broom by sweeping the broken flooring, office furnishings, and pieces of aircraft towards the core. Some of the debris passed through the array of core columns to the other side of the tower, and a landing wheel flew out of the tower, but a lot of the debris must have been caught in the array of columns. Some of this debris was flammable, so the center of the tower may have been provided with a lot of fuel, in addition to the jet fuel that was sprayed in the area.

Did the airplane destroy any of the core columns?

It is possible that most of the fuselage was shredded as it passed through 20 meters of flooring. By the time the pieces made it to the core columns, they may not have had enough kinetic energy remaining to do any significant damage. For all we know, the airplane did not actually break or bend any of the core columns. In such a case, the collapse of the tower would not have been due to damage of the core columns.

It is also possible that the airplane was sliced into halves, and the bottom half, which had the thickest metal components, slid across the floor, slammed into some of the core columns at high speed, and destroyed several of them. In that case the destruction of those core columns may have played a significant role in the collapse.

Since nobody inspected the rubble, nobody knows how many core columns – if any – were damaged by the airplane. This shows one of the reasons we have laws requiring that the rubble from such disasters be saved for scientific analyses.

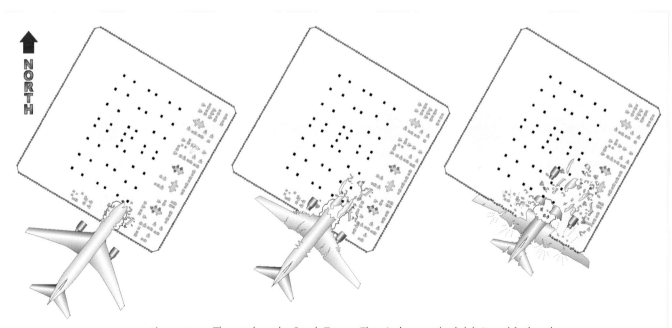

Figure 4-5 _The crash at the South Tower. The airplane pushed debris and fuel to the northeast corner. Not many core columns would have been damaged._

The North Tower survived the crash

The North Tower was quiet, stable, and motionless within a few dozen seconds after the plane crash. I am not aware of anybody making remarks about loud, creaking noises coming from the steel beams within the tower. Nor did anybody make remarks about loud noises caused by concrete floors breaking apart and falling down on the floors below it. The only noise was from the fire. There was no indication that the tower was in danger of collapsing. It appears that the airplane crash did not do enough damage by itself to cause the collapse. This would indicate that the collapse was due to the fires.

The South Tower is hit by an airplane

Flight 175 crashed into the South Tower at 9:03 AM, hitting between floors 78 and 84. This was 16 minutes after the North Tower was hit. This airplane hit near the edge of the tower at some unknown angle.

Figure 4-5 shows my speculation of what happened inside the tower. Photographs of the hole created by the plane show the point of impact, but photos do not show the exact angle of the plane, so the angle is my speculation. The diagram is merely to show what may have happened after the plane entered the tower.

The diagram shows the body of the airplane hitting two of the 47 core columns, but it is possible that the airplane hit only 1 column, or 7 columns, and it may have missed all columns. FEMA believes it "probable" that the airplane hit at least one column, but nobody knows for certain.

Regardless of the angle the plane hit, one of the engines entered the core area and may have damaged a core column. However, most of the aircraft entered the tower at a location where there were no core columns in its path, so

there was nothing to stop the pieces from flying through the office area. One engine and a piece of landing gear flew through the tower and came to rest several streets away. A portion of the fuselage (a piece with several passenger windows) flew through the tower and landed on top of Building 5.

The pieces of the airplane probably pushed office furnishings towards the northeast windows, as well as push flammable material into the core area. Jet fuel must have sprayed into the core area, also.

The Fireballs

The North Tower fireball

Some people assume the plane injected the North Tower with its full load of fuel, thereby creating an incredibly intense fire. However, a video taken at the time of the crash shows that a large amount of fuel burned outside of the tower. Figure 4-6 is a frame from that video. FEMA believes all the fuel entered the tower but some of it was blown out when it caught on fire inside the tower. Regardless of how the fireball was created, the photos show that some fuel did not contribute to the fires inside. It is also possible that some fuel went into elevator shafts and stairways, where it would not do much damage to the tower. Furthermore, the video shows a small fireball at the opposite side of the tower, which means some fuel passed through the tower.

The South Tower fireballs

This plane created two fireballs (or three, depending on how you count them). The smaller one was at the location where the plane hit the tower, and it was similar in size to the fireball at the North Tower. This would indicate that both fireballs consumed similar quantities of fuel.

The second fireball was along the "side" and "rear" of the tower. It actually began as two separate fireballs but quickly merged into one large fireball. Figure 4-7 shows the two fireballs after they merged.

How much fuel was lost in the fireballs?

FEMA does not go into much detail about the fireballs. Instead they assume each plane contained 10,000 gallons of fuel, and that all of the fireballs consumed perhaps 3,000 of the 20,000 total gallons. They do not bother to speculate on how much fuel remained in the South Tower, but their figures imply that an enormous amount of fuel remained inside both towers.

NAUDET JULES/GAMMA

Figure 4-6 *The fireball at the North Tower from the plane crash*

Despite the loss of fuel in fireballs, and despite any fuel lost down elevator shafts and stairways, an enormous amount of fuel remained inside the North Tower. This would create a fire much more severe than an office building normally experiences. Not surprisingly, photos of the North tower show fires and large quantities of smoke on several floors (Figure 4-8 is one example). People above the fire zone were jumping out of windows because the smoke was so thick and the fire so extensive that they could not use the stairways to get below the fire zone or up to the roof. It would appear as if the fires in the North Tower could support the theory that the fire damaged the structure of the tower, thereby contributing to or causing its collapse.

However, the situation with the South Tower was significantly different. Even if most of the fuel remained inside the South Tower, as the FEMA report suggests, photographs show that the fire never spread beyond a small section of the crash zone. The fires remained on one side of the tower, and only on a few floors. Compared to the fires in the North Tower, these were small fires. Rather than jump out of the windows, some of the people in the South Tower who were above the fire walked down the stairs. The fire was not their problem; rather, smoke and darkness was their problem.

The Raging Fires

Most experts believe fire caused both towers to collapse, but the fire in the South Tower does not appear to be any worse than hundreds of other fires in office buildings. Could such a small fire cause the South Tower to collapse when so many other office buildings survived fires that spanned more floors and which burned for a longer period of time? Or was the fire worse than it appears from the outside?

The North Tower fires were severe, but were they severe enough to destroy the tower?

Figure 4-7 *The South Tower fireball. The plane came in from the left side of this photo. The red arrow points to the Black Hole in the North Tower created by the airplane crash.*

The fires could melt aluminum?

Aluminum melts at 660°C. If FEMA's temperature estimates are correct, the interiors of the towers were _furnaces_ capable of casting aluminum and glazing pottery; they were not ordinary office fires. From the FEMA report:

> _The modeling also suggests ceiling gas temperatures of 1,000°C (1,800°F), with an estimated confidence of plus or minus 100°C (200°F) or about 900–1,100°C (1,600–2,000°F)._

> _Temperatures may have been as high as 900–1,100°C (1,700–2,000°F) in some areas and 400–800°C (800–1,500°F) in others._

Did the fires produce enough heat?

While the experts may be correct that the fire reached 1,100°C, a fire will not damage a building unless it can produce enough _heat_. Consider the difference between an

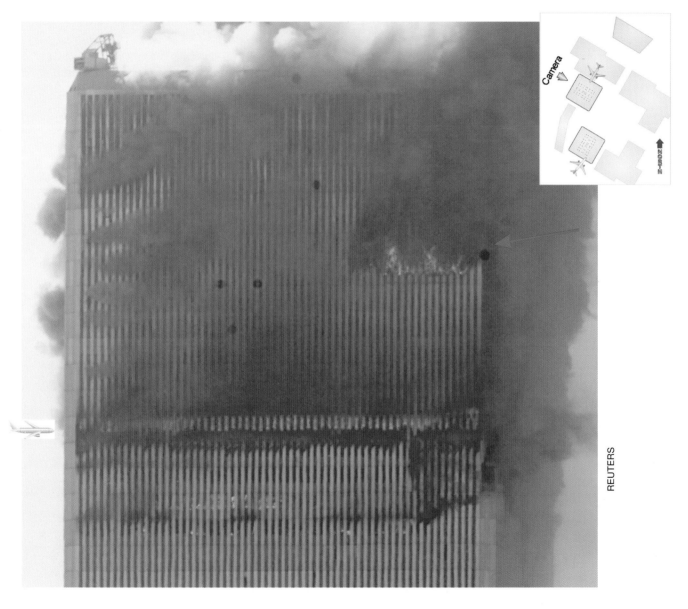

Figure 4-8   _The North Tower. The tiny airplane indicates the location of the crash and the direction the plane was traveling. The plane pushed debris and fuel to the other side of the tower (towards the right, in this view) This may be why the fires seem more extreme towards the right side. The red arrow points to the largest flames in the North Tower, but it is 6 or 7 floors above the crash zone. Why isn't the crash zone burning like that? Where are the flames from the 10,000 gallons of jet fuel?_

electric toaster and an electric light bulb to understand the difference between heat and temperature. Both devices send electricity through a metal filament in order to raise the temperature of that filament. The difference between them is that a lightbulb produces an extremely *high temperature,* whereas a toaster produces *a lot of heat.*

It is possible for a lightbulb to produce as much heat as a toaster if the lightbulb is very large or if 50 light bulbs are turned on at the same time. This shows that the quantity of heat can be increased simply by adding more sources of the heat. However, the temperature cannot be increased simply by adding more sources of the temperature. For example, a very large toaster will *not* produce the same high temperature as a lightbulb, nor will turning 50 toasters on at the same time produce the same high temperature as one tiny lightbulb.

The temperature of the fire in the World Trade Center was due to the chemical process involved in the oxidation of hydrogen and carbon. That chemical process occurs at a certain temperature regardless of how much fuel is burning. Increasing the quantity of fuel will *not* increase the temperature of that chemical process; rather, it will only increase the amount of heat that is being created. The only thing that affects the temperature of a fire is the material that is burning. For example, carbon produces a higher temperature than hydrogen.

The experts claim the fire raised the temperature of the steel to 340°C or higher. While the burning of hydrogen and carbon will produce temperatures that high, raising the temperature of dozens of massive steel beams to 340°C requires a lot of heat be produced for a long period of time. Consider a lightbulb to understand this concept. A lightbulb produces temperatures that are beyond the melting point of steel, but none of the steel beams melted when employees inside the World Trade Center turned on light bulbs. The reason is that a lightbulb does not produce much heat. A lightbulb does not even produce enough heat to melt itself.

On the morning of September 11th employees in the North Tower turned on hundreds of light bulbs on almost every floor. The filaments and plasmas in those bulbs produced temperatures of thousands of degrees, just as if they were tiny, extremely high-temperature fires. Those bulbs caused the temperature inside the tower to increase, exactly as fires raise the temperature. However, none of the steel inside the tower became weak from those high-temperature bulbs. The reason is that the bulbs did *not produce enough heat.*

The burning of jet fuel, office furniture, and carpeting will produce flames that have a temperature above 340°C. However, *the temperature of the flames is irrelevant.* The plasma in a fluorescent bulb is at a temperature beyond the melting point of every object in the universe, but none of that plasma has vaporized any of us yet. Likewise, the temperature of the flames in the World Trade Center is meaningless. The important issues are:

1) **How much heat** was generated.

2) For **how long of a period of time** was the heat in contact with the steel.

The burning of *one* office desk would *not* have damaged the structure of the North Tower. The tower was so massive that the burning of *two* office desks would not be able to weaken its structure, either, even if some carpeting and paper was also burned. In order for the steel structure to become 340°C, the fire would have to produce thousands of times as much heat as all the light bulbs, computer monitors, coffee makers, and microwave ovens that were turned on each day.

Another way to look at this issue is to consider that the burning of an office desk is equivalent to turning on a certain number of coffee machines or light bulbs. For example, the burning of a typical desk may be equivalent to turning on 60 computers for one hour. This makes it easy to realize that a lot more than one office desk must burn in order for a fire to damage a steel building. The burning of jet fuel is equivalent to brewing pots of coffee.

A possible reason some people are confused by these issues is that they assume a fire that is dangerous to people is also damaging to steel. The people who jumped out of the North Tower created the illusion that the fire was extreme, but people can be devastated by the smoke from a tiny fire of burning plastic, and temperatures of boiling water kill us quickly. However, an office fire would have to be phenomenal to damage thick steel beams.

Did the fires have enough time?

Let's assume there was enough jet fuel to completely melt the entire tower. Unfortunately, heat will not affect an object unless it is applied for a certain amount of *time.* You can see this effect if you have a stove that burns gas. The flames in a stove are much hotter than the fires of the North Tower because a stove mixes the fuel and air in perfect proportions, but you can safely pass your fingers through those hot flames if you move them quickly.

A lot of jet fuel was mixed with air when the planes crashed into the towers, and an enormous amount of heat was generated when it burned. However, that jet fuel burned so rapidly that it was just a momentary blast of hot air. The blast would have set fire to flammable objects, killed people, and broken windows, but it could not have raised the temperature of a massive steel structure by a significant amount. A fire will not affect steel unless the steel is exposed to it for a long enough period of time for the heat to penetrate. The more massive the steel beams are, the more time that is needed.

The South Tower fire was smaller and had less time

The airplane hit about 15 floors lower in the South Tower. The structural columns were thicker at this location, so the fire in the South Tower had to produce *more heat* than the fire in the North Tower in order to raise the columns to the *same temperature* as in the North Tower. However, the fires in the South Tower were *smaller*. Furthermore, the South Tower collapsed after the fires burned for only 56 minutes, whereas the North Tower fires burned for 103 minutes.

How did the small fires cause the South Tower to collapse in only 56 minutes while more intense fires in the North Tower burned for twice as long in an area where the steel was thinner? Also consider the 1991 Meridian Plaza fire in Philadelphia. That fire was so extreme that flames came out of dozens of windows on many floors, and it burned for 19 hours. The building was damaged, but it never collapsed.

Fire has *never* caused a steel building to collapse, so how did a 56 minute fire bring down a steel building as strong as the South Tower? It takes more than 56 minutes to cook a turkey. Only an incredible fire could destroy such a massive steel structure in 56 minutes. This implies that either the fire was indeed incredible but I am too much of a dimwit to realize it, or the fire had only a small effect on the collapse, if it had any effect at all.

Did any of the fireproofing function?

Both the core and exterior columns were protected with fireproofing materials. The airplanes certainly destroyed some of the fireproofing, but some columns would have retained all or most of their fireproofing. Also, gypsum drywall provides a small amount of fireproofing, and it was used throughout the tower. The fireproofing materials supposedly provide one or two hours of protection during "normal" fires. Although these were not normal fires, the fireproofing should have protected the South Tower from a 56 minute fire.

Since the North Tower fire burned for only 103 minutes, the columns that retained their fireproofing should have been protected to some extent. Only the few columns that were stripped of their fireproofing could possibly have reached a significant temperature from such a short-duration fire. The fire would have to be both high in temperature *and* producing an extremely large amount of heat in order to get through the fireproofing material in less than two hours.

Did the fires have enough fuel?

People on the ground smelled jet fuel because some of it never burned. Of the fuel that burned, a lot of soot was produced because of the lack of oxygen, which means some

of its energy was wasted. It also seems that much of the jet fuel burned up within a few minutes. This means that if the steel reached high temperatures, the heat had to come from the jet fuel that survived beyond the first few minutes, such as the fuel that soaked into carpeting and other items, and from the burning of office furnishings and airplane parts. Was there enough flammable material available to the fire to destroy the tower?

The companies that rented space in those towers could certainly come up with an estimate of the quantity of flammable material in the crash zone, and that would allow physicists to determine if there was enough energy in those objects to heat the steel structure to 340°C. It is possible that there was not enough jet fuel, wooden desks, computers, and other flammable objects in the crash zone to raise the temperature of the structure to even 120°C.

The debris suppressed the fire

As seen in Figures 4-3 and 4-5, a lot of debris from the broken flooring may have been pushed into the core area. Each airplane also added perhaps 80 tons of metal and glass to the inside of the towers. This large amount of nonflammable debris would significantly hurt the fires by interfering with the flow of air. For all we know, some of the hallways in the core had been packed so tight with debris that air barely moved through the area.

The debris would also absorb some of the heat from the fire, which would reduce the amount of heat available for the steel structure. If there were only a few tons of debris, it would be insignificant, but there was about 80 tons of nonflammable aircraft pieces, and perhaps many tons of broken flooring. The enormous quantity of aluminum would be an efficient heat sink, and the flooring pieces would absorb some heat, also.

Some people believe that the fire was producing so much heat that aluminum had melted. However, in order to melt a significant quantity of aluminum, the debris touching that aluminum would have to heat up to the same high temperature. This requires the fire to produce even more heat than would be necessary to melt only the aluminum.

Furthermore, if some of the heat from the fire was going towards the melting of aluminum, that means some of the heat was *not* going towards raising the temperature of the steel structure. Therefore, anybody who promotes the theory that aluminum was melting must explain how the fire could produce so much heat that it could both melt aluminum *and* raise the temperature of tons of debris, *and* still have enough heat remaining to raise the temperature of the steel structure. Where did this enormous quantity of heat come from? From the burning of a few dozen office desks, some carpeting, and some office papers? Many people believe that the jet fuel provided most of the necessary energy, but if the jet fuel was burning, where are the flames? Where is the light from the fire? How can 10,000 gallons of jet fuel burn without flames?

Why did the flames vanish so quickly?

The jet fuel created spectacular fireballs when the airplanes crashed, but within a few minutes most of the flames had vanished. Compared to the Meridian Plaza fire and other office fires, the fires in the towers had very few flames. Was the fire so deep inside the tower that the flames could not be seen?

The lack of flames is an indication that the fires were small, and the dark smoke is an indication that the fires were suffocating. The experts believe the fire was producing so much heat that it weakened the structure of the tower. However, the soot and lack of flames can be used as evidence that the fires were suffering from such a lack of oxygen that they were not capable of damaging such a massive steel structure.

The World Trade Center's "Black Holes"

Figure 4-1 (page 27) shows a close-up of the hole in the North Tower. While the photographer was far away and using a telephoto lens (which causes a fuzzy image), it lets us look into the tower to see what was happening in the crash zone. It lets us see how many of the concrete floors were broken, and how severe the fire was. Unfortunately, the hole is black, not brightly colored with flames of a fire. We cannot see inside the hole.

The photograph in Figure 4-9 was taken before the South Tower was hit, so it was less than 16 minutes after the airplane crashed into the North Tower, but the hole is black in that photo, also. Furthermore, every other photograph of the hole shows it to be black. There are only a few flames in few windows.

Figure 4-8 (page 32) shows a different side of the tower. Although a few flames are visible along one floor, most of the tower is dark. Could those fires be capable of melting aluminum and heating dozens of massive steel beams to 340°C or higher? Or was the fire raging in the center of the tower where we cannot see it?

When I first saw the Black Holes I dismissed them as the result of amateurs with inexpensive, automatic cameras. Figure 4-9 is an example. The image is tilted, blurry, and the photo was posted on the Internet without any identification of the photographer. This photo would bring me to the conclusion that the Black Hole was due to the lousy camera and the lousy photographer.

When I began putting this book together I started searching for the source of the photographs and I discovered that many are from professionals. However, the professional photographs do not show any more flames than the amateur photographs, and the holes are just as black. It is unlikely that every professional photographer made the same mistake in his aperture settings. These black holes, therefore, should not be dismissed as goofs by the photographer. There is a reason these holes are black; the reason is there is _no fire near the hole._

Another interesting thing to notice in these photos is that a breeze is blowing towards the hole. This would provide oxygen to the fire in the hole, which would allow the fire near the hole to burn better compared to the fires deep inside the tower. However, there is no sign of fire at this location. Since the fire was insignificant where oxygen is plentiful, what are the chances that a severe fire was burning around the core columns, where the smoke should be much thicker and where debris may have reduced the flow of air?

Flames can be seen along some windows, but not inside the tower. This could be a sign that the only significant fires were the ones next to broken windows. The fires deep inside the tower may have been barely surviving.

**Unknown **

Figure 4-9 *The South Tower has not been hit, so this Black Hole developed in less than 16 minutes.*

The North Tower fires were suffocating

It is commonly known that a fire can be extinguished by spraying it with water or certain chemicals, but it is not commonly known that an excellent method of suppressing a fire is to shut all the windows and doors to reduce oxygen and cause the smoke to accumulate. Another method of suppressing a fire is to dump nonflammable material on it, such as dirt, broken glass, and scraps of metal. The fire in the North Tower was suppressed in both ways:

- **Debris**. The aircraft dumped 80 tons of nonflammable aircraft pieces into the crash zone, and it busted some of the flooring into pieces, which created more nonflammable debris. This enormous quantity of debris must have absorbed significant amounts of heat, and it would have interfered with the flow of air.

- **Sealed windows.** The windows were sealed shut, so the only oxygen available to the fire was whatever blew in from the few broken windows and the hole created by the airplane. Some air would also have passed through the elevator shafts and stairways. There was obviously enough air flowing to keep a fire burning, but was there enough of a flow to maintain a fire so incredible that it could cause a steel structure to crumble?

The dark smoke and lack of flames is an indication that the fires did not have enough oxygen to burn properly. There were flames along some windows, but deep inside the North Tower, where the core columns were, the fire may have been barely surviving its own smoke, *if it was burning in the core at all*. For all we know, the fire in the core area was extinguished after ten minutes.

Where was the red light?

In an area that was not full of jet fuel there would be only a few scattered fires (Figure 4-10). In this diagram the air is cool because the fire has just started.

The smoke from the fire would cool down quickly as it spread along the ceiling because it would transfer its heat to the air and the ceiling. Items low to the floor, such as desks, would not be affected by the fire because they would be in the zone of cooler air. The steel columns would not be affected by the fire, either, because the smoke would be cool by the time it reached them. The columns that had been sprayed with jet fuel would be in close contact with high temperature flames, but even in that situation the hot flames would rise to the ceiling. My point is that the *air* and the *ceiling* would reach high temperatures before the columns.

As the air continued to heat up, items lower to the floor would eventually catch on fire, as illustrated by the burning computer (Figure 4-11). Flames would appear at more

windows. Every flammable object would eventually catch on fire. Therefore, photos should show the fires *spreading throughout the entire floor*. However, only one floor in North Tower appeared completely on fire (Figure 4-8). The fires on the other floors did not spread throughout the floor, nor were flames visible in many windows. Rather, the flames diminished over time. This implies the air temperature on all but one floor of the North Tower was *below the ignition temperature of plastic and paper*. Therefore, only the columns in that one floor are likely to have reached high temperatures.

As the fires continued to burn, the air along the ceiling would eventually be hot enough to roast the tops of the windows while the bottom of the windows remained considerably cooler. Since most windows are made of an inexpensive glass that cannot resist uneven temperature changes, windows tend to shatter from fires. Therefore, photos should show windows shattering as time passed. Photos do indeed show broken windows on many floors, but some of those windows broke from the airplane crash or the blast created by the fireballs. Some were also broken by people in a desperate attempt to get fresh air.

Only one floor of the North Tower shows signs of reaching a significant temperature. The tower was so tall that photos do not clearly show the windows of the crash zone, so it is possible that many of the windows along that floor (Figure 4-8) were shattered by the fire. However, photos of the front of that floor (e.g., Figure 4-1) do not show signs of windows shattered from high temperatures. Since the fire could not even crack the glass through the entire floor, and flames cannot be seen in the hole, how could the fire have produced enough heat to cause a steel structure to crumble?

If FEMA's 1,000°C estimate is anywhere near correct, all aluminum objects near the ceiling would have melted, and so would many aircraft pieces. Pottery furnaces operate at that temperature. There should have been pools of molten aluminum inside the towers. However, if the fire did not have enough time to melt aluminum, or if the fire did not produce enough heat to melt aluminum, how did the fire have enough time and heat to raise the temperature of the thick steel columns to such an extreme that the tower crumbled?

Finally, objects at 1,000°C glow such a bright red that the red light is clearly visible in sunlight, and they produce enormous amounts of infrared radiation (heat). Therefore, photos should show the ceiling glowing red, and the infrared radiation would roast everything in the area. Since each ceiling was also a floor, fires should break out on the floors above. So why does the inside of the tower appear black instead of red? How can such extreme temperatures be so invisible? Why didn't the fire spread to other floors?

FEMA's estimate of 1,000°C at the ceiling may be correct for the first few seconds when the jet fuel ignited, but there is

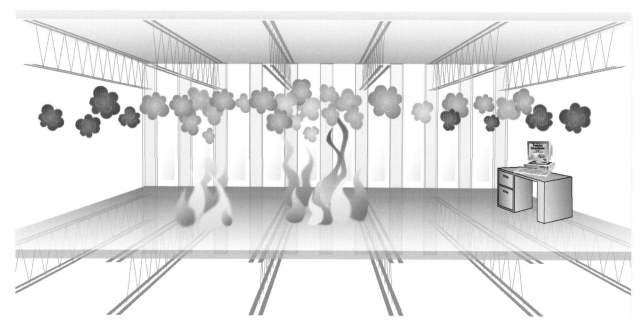

Figure 4-10   *Everything in the room was cool when the fires started. The hot smoke cooled down quickly as it warmed the air and ceiling. Objects near the floor remained cool.
(The cool temperature of the smoke is illustrated with a dark color.)*

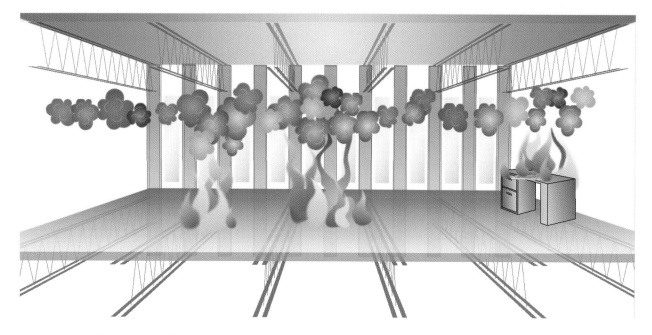

Figure 4-11   *Over time the temperature of the air in the crash zone would increase, and so would the ceiling.* **The fire should spread as a result.**

From the FEMA report: "The modeling also suggests ceiling gas temperatures of 1,000°C (1,800°F)"
Such a high temperature would melt aluminum and cause everything to **glow a bright red that is visible in sunlight.** *Why didn't the windows shatter from such an intense fire? Why don't photos show any of the red light?*

no evidence that such high temperatures persisted for any significant period of time. There is not even any evidence to support the estimates of 600°C.

The Exterior Columns remained cool

A significant amount of the strength in the towers came from the exterior columns. Considering that only one of their four sides was in contact with the inside of the tower, and considering that the fires near the windows were small, it is unlikely that the exterior columns could have reached a high temperature. This means that the exterior columns would have retained their strength throughout the fire. This in turn means the breaking of the exterior columns cannot be blamed on the fire.

The South Tower fires seem insignificant

Photos of the South Tower show fires that are much less intense than those of the North Tower. Despite this, FEMA suggests the possibility that something melted:

> *This videotape suggests that, in the minutes immediately preceding the collapse, the most intensive fires occurred along the north face of the building, near the 80th floor level. Just prior to the collapse, a stream of molten material—possibly aluminum from the airliner— was seen streaming out of a window opening at the northeast corner at approximately this level.*

The video that FEMA refers to was taken at the offices of Skidmore, Owings & Merrill LLP (SOM) at 14 Wall Street, which is just a few blocks away from the South Tower. FEMA was allowed to view this video, but when I sent an e-mail request to SOM to buy a copy of the tape, the curt response was:

> *We need to know for what is it going to be used.*

I never heard from them again. Why the secrecy for a video that supports our government's theory that a fire caused the collapse?

FEMA says the molten material came out of the *northeast corner* of the tower. As Figure 4-5 shows, the airplane swept a lot debris to the northeast corner, including lots of airplane pieces. There would be plenty of aluminum in the area to melt, but I do not see any evidence in the photos of a fire capable of melting visible quantities of aluminum. However, there would be more than 2,300 kilograms of human body parts in that corner from both the airline passengers and the office workers. Their body fluids and fat could explain

FEMA's "stream of molten material," and it would explain why the video is a secret.

Why didn't fires spread in the South Tower?

In order for the fires in the South Tower to heat the core columns to a significant temperature, a lot of hot gas from the fire had to travel along the ceiling to the core columns. Since the columns were thick, the flow of hot gas would have to continue for some period of time. However, a large flow of hot gas would set fire to everything flammable in the ceiling (such as the plastic of electrical wires, lights, and cables). The hot gas would eventually set fire to papers and other objects that were near the ceiling, and later it would set fire to items lower to the floor, such as the plastic in computers monitors (Figure 4-11).

Photographs of the South Tower should show the fire spreading throughout the area as time passed. However, photos show the spectacular flames vanished quickly, and then the fire remained restricted to one area of the tower. Rather than spreading throughout the area, the fires slowly diminished. How could a fire produce such incredible quantities of heat that it could destroy a steel building, while at the same time it is incapable of spreading beyond its initial starting location? The photos show that *not even one floor* in the South Tower was above the ignition temperature of plastic and paper!

Why didn't the windows around the crash zone break from this incredible fire? The photos show the fire was not even powerful enough to crack glass!

Why do photos show only sooty smoke and black holes, such as Figure 4-12? Why is there no evidence of an intense fire in *any* photograph? How can anybody claim the fires were the reason the South Tower collapsed when the fires appear so small?

Fire has *never* caused a collapse

The fire in the office building at One Meridian Plaza in Philadelphia in 1991 was so intense that it damaged the structure of the building. As FEMA's 1991 report describes it:

> *After the fire, there was evident significant structural damage to horizontal steel members and floor sections on most of the fire damaged floors. Beams and girders sagged and twisted —some as much as three feet —under severe fire exposures, and fissures developed in the reinforced concrete floor assemblies in many places. Despite this extraordinary exposure, the columns continued to support their loads without obvious damage.*

The Meridian Plaza fire was extreme, but it did not cause the building to collapse. The fire in the South Tower seems insignificant by comparison to both the Meridian Plaza fire and the fire in the North Tower. How could the tiny fire in the South Tower cause the entire structure to shatter into dust after 56 minutes while much more extreme fires did not cause the Meridian Plaza building to even crack into two pieces? And why did the North Tower handle a larger fire for twice as long?

There is no support for the "Hot Fire Theory"

The most popular theory is that fire destroyed the towers by weakening the steel with high temperatures. The point of this chapter is that the fires seem too insignificant to support such a theory.

Many people believe the fire destroyed the towers when the naked steel beams were exposed directly to intensely hot flames. First, the columns were not naked. Rather, most of them were protected against such small, short duration fires. Figure 4-5 shows that flying debris in the South Tower may have destroyed some of the fireproofing around some core

Figure 4-12 *This photograph was taken slightly before the one in Figure 4-7. There are only a few flames in the North Tower, and the smoke is very dark. The fires have been burning for only 16 minutes but already most flames have vanished. Why didn't the fire grow over time?*

columns, but most columns certainly retained all of their fireproofing. Therefore, only a few core columns are likely to have become warm from a 56 minute fire.

Second, the fires were not producing much heat. Even if every core column had been stripped of its fireproofing, massive steel columns will not reach high temperatures in only 56 minutes from fires that are incapable of spreading to other flammable office furnishings. If the fires were capable of raising steel beams to a high temperature, the fires would have also raised the computers, wooden desks, and other flammable materials to high temperatures, which would have caused fires to spread throughout the floor.

The sooty smoke and the black holes in the towers cannot be dismissed as interesting aspects of the fires, nor as problems with the photography. Rather, they are signs that the air flow was so restricted that the only significant fires were near broken windows. The fires in both towers were probably coating the columns with soot rather than heating the columns to a high temperature.

It does not appear that the fire in *either* tower was capable of raising the temperature of the core or exterior columns to a high enough temperature to cause the steel to lose strength. The flames are nearly invisible even when a photo is brightened (Figure 4-13).

Damage from thermal expansion is possible

Thermal expansion is a serious problem for many products. Bridges, sidewalks, and buildings are designed to cope with it, but only to a certain extent. If some steel beams in the towers increased to 90 or 140°C they would not have lost any strength, but they would have expanded, which would cause them to push against other beams. If they expanded more than the structure was capable of dealing with, then the fire would have damaged the structure.

Thermal expansion can cause a structure to break into pieces but, as the next chapter shows, the towers shattered into dust rather than cracking into pieces. Therefore, the *Collapse by Thermal Expansion* theory seems unlikely.

AP/Wide World Photo

Figure 4-13   *The North Tower 30 seconds before it collapsed. The only serious fire is the same fire the red arrow points to in Figure 4-8. This fire is high above the crash zone, and only in one small section of that floor. The crash zone is darker than it ever was, and I brightened the image to make the flames more visible.*

Three Buildings Collapse

5

Did the South Tower collapse sooner due to the heavier load?

Both towers survived the airplane crashes, and slowly the flames were replaced by wisps of dark smoke. With hundreds of firemen rushing into the towers it seemed that the fires would soon be extinguished and the nightmare would be over. However, the South Tower suddenly collapsed 56 minutes after the airplane crash. About 40 minutes later the North Tower suddenly collapsed, which was 103 minutes after the airplane crashed into it. Why did the South Tower collapse so soon after the airplane crash?

The portion of the tower above the crash zone was about twice the size in the South Tower (Figure 5-1). Many people, FEMA included, believe the weight of this section caused the South Tower to collapse first. However, the steel columns in the crash zone of the South Tower were thicker in order to handle the heavier load above them. Therefore, the increase in weight above the South Tower's crash zone should have been compensated for by the increase in thickness of the steel columns.

A computer simulation might help us understand this issue. The MSC Software Corporation performed a

Figure 5-1

The section above the crash zone was twice the size in the South Tower; about 30 floors compared to 15 floors in the North Tower.

Flames are visible in this photo, but the hole in the North Tower is already black.

simulation, and a few of their images (Figure 5-2) ended up in the report produced by the House Science Committee on March 6, 2002. Unfortunately, as with most of the investigation, their analysis was not funded, so they used what was readily available to them, which happened to be a 747 crashing into a structure that had floors taller than the airplane. Since their simulation doesn't help us understand what happened when the 767 airplanes hit the World Trade Center, why were they included in the report? Was somebody trying to impress us?

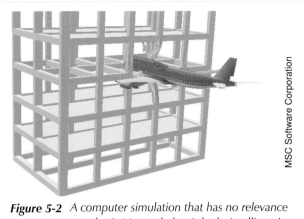

Figure 5-2 *A computer simulation that has no relevance to the 9-11 attack, but it looks intelligent!*

What caused the South Tower to collapse?

FEMA does not explain the collapse of the South Tower. Rather, they have a vague remark that the collapse was probably similar to the North Tower:

> *The same types of structural behaviors and failure mechanisms previously discussed are equally likely to have occurred in WTC 2*

So let's look at FEMA's explanation of the collapse of the North Tower.

The Pancake Theory

FEMA agrees with many experts who believe the collapse began when fire caused steel beams to expand, which then lead to the breaking of joints. FEMA has two diagrams in their report to explain this. The first diagram (Figure 5-3A) has the title *"Expansion of floor slabs and framing results in outward deflection of columns and potential overload."* It shows the fire heating the floor above it, and the expansion of that floor is pushing against the exterior and core columns, causing them to deflect.

How many millimeters did the columns deflect? The towers were designed to be flexible enough to sway in storms, so a small deflection would be insignificant. Was the deflection beyond the design limits of the tower? Unfortunately, FEMA does not provide such details, nor any supporting evidence for their diagram.

FEMA's second diagram (Figure 5-3B) shows a floor falling down. This diagram makes it appears as if the floor was held to the columns at only two locations, but the floors were *grids of steel* (Figure 3-12). In order for a floor to fall, *hundreds* of joints had to break almost simultaneously on 236 exterior columns and 47 core columns. FEMA does not bother to explain how this could occur.

FEMA believes the first floor to break started a chain reaction when it hit the floor below it by breaking the joints holding that floor. This resulted in two floors that were falling, which then broke the floor below them, and so on. FEMA refers to this as *"a pancake-type collapse of successive floors."* (Professor Bazant promoted this Pancake Theory for the North Tower, so maybe FEMA got the idea from him.)

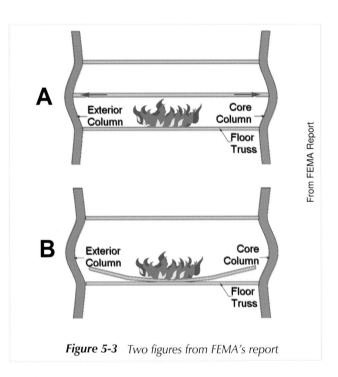

Figure 5-3 *Two figures from FEMA's report*

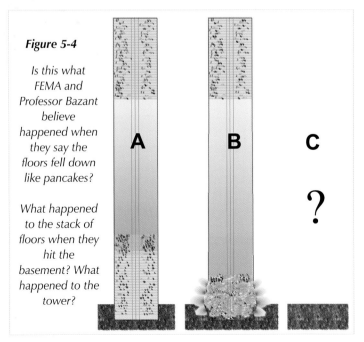

Figure 5-4

Is this what FEMA and Professor Bazant believe happened when they say the floors fell down like pancakes?

What happened to the stack of floors when they hit the basement? What happened to the tower?

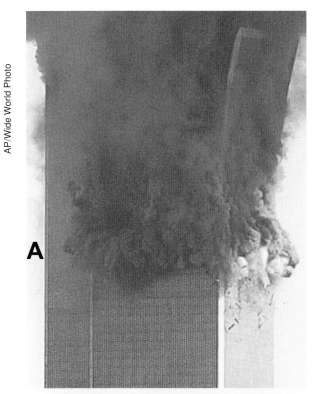

A

B

C

Figure 5-5 *The South Tower tips*

FEMA does not explain what finally happened to the stack of floors when they hit the basement, so it is up to us to fill in the missing details. Figures 5-4A & 5-4B show my guess at what FEMA's next two diagrams would look like if they had bothered to adequately explain their Pancake Theory. My guess is that the stack of floors broke into pieces and spread out into the basement and onto the ground. I leave it to the readers to guess at what Figure 5-4C would look like.

The top of South Tower cracks and tips

The first visible event in the collapse of the South Tower was the tipping of the top section towards the crash zone (Figure 5-5). This top section is about 300 feet tall. This enormous section begins falling over.

It appears as if the process began when some columns near the crash zone broke or buckled. This is shown in Figure 5-6A as a large crack. (The three vertical, red lines in the center of this tower represent the core columns.) The exterior columns on the other side of the tower were probably intact at that moment in time. The end result was an unbalanced force which caused the upper portion to tip towards the crash zone (Figure 5-6B).

Photographs of this tipping of the South Tower do not support the Pancake Theory. Furthermore, photos of the rubble do not show a pile of flooring anywhere, nor any large pieces of flooring, concrete, or steel trusses. All steel in the trusses broke at their joints, and all the concrete shattered into small particles. The rubble does not even show signs of office desks, furniture, or computers. Why would FEMA claim the collapses of the North and South Tower are similar when photos show them to be different? Why would FEMA claim the floors fell like pancakes when photos show otherwise?

Does the Pancake Theory explain the collapse of the *North* Tower? How would we know when FEMA doesn't bother to adequately explain it? Is FEMA trying to explain the collapse, or are they merely trying to pacify us? Or did somebody interfere with their investigation?

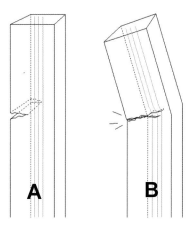

Figure 5-6

The South Tower tipped when columns on one side broke.

A　　**B**

The top section is severed from the base

When the tipping first started, the core and exterior columns on the opposite side of the crash zone were intact, so the tower was still in one piece. However, the top section began falling downward almost immediately after the tipping had begun. The only way the top could fall is if all the remaining columns had broken a few moments after the tipping began (or the joints connecting the columns had broken). The top section then became an independent object that fell onto the base (I will refer to the bottom portion as the "base"). I would have expected the top section to fall off and hit the ground (Figure 5-7), but Figures 5-8 and 5-9 show the top section disintegrated at the junction between itself and the base.

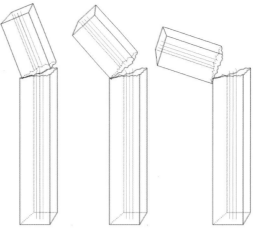

Figure 5-7 *If the columns broke at the crash zone I would expect the top to fall off.*

Figure 5-8 *The top section of South Tower is shattering into dust*

Clouds of concrete

Prior to the collapse only small wisps of black smoke were seeping from the tower and rising upward. When the top section began to tip, enormous clouds were expelled horizontally out of the tower, all around the crash zone. These clouds were not the smoke of a fire. Rather, something was occurring inside the tower to create large amounts of powder, and then expel that powder at high velocity. What could the powder be?

The US Geological Survey analyzed the powder on the streets of Manhattan after these buildings collapsed. Their analysis showed the powder to be primarily concrete and gypsum.

What was occurring at the crash zone to convert the concrete and gypsum to powder? Gypsum is a soft material so it is easy to believe that the gypsum was crushed to powder during the collisions of such massive pieces of building, especially the gypsum that was roasted in the fire. However, concrete does not turn to powder very easily, even if it is roasted in a fire.

AP/Wide World Photo

Figure 5-9 *About ½ of the top section of South Tower has shattered*

Figure 5-10 *The top section of the South Tower has tipped to about 22°. The top of the tower is hanging over the base by about 23 meters in this photo.*

Light and dark clouds of concrete

The clouds of dust in Figures 5-8 and 5-9 are almost all the same shade of gray. These clouds are coming from the "back side" of the tower (the side opposite the crash zone). Photos that give a better view of the crash zone (Figure 5-10) show the clouds above the crash zone are dark, and the clouds below are light.

The upper clouds are mixed with the black smoke from the fire, while the lower clouds are pure concrete, gypsum, and whatever else has been pulverized. The white clouds show that the pulverizing process is occurring in the portion of the tower that is below the fire zone. This was the area of the tower that was cool, so the steel and concrete in that area were still at their maximum strength, but the structure shattered anyway.

The disintegration went to the ground

The tilted portion of the tower was about 30 floors tall, so it was massive; Professor Bazant estimated it was 87 million kg.† A popular explanation for what happened is that the collision of these two massive structures caused all steel beams to break at their joints and a lot of concrete to shatter into powder. However, while dropping such a massive piece of building onto another building is certain to create incredible destruction, I would expect the top to fall off, as in Figure 5-7.

The top did not fall off; instead, it shattered, as if it were made of talcum powder. In Figure 5-10 the top section has disintegrated to perhaps half its original size. Since the disintegration is occurring only at the junction where the base and the top section are colliding, the people inside the top section were still alive when that photo was taken.

I would expect the disintegration to stop as soon as the top section had completely shattered. After the dust settled I would expect to see a jagged base with a pile of dust and rubble on the top. However, the base did not remain standing; rather, it continued to shatter until the entire structure was gone. Obviously, once the disintegration process got started, nothing was going to stop it.

By the time the photo in Figure 5-10 was taken, millions of kilograms of debris from the top section had fallen onto the base. A popular explanation for why the base disintegrated is that the enormous weight of the debris shattered the floors of the base section, and as each floor shattered, the debris accumulated, making it easier to shatter the next floor.

---

† To understand how large the top section was, a 30 story building that is 63 meters (207 ft) on each side would be considered *enormous* if it were placed in most cities. Yet this was just the upper portion of the South Tower!

The experts don't explain the South Tower

The FEMA diagram of one floor falling down, thereby starting a chain reaction (Figure 5-3B), is how most people explain the collapse of the towers, but this does *not* adequately explain what happened with the South Tower. A floor in the South Tower *may* have fallen onto another floor, but there was more going on inside the South Tower than that.

The floors in the South Tower did not simply "fall down" like a stack of pancakes; rather, every one of the hundreds of columns near the crash zone broke, which caused the top section to tip over and fall down, and then the two sections of tower shattered into powder at the junction between them.

Why do FEMA and other experts promote the Pancake Theory? Why don't the experts explain the *tipping* of the South Tower? Why don't they explain the *powdering* of the concrete? How did the small fires in the South Tower cause hundreds of steel columns to break? If the fires did not cause the tipping, what did? Is the crash of the airplane responsible?

If the experts are baffled by these issues, why are they producing reports that try to convince us that a hot fire caused the collapse? If they cannot explain the collapse, they are not experts, and they should quit promoting themselves as experts.

Professor Bazant explains the South Tower

Professor Bazant is perhaps the only official expert who has bothered to explain the tipping of the South Tower. His diagram is Figure 5-11. According to his theory, the fire heated some of the core columns to such a high temperature that they lost strength and could not hold the weight above them. Those particular columns buckled. This caused the top of the tower to tilt towards the crash zone. The other core columns were still intact and holding onto that top section, thereby preventing it from falling off. However, the fire caused all of the core columns to become soft, so after a brief period of time all other columns buckled in the opposite direction. The end result was that the top section rotated at approximately its center point. After a brief rotation all of the core columns snapped. The rotation stopped at this point and the top section began to fall downward.

I don't think Bazant's theory explains the collapse of the South Tower for two main reasons:

- The photographs do not indicate to me that the top rotated; I see only a tipping motion.

- His theory requires the piece of tower to tip, rotate, and then stop rotation within a second or two, which requires extremely high rates of acceleration and deceleration; i.e., lots of energy.

While this can easily occur in sketches, I cannot believe it can occur to an 87 million kg structure when the only force acting on it is gravity.

The professor published his theory two days after the attack, so I doubt he saw the photos that are in this book. His theory is probably based on television reports, which are much lower resolution.[†]

The photos in this book show the top continuously tipping as it fell. The top never rotated, and it never stopped tipping. This follows the laws of physics. As Issac Newton explained, once an 87 million kg object starts to tip, only an equally incredible force in the opposite direction will stop the tipping. But there was no force up there except gravity, so there was nothing to stop the tipping.

The top section is tilted about 22° in Figure 5-10. It tipped a bit more after that, and then it became completely hidden by dust.

Where did the overhanging section go?

Photos show both the top section and the base disintegrated as they collided, but we cannot see what happened at the junction because the clouds of powder block our view.

Figure 5-12 shows what might have been happening behind the powder. Since the top section is tipping over as it drops, about ¼ (by volume) of the top section will never collide with the base. This large section should hit the ground. (It would also hit Building 4, which was directly underneath it.) The overhanging portion was probably more than 20 million kilograms. What happened to that overhanging portion?

The section of Building 4 that was directly under the overhanging section was *completely* crushed, and there is a large pile of rubble in that area. Also, the rubble is full of the columns that were along the outside of the South Tower. This implies that the overhanging section did indeed crush the portion of Building 4 that was under it. A question none of the experts bother to answer is: Did that overhanging section hit Building 4 in one big chunk, as Figure 5-12 shows?

I have not seen any photographs or video that show large chunks of the tower falling down. If a large chunk had fallen, it would have passed out the bottom of the clouds of powder (objects fall faster than powder in an atmosphere). This means that if the overhanging section fell as one large piece, none of the photographers or video cameras caught it as it fell, which is unlikely considering how many people were taking photos at the time. This implies that Figure 5-12 is incorrect.

Photos of the rubble show only short pieces of steel and dust in the area where Building 4 once stood. This means if the overhanging section hit the ground as one large piece, it somehow shattered into dust and small pieces when it hit, and then the pieces scattered in such a manner that nobody realized that a large piece hit.

Figure 5-13 shows another possibility. Perhaps the overhanging section shattered into pieces as the top section collided with the base, even though it never actually contacted the base. This diagram brings up two issues:

- The **contents** of the overhanging section should fall out.

  The office desks, people, computers, and other items in the overhanging section should fall out and land on both the ground and on top of Building 4, rather than fall on top of the base. The tilting probably caused many of the items inside the top section to roll towards the overhanging section, so there should be hundreds of objects in that section.

- Pieces of the overhanging **structure** should fall down.

  About ¼ of the top section was overhanging the base; therefore, when that section disintegrated into pieces, hundreds of steel beams, pieces of concrete, and windows should fall through the air rather than hit the base.

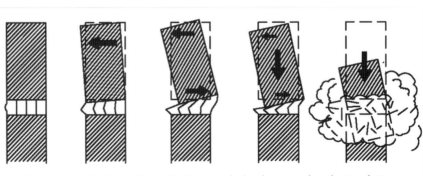

Figure 5-11   *Professor Bazant's diagram of what happened to the South Tower.*

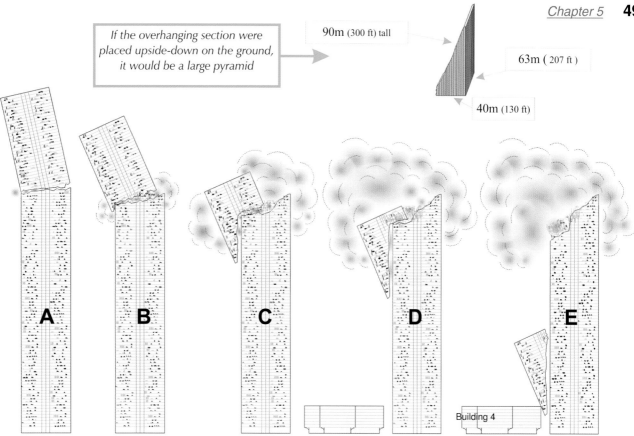

If the overhanging section were placed upside-down on the ground, it would be a large pyramid

90m (300 ft) tall

63m (207 ft)

40m (130 ft)

Figure 5-12 If the top section disintegrated because it collided with the base section, then the portion that was overhanging should have remained as one piece, and then dropped on top of Building 4.

Since no overhanging section can be seen falling in the photos, and no large piece of the tower was found on top of Building 4, this diagram does not explain what happened.

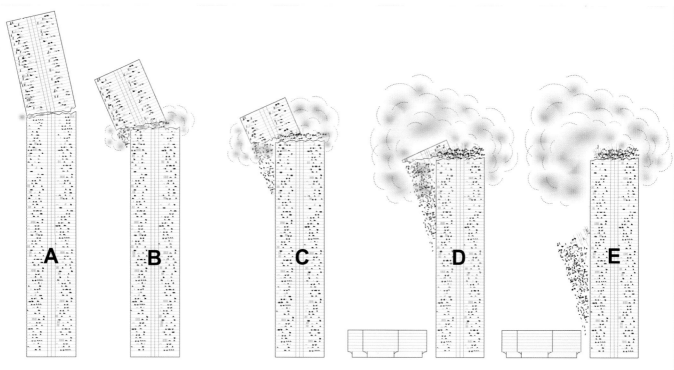

Figure 5-13 In this diagram the overhanging section shatters. Steel beams, pieces of flooring, and the contents of that section should fall on top of Building 4.

Since no debris can be seen falling in the photos, this diagram does not explain what happened, either. So what happened to the overhanging section?

Even if the top section was overhanging by only 1/6th, there should be hundreds of pieces of office furniture, computers, people, and steel beams falling through the air. With about 30 floors in that top section, even an overhang as small as 1/10th would drop hundreds of objects.

Furthermore, there were exterior columns every meter along the outside of these towers, so even an overhang as small as 1/20th would cause hundreds of those columns to drop through the air rather than hit the base.

Objects that fall through air will hit the ground first

Objects that fall through air rather than crash into the base would reach a very high velocity. They would be the first objects to hit the ground. Since the top section was overhanging only on one side, the other three sides of the base would have "normal" levels of debris passing out of the dust clouds. Therefore, if Figure 5-13 is correct, photographs will show that one side of the building is dropping hundreds of steel columns, along with a lot of office furniture, carpeting, and people. The side *opposite* the overhanging section should have hardly any debris, and the remaining two sides will have some debris but not nearly as much as the side with the overhang.

However, none of the photographs or video that I have seen show objects falling out of the dust from the side that is overhanging. There is a small amount of debris falling from all four sides, but there is no significant amount coming from the side that is overhanging. Therefore, Figure 5-13 is certainly incorrect. So what happened to that overhanging section? How can 20 million kilograms of steel and concrete vanish? And what happened to the thousands of kilograms of people and office furnishings that were inside that overhanging section?

The Pigpen Theory

Another possible explanation is that the entire overhanging section (as in Figure 5-12), or the debris from the overhanging section (as in Figure 5-13), dragged dust as it fell, and pushed dust ahead of it, thereby remaining hidden behind dust (Figure 5-14). I will call this the "Pigpen Theory" after the character in the *Peanuts* comics who was partially engulfed in a cloud of dust.

If the Pigpen Theory is correct, the 20 million kg of dusty objects from the overhanging section would form a large, wedge-shaped cloud of dust. Figures 5-15 to 5-18 do indeed show a wedge-shaped cloud in the correct location. However, this dusty wedge does not drop any faster than the clouds on the other three sides of the tower. This implies that the other three sides of the tower are also dropping so many dusty objects that the entire tower is surrounded by dusty debris.

The Pigpen Theory explains why the overhanging section cannot be seen, but it creates the dilemma of explaining how the dusty objects could push enough dust *ahead* of themselves to remain completely hidden the entire time they fell. While a comic character can easily push dust ahead of itself, note that in Figure 5-18 a dusty object is falling, but the object is visible to us because the dust is trailing *behind* it, not preceding it. Is it possible for debris to fall in such a manner that dust is *pushed ahead* of the debris?

The South Tower fireworks display

Figures 5-12 to 5-14 could give you the impression that after the top has completely disintegrated, the base will remain standing, and there will be an enormous pile of debris at the top of it. However, subsequent photographs show that the base of the tower did not survive. Rather, by the time top section finished its disintegration, the base portion began disintegrating at an increasingly rapid rate.

The sequence of photographs in Figures 5-15 to 5-20 show the disintegration of the base. The ejection of dust was so extreme that the tower appeared to be a fireworks display.

The overhanging section is towards the left in Figures 5-15 to 5-20, as in the sketches of Figures 5-12 to 5-14. Therefore, the objects that fall out of the overhanging section should be falling along the left side of the tower in these photographs. However, I cannot see any evidence in these photos that *anything* from the overhanging section fell.

Photographs show a few objects falling along all four sides, but Figures 5-12 and 5-13 show that hundreds of *exterior* columns should be falling, not just a few dozen. Also, depending on the degree the overhanging section was tilted, dozens of pieces of *core columns* that were at the top of the overhanging section would have fallen through the air, also. How did all of those massive core columns vanish?

Figure 5-17 shows two, truly heavy objects falling out of the clouds and dragging dust with them. However, both of them are in the wrong area to be from the overhanging section. The overhanging section had 20 million kg of material, but those 20 million kg were *as invisible as the ravaging fires*. This certainly was a strange collapse!

The rubble from the South Tower

When the collapse was over, there was nothing remaining on the ground except short sections of steel beams and a few small pieces of concrete. Almost every piece of steel in both towers broke at the joints. Virtually every piece of concrete shattered into dust. All telephone wires broke into pieces, and all office furniture shattered. Even the toilets and sinks shattered. All of the corrugated steel sheets that held the concrete floors were shredded into small pieces. Photographs of the rubble do not show any large pieces of anything. Figure 5-19 is a portion of a gigantic photo taken by NOAA from an airplane that flew over the site on September 23rd. Parts of the image seem blurry because smoke and/or steam was still seeping out of the rubble at the time.

As is true of all other photos of the rubble, all we can see is dust and pieces of steel. Also, no section of the rubble resembles a stack of pancakes. Obviously, when these towers collapsed, the tower and every object inside was shredded, pulverized, and/or burned to ash.

Nobody knows exactly how large the overhanging section was, but the dashed rectangle in Figure 5-19 shows its approximate position and size when it reached it maximum tilt. Within that dashed rectangle should be

hundreds of office desks, human bodies, computers, and pieces of carpet, in addition to about 20 million kg of tower pieces, but there does not appear to be anything in that area except dust and short pieces of steel.

A proper investigation of the rubble would explain what happened to the overhanging section. The columns at the top of the tower were thinner than the columns at the bottom of the tower, and some columns had markings from the factory, so investigators would be able to deduce which columns came from the overhanging section, and which were from other sections of the tower. This could help us understand what happened to that overhanging section.

Unfortunately, the debris was removed so quickly that nobody had a chance to study it. The photograph in Figure 5-19 was taken 12 days after the collapse, but crews had already removed an enormous amount of the rubble that had landed on top of Building 4. They also removed a lot of the rubble that was part of Building 4 itself. This is why the

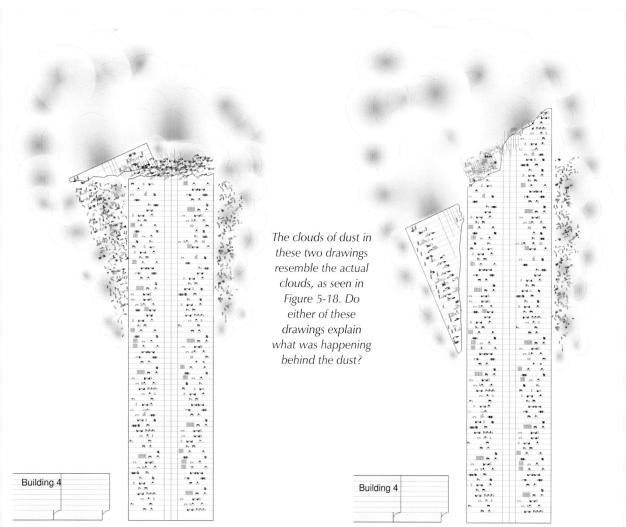

The clouds of dust in these two drawings resemble the actual clouds, as seen in Figure 5-18. Do either of these drawings explain what was happening behind the dust?

Figure 5-14   *Did the overhanging section (or its contents) push dust in front of it*
as it fell, thereby remaining hidden from us the entire time?
*Is it possible for an object to push dust **ahead of itself**?*

REUTERS

Figure 5-15   *This photo shows a level of disintegration that corresponds to Figure 5-12C or Figure 5-13C.*

*The side with the overhanging section should have **thousands** of times as much debris as the other three sides, but somehow the dust is so extreme that 20 millions kilograms of material is hidden at all times.*

REUTERS

Figure 5-16   *The red arrow is pointing to puffs of dust. The significance of the dust will be discussed in Chapter 7*

Figure 5-17   _The red arrows are pointing to objects that have fallen below the clouds. Since these objects fell out of the clouds, why not pieces from the 20 million kg of the overhanging section?_

REUTERS

Figure 5-18   *The red arrow is pointing to the perfectly horizontal base of the dust cloud.*
The significance of the horizontal base will be discussed in Chapter 7

Figure 5-19   _Photo taken from an airplane on September 23._

The dashed rectangle below the South Tower and on top of Building 4 is approximately where the overhanging section landed. (See Figures 5-13 and 5-14)

Figure 5-20 *The clouds of dust and debris were ejected to perhaps 3 times the width of the tower*

lower left portion in the outline of Building 4 is lacking rubble.

The North Tower starts to collapse

The North Tower stood stable and motionless for 1 hour and 43 minutes. Photos taken at 10:29 show puffs of dust coming out of the tower along the crash zone, which quickly became horizontal ribbons of dust (Figure 5-21). The ribbons did not rise upwards, as smoke does. Rather, they came out of the windows horizontally, which implies they were forced out due to high pressure. The collapse is occurring at the ribbons of dust, but there are not many flames.

Where did the puffs of dust come from?

The official explanation for what happened to the North Tower is that the floor directly above the fire broke and fell down (the Pancake Theory). However, if the floor had cracked into pieces before falling, those pieces would have fallen through the air without blowing smoke out of the windows. This leads us to conclude that the floor did not break into pieces before falling.

Perhaps the floor fell in one large piece. Then, like a piston pushing air in a cylinder, it squeezed smoke out the windows (Figure 5-22). However, if the floor acted like a piston, the air that was pushed *out* of the windows should exactly match the volume of air that rushes *in* to replace the air above the falling floor. Therefore, the photos should show a corresponding vacuum that sucks air into the windows to

Figure 5-21 *The top of the North Tower has dropped a small amount, which means the entire top section has been severed from the base.*

Time: 0 seconds

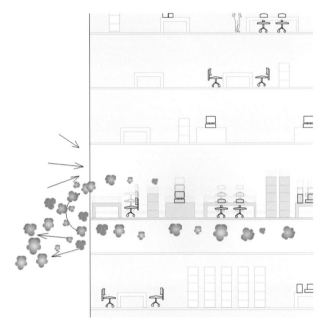

Figure 5-22 *If a floor truly fell down in one piece, dust would be sucked back inside*

Figure 5-23 *1/3 seconds*

Figure 5-24 *2/3 seconds*

replace the air that was forced out. The effect would be the same as a cigarette smoker who blows smoke out of his mouth while inhaling through his nose.

The video shows clouds of dust forced out at a high velocity, but no dust gets sucked back in. Therefore, Figure 5-22 does not explain what is happening in Figure 5-21. While it is possible that a floor actually did fall down like a piston, this particular section of the video is not showing such an event.

It is impossible to realize it by looking at Figure 5-21, but the top of the tower has dropped slightly from its normal height. The only way the top could drop is if the top section has completely separated from the base. This requires *hundreds* of core and external columns to break.

The experts claim that the collapse started when a floor above the fire broke and fell to the floor below it. Perhaps they are correct that the very first event in the collapse was the breaking of joints that held up a floor. However, at 10:29

the entire top section of the North Tower had been severed from the base and began falling down. If the first event was the falling of a floor, how did that progress to the severing of hundreds of columns?

Figure 5-27 shows the columns that held up the top section have broken. As the top section collided with the base, it disintegrated into dust. Ribbons of dust and smoke were squeezed out of the junction at a high velocity. A vacuum would be created at the top of the tower rather than near the crash zone. This would explain why dust was blown out of the crash zone but none of that dust was sucked back inside.

The airplane crashed into the 96th floor, so there were approximately 15 floors in this top section. (A 15 story building that is 200 feet on each side is *enormous* but it seems small in these photos because the tower was so large. When looking at Figures 5-21 to 5-26 it is easy to forget that

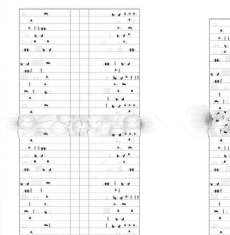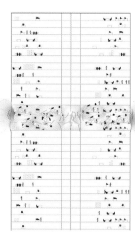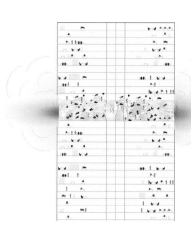

Figure 5-27 *The top of the North Tower fell down without tipping. This required **hundreds** of columns to break in a balanced manner. Then, after breaking, the top fell down onto the base, shattering into dust in the process. Why would a steel structure shatter after falling such a short distance?*

Figure 5-25 *1 ½ seconds*

Figure 5-26 *2 seconds*

we are viewing the disintegration of *millions* of kilograms of steel and concrete.)

Flames appear in the dust as the top section fell. Perhaps flames that were deep inside the tower were blown out the windows, which brought them into our view. Or perhaps the smoldering material inside the tower bursts into flames when it was pushed outside and finally reached enough oxygen to burn properly.

Photos show the top of the tower fell downward without any tilting motion. If the columns on one side of the tower had broken before the columns on the other side, the top section would have tilted, as occurred with the South Tower. Since there was no tilting of the North Tower, every column in the crash zone broke in a perfectly balanced manner, as illustrated in Figure 5-27.

There were 47 columns in the interior and 236 columns along the outside. Since the crash zone of the North Tower was near the 96th floor, the columns in this area were thinner than the columns near the ground level. However, they were still so thick that it would require a significant amount of energy to break them. How did the fire break so many columns? Did one column break, which then caused another column to break, and so on? If so, it is an amazing coincidence that the columns separated and/or snapped in such a perfectly balanced manner that the top never tilted.

** Unknown **

Figure 5-28 *The North Tower is starting to spew streamers of debris. The red arrow points to a large plume that is almost horizontal. What force was blowing debris such a distance?*

For now let's just assume that the fire heated all the core columns to approximately the same temperature, and then they all snapped about the same time. Once those core columns snapped, the exterior columns were no longer able to hold the weight above them, and they all snapped at nearly the same moment in time. This caused the top section to become an independent object, and it fell down onto the base.

Regardless of what caused the top section to separate, it fell only a few feet to the base, so when it hit the base it would be traveling at a low speed. Why didn't it simply break a few floors, bend a few steel beams, and then come to rest on top of the base? Why did it disintegrate into dust at the junction? And how did it start a chain reaction that caused the entire tower to shatter? (Figures 5-28 and 5-29) What was occurring at the junction to create such large volumes of dust? Were these towers unusually fragile? Was the concrete defective? Or is this the way all steel buildings behave after airplanes crash into them?

The North Tower fireworks display

After perhaps a second of collapsing, the North Tower became another monochrome fireworks display, spewing

** Unknown **

Figure 5-29   *The tower is 63 meters (207 ft) wide. The red arrow points to pieces of the tower that have been thrown **at least 70 meters**. Why didn't the pieces simply **fall down**? Why were they **ejected** with such force?*

dust hundreds of feet from the towers. As with the South Tower, all parts of the building turned into dust and short pieces of steel before any of it hit the ground.

Fires break out in Building 7

CNN and other news agencies have a time line of events on September 11, and they report Building 7 on fire at 4:10 PM, but FEMA and some newspaper reports claim fires burned for 7 hours, and one report claims 8 hours. Since everybody agrees that Building 7 collapsed at 5:20 PM, if the fires burned for 7 hours, that means the fire started about 10:30 in the morning. The North Tower collapsed at 10:29, so this implies the collapse of the North Tower caused fires to break out in Building 7.

The FEMA report contains photographs of Building 7 that were taken shortly after the collapse of the North Tower, and the photographs show a small amount of damage to the exterior of Building 7 as a result of flying debris. However, FEMA has no idea how this small amount of damage started fires inside the building. There were other buildings near the North and South Towers that were also damaged by debris, but they did not suffer catastrophic fires or collapses. Why would Building 7 be any different?

What was burning in Building 7?

Did the diesel fuel inside Building 7 have anything to do with the fires? There is so much secrecy about Building 7 that you may not be surprised to learn that nobody has an explanation for *what* was burning. Some people suspect the diesel fuel was burning, but nobody can explain *how* the fuel caught on fire. The FEMA report even admits in several places that they have no idea what happened:

> *The specifics of the fires in WTC 7 and how they caused the building to collapse remain unknown at this time.*

Their remark that the fires and collapse is *"unknown at this time"* implies that at some later time they may figure it out. However, by the time they published their report, all the rubble for Building 7 was gone. Therefore, they knew there was no possible way they could analyze the rubble and explain what caused the building to collapse. They would have been more honest if they had written their statement as follows:

> *The specifics of the fires in Building 7 and how they caused the building to collapse are unknown, and will never be known because all the evidence has been destroyed. Case closed.*

The FEMA report avoids mentioning that all of the rubble was destroyed. Instead, they create the impression that they are still investigating, and that a future report will fill in the missing details. On the title page of their report, in a very large size is: *"Data Collection, Preliminary Observations, And Recommendations."* The remark about the *preliminary* observations implies that there will be *final* observations later on. But FEMA knew there would be no final report.

Some people assume that the diesel fuel inside this building caught on fire. The FEMA report mentions that about 20,000 gallons of diesel fuel was recovered after the collapse because several tanks survived intact and still contained their fuel. However, thousands of gallons were missing, so a lot of fuel may have burned. But how did the diesel fuel catch on fire? The tanks were surrounded by fireproof enclosures, and the pipelines were protected by a double-wall steel pipe. If the fireproofing and the double-wall pipe protected the diesel fuel, that means the fire started in something else. Was there other flammable material in that building that nobody wants to admit to?

The nearly invisible fires in Building 7

Figure 5-30 shows the rear of Building 7. The front of Building 7 (where the main entrance was located) faced the North Tower. The North Tower would be directly on the other side of the building in this photograph (also in photos Figures 5-31 to 5-33). The front of Building 7 has some broken windows and other minor damage from falling debris, but the sides and rear of the building have no damage and only a few fires.

Every photo taken of Building 7 shows only a few tiny fires in only a few windows. The fires appear so insignificant that I would expect the sprinkler system to put them out. Since these fires were burning all afternoon, the sprinkler system had plenty of time to spray water on them. Was the sprinkler system defective? Of course, if diesel fuel was burning, the sprinkler system would not be able extinguish the fires. Or, if they were magnesium fires, or fires from an experimental weapon system, the sprinkler system would not do much good, either.

The firemen also had many hours to extinguish these fires, so why didn't they? Since hundreds of firemen were killed when the towers collapsed, it is possible that there were not enough firemen remaining to deal with Building 7. Or perhaps the firemen – who had complained about the dangers of Building 7 – were afraid to go into that building because of the giant transformers, 13,800 volts, and tanks of diesel fuel.

Figure 5-30 *The fires in Building 7 at 3pm. The red arrows point to east edge of Building 7; the west edge cannot be seen. The only fires are on the 7th and 12th floors (in the reflection of a smaller building).*

Building 7 collapses

At 5:20 in the evening the building suddenly collapsed. Figures 5-31 to 5-33 show how the collapse occurred.

Building 7 collapsed in a different manner than the towers. The towers shattered into huge clouds of powder starting near the crash zone and working downward to the ground, causing the towers to resemble fireworks. But Building 7 collapsed at its bottom, causing it to resemble the typical demolition of an old building. While a lot of the concrete in Building 7 turned to powder, this building did not break down as thoroughly as the towers.

Figure 5-34 is the portion of the photo taken by NOAA on September 23 that shows the rubble of Building 7. This building was reduced to a tiny pile of rubble, although large pieces of the exterior survived. Those large sections fell on top the rubble in the manner seen in the photo; i.e., the cleanup crews did not put them into those positions. When Building 7 collapsed, the interior fell first, and that caused the outside of the building to move inward, as if the insides were being sucked out. The result was a very tiny pile of rubble, with the outside of the building collapsing on top of the pile. This is how conventional demolitions operate.

Underneath the pile of rubble are ten giant transformers. If it were not for those transformers, the pile would be even lower to the ground.

Incidently, the electrical power substations are going to be rebuilt in the same location, and a new building will be put over them, creating the same situation as before. However, reports have not yet specified whether this new building will also contain 42,000 gallons of diesel fuel and the CIA.

Incredible fires should be visible

The fire in Building 7 was supposedly so extreme that it caused a steel building to crumble. However, all photos show only a few tiny fires in only a few windows, and only tiny amounts of smoke were produced.

I would think that a fire of the magnitude necessary to collapse a steel building would have set fire to a lot of the office furniture, carpeting, and other flammable objects. This in turn would have caused a lot of flames to be visible in a lot of windows. Also, such a large fire would produce a lot of smoke. I also suspect that such a large fire would have caused many windows to shatter. How could an incredible fire burn in the building without any photos showing evidence of large flames or tremendous plumes of smoke?

Compare the fires in Building 7 to the fires in Buildings 4, 5, or 6 (Figure 6-2). The fires in Building 7 were so small that you could safely roast marshmallows over them. Apparently, the smaller the fire, the more destructive it is!

Somebody knew Building 7 would collapse

Tom Franklin, the photographer who took the famous "Iwo Jima flag raising" photo on September 11th, was near Building 7 at about 4 PM. In his description of how that photograph came about, he makes an interesting remark about Building 7:

> *"Firemen evacuated the area as they prepared for the collapse of Building Seven.*
>
> *We were catching our breath, drinking water and juice, when I decided to walk back toward the debris. It was between 4 and 5 p.m.*
>
> *I would say I was 150 yards away when I saw the firefighters raising the flag."*

Franklin's remarks shows that somebody told the firemen by about 4 to 5pm to stay away from Building 7 because *it was going to collapse.* Franklin obeyed and walked away from the area, but he did not bother to take photos of the raging fires. How could he walk away from a 47-story building that was engulfed in flames and about to collapse on him without taking a few photos? He should have been able to feel the heat on his head. How could he ignore the first fire ever to destroy a steel building? Or did Franklin look at Building 7 but not see any flames?

Several people took photos of the side and rear of the building because they saw a few flames, but apparently nobody took a photo of the front of the building. I suppose there was *not even one flame* on the front side.

More interesting, what evidence could anybody have that Building 7 would collapse? Considering that no fire had ever caused the collapse of a steel building before, why would anybody believe Building 7 would crumble from a few tiny fires? Who were those people who told the firemen to stay away?

New business opportunity: *Fire Demolitions, Inc.*

If our government and university professors are correct that a fire can cause a building to collapse in the exact same manner as a demolition company destroys buildings with explosives, then I would like to start a new business: the *Fire Demolition Company, Inc.* This company will demolish buildings by setting a few small fires inside, rather than by installing hundreds of packages of explosives. A demolition by fire will be significantly less expensive than a demolition by explosives. It is also quicker. For example, *Fire Demolition Inc.*, can take down a 110 story building in 56 minutes simply by setting a few small fires on a few floors. By comparison, a conventional demolition company would spend days just wiring the building with explosives.

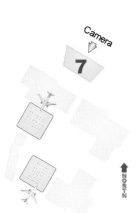

All three of these Bldg 7 photos seem to be by Roberto Rabanne

Figure 5-31
According to FEMA, this shows Building 7 as it begins to collapse, at 5:30 PM

Unlike the towers, but like a conventional demolition, this building crumbled at the ground.

Most of the dust was produced at the ground, rather than high up in the air.

Where is the fire that is causing this building to collapse?

Figure 5-32   *A few seconds after Figure 5-31*

Figure 5-33   *A few seconds after Figure 5-32*

Figure 5-34   *The rubble of Building 7 is in the center. Figure 5-19 is another portion of this same photo.*

Large pieces of the exterior fell on top of the rubble, as if the insides were sucked out. This is how a conventional demolition works.

Is it a coincidence that a nearly invisible fire caused this building to collapse in exactly the same manner as demolition companies get rid of old buildings?

After the collapse

6

The World Trade Center Volcano

By the end of the day the area around the World Trade Center was covered with concrete and gypsum powder up to several inches thick, as if a volcano has erupted nearby (Figure 6-1).

The significance of the thick coating of powder becomes more apparent when you look at the collapses, burnings, and bombings of other buildings. When has a building produced such large volumes of powder? This was not a typical collapse.

Forest fires produce large amounts of ash, but that ash is from the burning of wood. The streets of New York were full of powdered concrete and gypsum, not ash from burned office materials.

Only metal survived

Every photo of the rubble of shows that nothing but steel remained. How can buildings fall down without at least some of the office furniture, plumbing fixtures, and concrete surviving? How is such total annihilation possible?

We are suppose to believe that the people who designed the World Trade Center never provided enough of a safety margin to handle a rise in temperature caused by a serious fire. This could be true, but that does not explain why the entire building *turned into powder* and small pieces of steel. Rather, it would only explain why some of the steel beams buckled under the stress, and it could explain why some of the joints broke. It would not explain why *every* concrete floor disintegrated into tiny particles before it hit the ground.

Courtesy of Terry Schmidt

Figure 6-1 *Is there a sensible explanation for why the towers produced as much dust as a small volcano?*

Figure 6-2   *Both Buildings 5 and 6 suffered from extreme fires. These were "conventional" fires; i.e., giant flames were visible, even through dark smoke, and windows shattered.*

Figure 6-3   *Building 6 survived the intense fires without crumbling. The debris from the tower crushed some of this building; the fire did not do that damage. (See Figure 6-4 to understand what this photo shows.)*

Why did Buildings 4, 5 & 6 hold together?

The two buildings with the address of 4 and 6 were close to the towers, and Building 5 was a bit further away. Fires were extreme in these buildings (Figure 6-2). Buildings 4 and 6 were also bombarded with debris from the towers. However, none of these buildings shattered into dust. They were damaged, but their steel structures held together (Figure 6-3).

The steel beams in these smaller buildings were much thinner than the beams in the towers and in Building 7. However, these thin beams survived extreme fires and bombardment by debris better than the much thicker beams in the towers and Building 7. Do small buildings survive fires better than large buildings?

Incidently, Figure 6-4 shows pieces of aluminum scattered on the rooftops and the rubble, as if the area had been decorated with tinsel. The aluminum coverings of the exterior columns (Figure 3-6) were shredded into short pieces and blown as far as several hundred feet from the towers. The metal in the towers appears to have been put through a shredding device, and the concrete appears to have been put through a pulverizing device. How can a building "fall down" in such a manner?

Thermal images

As far as I know, nobody inserted probes into the rubble to determine the temperature inside. However, on September 16, five days after the buildings collapsed, NASA flew an airplane over the World Trade Center to create a thermal map. The airplane recorded the infrared radiation coming from the ground, so it gave an indication of the surface temperature of the rubble.

James R. Tourtellotte

Figure 6-4 *The blue arrow shows approximately the angle of the photo in Figure 6-3. Building 7 is the pile behind Building 6. There are two holes in Building 6, and one in Building 5. The red arrow points to a hole in Building 5.*

The US Geological Survey put a report together based on NASA's data. They analyzed the infrared data from the eight hottest locations to determine the actual temperature of the rubble at those points (Figure 6-5). This map was created after firemen and cleanup crews had spent five days spraying water on the rubble and hauling rubble away. Therefore, it is possible that the eight hottest spots would be in different locations if the thermal map had been created the day after the attack rather than five days later.

The location marked with the letter **H** is in the location of Building 4 but, as Figure 5-13 shows, about 20 million kilograms from the overhanging section of the South Tower fell towards this area. Therefore, the high temperature of the spot marked as **H** may be due to the rubble from the South Tower, not the rubble from Building 4. Also a portion of Building 4 remained standing near that location (Figure 6-6), so if there were still fires burning inside then it may be the temperature of the flames, not the rubble.

The two highest temperatures at locations **A** and **G** are beyond the melting point of aluminum. The firemen sprayed water on much (maybe all) of the rubble for an unspecified number of days. The firemen sprayed so much water that shallow pools can be seen in some photographs of the rubble. This means that even after five days of being cooled by water the rubble was still hot enough in some locations to melt aluminum.

The high temperature of the rubble explains why smoke and steam seeped out of the rubble for *months*. Furthermore, if the surface of the rubble was capable of melting aluminum after five days, what was the interior of this rubble capable of doing immediately after the collapse? Was it capable of melting copper?

Photographs of the rubble show only steel and dust. NASA's thermal map could explain this odd situation. Specifically, only steel and a few other materials could survive such extreme temperatures. The flammable office materials and people would become ash in such an inferno.

Why was the rubble so hot? The fire was confined to small areas of the tower, so it is unlikely that the fire could have created so much hot rubble. Was the heat created when the rubble hit the ground (which converts potential energy into thermal energy)?

The World Trade Center odor

Further evidence of the rubble's high temperature comes from the people in Manhattan who complained about the peculiar, unpleasant odor in the area.

If the rubble had been cool, not much smoke or steam would have come from the rubble. The paper, plastic, and carpeting trapped in the dust and steel would have remained unburned. The dead people trapped in the rubble would have slowly decayed, creating bad smells. However, if the rubble was hot, the 2000 to 3000 people trapped in the rubble would cook, sizzle, and burn. Their muscles would produce familiar meat-like odors, but the contents of their intestines would not produce such pleasant odors, nor would their fat or hair.

If there had been only *two* bodies in the rubble, their odor would have been dominated by the smoke from burning paper and plastic, but there were *130,000 kilograms* of body parts in that rubble. There would have been a large volume of unpleasant odors coming from those bodies for many days.

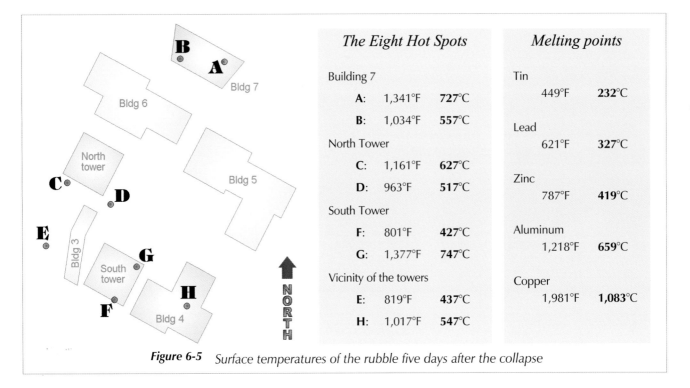

Figure 6-5   *Surface temperatures of the rubble five days after the collapse*

We are blind without data

Because NASA collected data on the temperatures of the rubble, including the longitude and latitude of the points they collected the data for, we can make specific, detailed statements such as:

> *The temperature at the surface of the rubble of the North Tower at 40°42-39.94" N latitude, 74°00'45.37" W was 747°C five days after the collapse.*

If nobody had bothered to collect thermal data, we would have to observe photographs of the rubble and guess at the temperature based on the production of smoke and steam. We could deduce that the rubble is "hot" because steam came out for weeks, but we would not know the actual temperature. Without data to work with, we are blind.

Now imagine the other extreme in which NASA did more than fly over the site five days later. Imagine that on September 12th scientists inserted temperature probes into the rubble. This would allow them to determine the temperatures at different depths within the rubble. This in turn would allow them to estimate the total energy content of the rubble. Once they know the energy in the rubble they can make a good guess as to whether explosives were used to bring the buildings down because they would know whether there was more energy in the rubble than the building had in potential energy.

The point is that if we do not collect evidence in crimes or fires, we cannot be sure exactly what happened. To rephrase that, when you want to avoid getting caught for a crime, destroy all evidence before it is inspected.

Increasing the rate at which evidence is destroyed.

On September 23, the government agency NOAA sent an airplane over the World Trade Center for several hours to create three-dimensional elevation maps of the area (Figure 6-6 is one of them). The darkest green spots are below the ground level. Christopher Bollyn of *The American Free Press* points out that the hole in Building 6 is one of those deep holes; i.e., the dark green color inside the hole is not a "shadow." There are *no shadows* in an elevation map. This means the hole in Building 6 is below ground level.

Furthermore, the hole in Building 6 was full of the rubble from the 8 floors above the hole, which means that if the

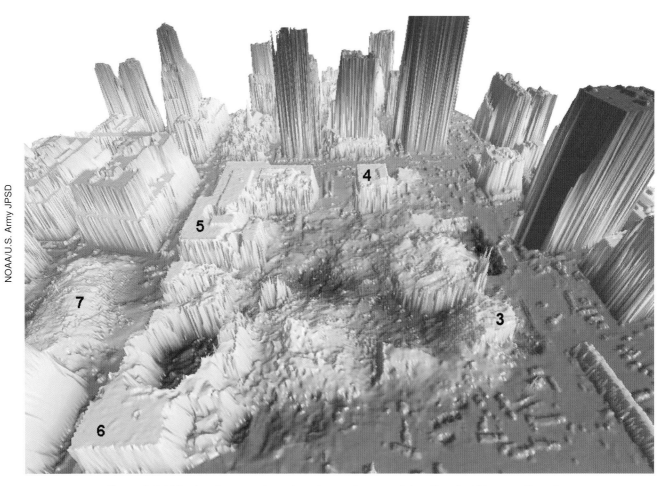

NOAA/U.S. Army JPSD

Figure 6-6 *This elevation map shows how low to the ground the piles of rubble were. There is no support for a "Pancake Theory" in this image. The towers shattered into dust; the floors did not fall down like a stack of pancakes. Only a small corner of Building 4 survived the bombardment of debris from the overhanging section. Building 3, the hotel, was also crushed.*

rubble had been removed from the hole *before* the elevation map had been made, the hole would be even deeper. Did pieces of the North Tower crush *only* the center of Building 6? If so, it crushed it so deeply that it was below ground level after the rubble from eight floors fell into it. Or did something in Building 6 explode, in which case we could explain the smoke in Figure 1-1? Building 6 was the US Customs building. What was inside that building?

Getting back to Figure 6-6, NOAA said the purpose of the elevation maps was to help crews identify the original foundation structures, basement areas, underground utility connections, and elevator shafts. Was NOAA helping the investigators understand what happened? Or were they helping clean-up crews to remove the rubble?

No photos! Get out or be arrested!

There is a site on the Internet (cryptome.org) that contains photographs that were taken on October 3, 2001 (Figure 3-6 is one of them). According to the story of how these pictures were taken, the photographer went to the World Trade Center to take pictures. He found barricades and security guards surrounding the area (except for one location where the guard may been busy somewhere else). He walked around the site, stopping every so often to take a photo.

After taking dozens of pictures he encountered a police officer who asked him if he had authorization to take photographs of the area. When he told the officer he did not, other officers came over and told him he was in a crime scene and was not allowed to take photographs. An officer asked to see his digital camera and the photographs he had taken. After briefly looking at his camera the officer gave it back and told him to stay away from the site or he would be arrested. When the photographer got home and tried to view his photographs he discovered that they had been deleted from the camera's flash memory by the officer.

The officer who deleted the photos may not have understood that when a computer deletes a file, it does not actually delete the *file*. Rather, it deletes the *entry* for the file in what could be called its "table of contents." Since the photographer understood this, he restored his camera's table of contents with some software specifically designed to restore deleted files. He then posted the forbidden photos on the Internet, and I put one of them in Figure 3-6.

The point of this story is that the police blocked off the World Trade Center on the same day the attack occurred. They stopped people from taking photographs of the area, and they interfered with the engineers who were trying to investigate. However, they did not stop the crews from destroying the rubble, selling the rubble as scrap metal, or tossing the rubble into garbage dumps. They only stopped people from collecting information about the collapse.

Of course, I suspect that most of the individual police officers were simply following orders. People further up in the government hierarchy certainly made the decision to destroy the rubble and block investigations.

The area where Flight 93 crashed was also off-limits to photographs. According to a Pittsburgh television news report:

> *Also on Thursday, the Pennsylvania State Police arrested two photographers for breach of security. A police officer said that two stringers from New York City were given permission to take pictures of one portion of the crash scene, but they went into a restricted area and immediately were arrested.*

What was in the restricted area that nobody was allowed to see? What portion of *any* airplane crash could possibly need such secrecy that tax money needs to be spent on the arrest of photographers? Were the photographers trying to get photos of the dead bodies for some idiotic purpose? Or were they merely trying to document the plane crash?

Destroying evidence is an admission of guilt

Destroying evidence, hiding evidence, and preventing the gathering of evidence should be considered an admission of guilt. Nobody destroys evidence if it shows their innocence. The FBI, CIA, police, FEMA, and other agencies knew they should investigate the World Trade Center collapse. The police and FBI routinely block off crime scenes, guard the evidence, and refuse to let people into the area until it is inspected and photographed. The FBI would never allow crews into a "real" crime scene with torches to cut up and sell the evidence. The FBI deliberately allowed that rubble to be destroyed.

The police helped destroy the evidence

Police are supposed to keep people away from crime scenes to *protect the evidence* so that it can be inspected. In the case of the 9-11 attacks the police did the exact opposite; i.e.; they kept people away so that the e*vidence could be destroyed* before anybody could inspect it. If this is not a sign that something is seriously wrong with our government's behavior in regards to this 9-11 attack, what would be?

Can Explosives Explain It?

How could the towers disintegrate so easily?

For 30 years the steel framework of the towers survived winds that put a lot of stress on the structure. According to the engineering sites that describe these towers, the shaking and stress from a severe winter storm was more intense and of a much longer duration than the stress produced by the airplane crashes. If those engineers are correct, the towers were not flimsy, and the design limits of the towers were not exceeded by the airplane crashes. That would explain why both towers survived the airplane crashes; the airplanes did nothing more than shake the towers for a brief moment.

As Chapter 4 explained, the fires did not seem severe enough to explain the disintegration of the buildings. So if not the fires or the airplane crashes, what would cause the towers to shatter?

FEMA and other "experts" promote the theory that the floors fell down like pancakes, but none of the floors simply "fell down." Hundreds of corrugated steel pans were shredded during the collapse of the towers, and thousands of steel beams were broken at their joints. What can cause such total destruction of hundreds of thousands of tons of steel assemblies and concrete?

The concrete turned to powder in the air

When the upper portion of the North Tower fell down onto the base (Figure 5-21) it fell a distance of only one or two floors. It would not be traveling very fast when it hit the base. I can understand that it might crack the floors, bend some steel beams, and even bust a few holes in the flooring, but how could it shatter into dust after falling such a short distance? And how could it start a reaction in which the entire tower shatters? And how could the powder be ejected with such a high velocity that the clouds reached perhaps 200 to 400 feet wide? Throwing dust any significant distance requires a lot of energy. (Figure 5-29 shows the tower throwing streams of dust an enormous distance.)

How could the towers disintegrate in 8 seconds?

There were thousands of massive steel beams in the towers, and they hit the ground at a high velocity. This created shocks that seismic stations picked up. According to the Columbia University Seismology Group, the North Tower created a shock of magnitude 2.3 (Figure 7-1), while the South Tower created a shock of 2.1. Their report also shows that the South Tower collapsed in 10 seconds and the North Tower collapsed in 8 seconds. Video images also show the towers collapsing within 8 to 10 seconds, verifying the seismic data.

Figure 7-1 shows the shocks increased during the first 5 seconds (red) then dropped abruptly to a lower level for about 3 seconds (blue), and then slowly tapered off (green). The seismic data of the South Tower showed the same pattern, although the red section peaked a bit higher in the North Tower. The significance of this seismic data will be explained later.

Figures 5-13 and 5-14 illustrate a flaw in all official theories of the collapse of the South Tower. Specifically, the steel beams in the overhanging section fell through the air, so they should hit the ground before the beams that had to crash through the base section. There is no possible way that a steel beam that hits dozens of steel and concrete floors will reach the ground as quickly as a beam that falls through the air. Hundreds of exterior columns from *both* towers should also have fallen on all four sides, but only a few are visible.

The beams that fell through the air would fall at 32 feet per second, per second; the rate at which all objects fall in the earth's gravity. The towers were about 1300 feet tall. If a object is dropped from 1300 feet, it will hit the ground about 8 seconds later. Notice that the North Tower collapsed in 8 seconds. That means pieces of the North Tower fell down as fast as objects fall through air. How could the debris crush 100 steel and concrete floors while falling as fast as objects that fall through air?

The video shows that the collapse occurred at the same rate as if somebody had dropped the steel beams in air from the top of the building. It *aint possible* for steel beams to bust through all of those floors without slowing down!

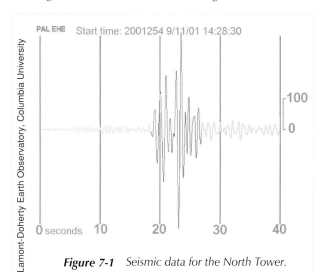

Figure 7-1 *Seismic data for the North Tower.*

Were explosives detonated by a computer via radio links?

One way to explain the rapid collapse of the towers (and other odd aspects of the collapse) is that explosives were placed in these buildings before the airplanes hit them. Explosives easily explain the dust that flew out of the towers (Figure 7-2). However, for those of you who are unfamiliar with computers, let me begin by explaining how the explosives could be controlled.

Packages of explosives could be installed on nearly every floor, in the areas used by maintenance personnel. A few packages may have been connected together with wires so that they detonate simultaneously, thereby acting as one package. Each package would have a battery powered radio link that connected it to the main computer. This master computer would be able to detonate specific packages of explosives at specific times simply by sending signals to the packages.

Think of cellphones to understand this. Imagine 100 cell phones spread out on a table. You could trigger the ringer on any one of them simply by dialing the number to that particular phone. Now replace the ringer with the detonator of an explosive; you would then be able to detonate any explosive simply by dialing that phone. Now replace your manual dialing of the phone with a computer that calls the phones in a certain sequence and according to a certain time table.

After determining that the airplane hit the 77th floor of the South Tower, the master computer would be set to detonate the explosives on the 77th floor, and then 250 milliseconds later the explosives on the 76th floor, and then 180 milliseconds later the explosives on the 75th floor, etc.

Figure 7-2   *This view shows the puffs of white dust coming out of the base section. These puffs always come out in a horizontal line, and they appear before that section of the tower breaks away from the building. Explosives easily explain this; i.e.; the high pressure gas forced dust out of the windows.*

The puffs and ribbons of dust

Since the airplane hit the South Tower on one side, the collapse was initiated by detonating explosives near the crash zone (Figure 7-3). This caused the tower to tilt toward the crash zone, creating the illusion that the columns in the crash zone had become weak from the fire and the airplane crash.

Within milliseconds other explosives along the crash zone were detonated to break all the columns along the crash zone (Figure 7-4). This instantly disconnected the top section without altering its position or orientation. (You can see this effect if you place a block of wood on top of another block, and then knock the lower block out from under it very quickly. This will cause the top block to fall down without changing its orientation. Or, if you rapidly pull a tablecloth out from underneath objects, those objects will drop vertically to the table without changing their orientation or position.)

Once the top section was severed, it began to fall downward at the rate at which all objects fall due to the force of gravity. It also continued to tilt towards the crash zone as it fell (Figures 7-5 to 7-10).

Photographs show ribbons of dust coming out of both towers as they collapse. Two suspicious aspects of these ribbons are:

1) The dust comes from a floor while that area of the tower still appears structurally intact, rather than forming at the location where the tower is in the process of crumbling. (One of these ribbons has just formed along the left side of Figure 7-2. The floors immediately above the ribbon seem intact. The area that is collapsing seems to be many floors higher up.)

2) The dust comes out very precisely. Specifically, almost the same quantity of dust comes out of each window, and only along one floor at a time, as opposed to appearing haphazardly in different windows along different floors. (Look back at the red arrow in Figure 5-16.)

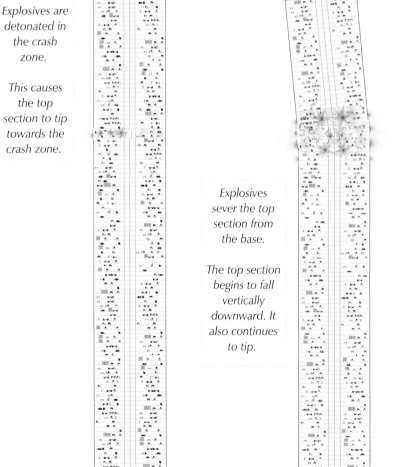

Explosives are detonated in the crash zone.

This causes the top section to tip towards the crash zone.

Explosives sever the top section from the base.

The top section begins to fall vertically downward. It also continues to tip.

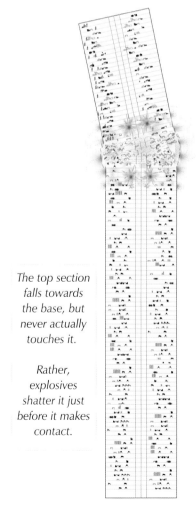

The top section falls towards the base, but never actually touches it.

Rather, explosives shatter it just before it makes contact.

Figure 7-3   *Start*   **Figure 7-4**   *½ second*   **Figure 7-5**   *1.0 seconds*

The precision of these ribbons is most obvious in a video taken by an amateur photographer who was standing under the South Tower (Figure 7-11). I doubt such a perfectly balanced increase in pressure could be due to the random falling of debris from the floors above. Rather, explosives were being set off inside the building. The ribbons are horizontal and precise because the explosives were detonated one floor at a time.

After a ribbon blows out of the building it grows into large clouds. Meanwhile a new ribbon forms underneath it.

The rate of disintegration increased over time

A few floors shattered during the first second, but that rate of disintegration did not hold steady. Rather, the number of floors shattering each second increased each and every second. The reason is that objects falling in gravity continually increase in speed, so the explosives were detonated at an increasingly faster rate in order to stay ahead of the falling objects.

- The top section of the tower did not collide with the base; rather, the explosives shattered it just before it would have made contact.

- The debris did not contact the base portion; rather, the explosives were always staying a few microseconds ahead of it.

- The overhanging section cannot be seen falling down in photographs in one large chunk because it was shattered by explosives. Its debris fell down at the rate objects fall in gravity, but none of the debris can be seen in photographs because the base was destroyed at the same rate; therefore, the base was always a few microseconds ahead of that debris.

The steel beams fell much faster than the dust, so the steel beams were actually passing through the clouds of dust. However, new clouds were created at the same rate at which the debris was falling. Therefore, as soon as a steel beam fell below one particular cloud, it entered a new cloud that had just been created a few microseconds earlier. By the time it fell below _that_ cloud, another cloud had been created below it. The end result was that all of the falling objects were always hidden by clouds of dust.

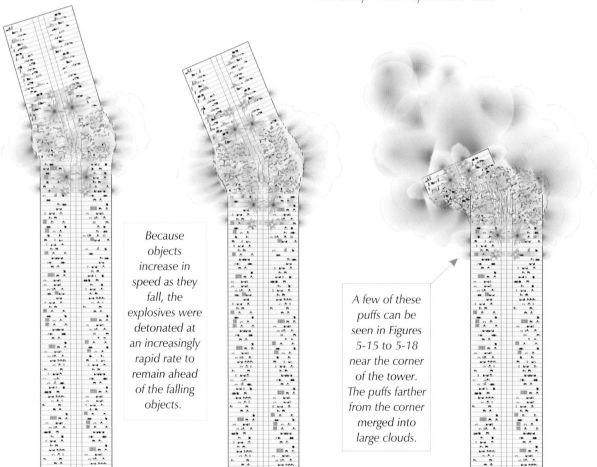

Because objects increase in speed as they fall, the explosives were detonated at an increasingly rapid rate to remain ahead of the falling objects.

A few of these puffs can be seen in Figures 5-15 to 5-18 near the corner of the tower. The puffs farther from the corner merged into large clouds.

Figure 7-6   1½ seconds   **Figure 7-7**   2.0 seconds   **Figure 7-8**   2½ seconds

The clouds of dust expanded to perhaps two or three times the diameter of the building because the explosives created a high pressure inside the tower. The 20 million kg of debris from the overhanging section eventually hit Building 4, but we cannot see that debris as it fell because the clouds of dust were so phenomenal. The only objects that can be seen falling are some of the outer pieces of the tower that were blown off as the explosives were detonated.

Figure 6-4 shows shiny objects scattered on the rooftops in the area. These objects are pieces of the aluminum coverings along the exterior columns (Figure 3-5, page 24).

The explosives shredded the covers, and the gas pressure was so high that some of them were blown all over the neighboring buildings.

The final explosions at the base of the tower and in the basement had to break joints on columns made from 100mm thick steel, so they were **powerful** explosives. The seismic data peaked when the explosives in the basement were detonated. Then the explosions stopped and the rubble continued to fall for another couple of seconds, resulting in smaller seismic tremors (the blue section of Figure 7-1)

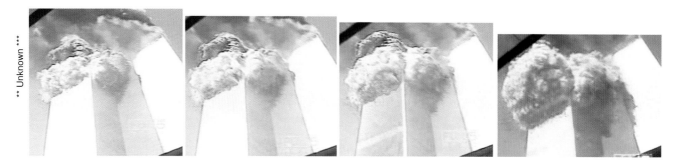

Figure 7-11   *Four frames of video show the collapse progressed floor by floor in a nearly perfectly balanced manner.*

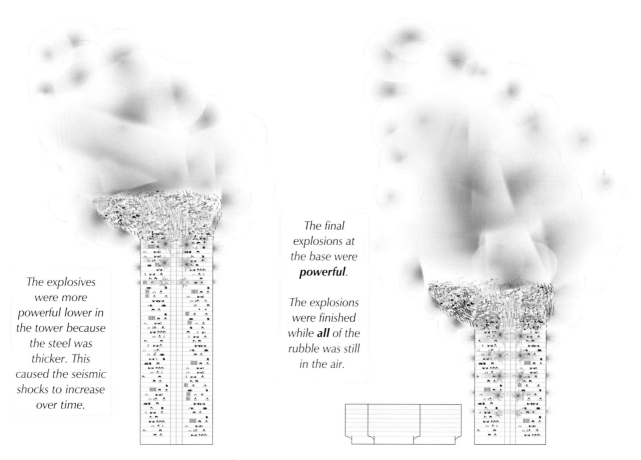

The explosives were more powerful lower in the tower because the steel was thicker. This caused the seismic shocks to increase over time.

*The final explosions at the base were **powerful**.*

*The explosions were finished while **all** of the rubble was still in the air.*

Figure 7-9   *4.0 seconds*

Figure 7-10   *4½ seconds*

No "potential energy" needed

Objects above the ground have "potential energy" due to the force of the gravity. The experts claim that the potential energy of the towers was the source of the energy that shattered the towers into dust. However, the only sensible explanation for the collapse is that explosives were detonated at a rate that matched the acceleration due to gravity. Each floor was shattered *before* the debris above it was about to make contact. The end result is that the debris *never collided with the floors*. Rather, all debris was in free-fall..

By the time the debris hit the ground, the fastest moving debris (the debris from the top of the tower) was traveling up to 190 mph. Since none of its potential energy was used to shatter the towers, all of its energy was available to become heat. There was more than 200,000 tons of steel in these towers, and it was at an average height of 200 meters, so a lot of energy was available for heat production. The explosives added even more heat to the beams. This would explain why the rubble ended up with such a high temperature.

The explosives would also explain why photos of the rubble show only dust and pieces of steel; namely, the concrete, carpeting, and office furniture were pulverized by the explosives. Only steel can survive such abuse.

The seismic data of the towers shows that the South Tower required about two more seconds to collapse than the North Tower. The extra two seconds was because the South Tower started to collapse by forming a crack, and then the tower was severed into two pieces. Each of those two pieces were separate, independent demolitions, but both of them occurred at the rate an object falls in gravity. By comparison, the North Tower disintegrated in almost one, continuous motion.

Have you ever tried to break concrete?

I suspect that many of the people who refuse to believe explosives were used have never tried to bust a concrete slab. Most people seem to believe that concrete has about the same strength as chalk, but if concrete was as fragile as the typical person believes, it would not be safe to use it in bridges.

Breaking concrete into pieces is a common procedure around the world. Pneumatic jack hammers are designed specifically for this purpose. The jack hammers do not pulverize the concrete into powder; rather, all they do is crack it into pieces. Only a small amount of powder is created in the process. In order to pulverize concrete into powder, explosives must be used. Concrete will not turn into powder simply by falling down onto another piece of concrete.

Some people have made the remark that the buildings were very tall, and therefore a piece of concrete falling from such a height could easily shatter into powder. However, the concrete shattered in the air, not when it hit the ground. If a piece of concrete is 1,000 feet in the air and shatters into powder after falling to 990 feet, that means it shattered into powder after falling only 10 feet. This is exactly the same as dropping a concrete block from a height of 10 feet above the ground.

Building 7 was a conventional demolition

Videos show Building 7 collapsing in perhaps eight seconds. Building 7 was about half the height of the towers, but it collapsed in about the same amount of time.

Figure 7-12 shows the seismic data of its collapse. The first thing to notice is that the vibrations are one tenth the magnitude of the North Tower. Therefore, the background noise is much more noticeable. The background noise is so significant that it is difficult to figure out exactly when the collapse began and when it finished.

The next thing to notice is that there appears to be three phases to the collapse of Building 7. The first may be the building falling down (red); next is a few seconds where perhaps the rubble settled (blue), and finally the vibrations increase significantly (green).

It is possible that the second and third phases (blue and green) are not even part of the collapse of Building 7. Maybe an earthquake coincidentally occurred at that moment in time. The seismic sensors pick up vibrations, but they do not identify the source of those vibrations. Only a serious scientific analysis from a variety of seismic centers could pinpoint the source, but our government has not bothered with such an analysis.

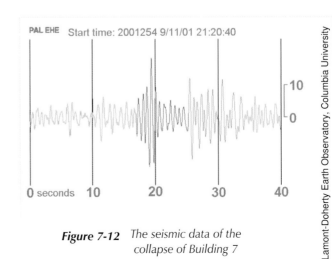

Figure 7-12   *The seismic data of the collapse of Building 7*

The third phase (green) is the confusing part of the graph. If those vibrations belong to Building 7 it could mean that explosives were set off *after* the building had collapsed.

It should be noted that the "experts" claim that Building 7 collapsed in 18 seconds, which would mean all three phases of that seismic data are of the "collapse." However, the low quality video I found on the Internet shows the building collapsing in about eight seconds. Do the experts have a more accurate video? Or are they making the mistake of measuring from the start of the red phase to the end of the green phase and then assuming that entire span of time is the collapse?

How could the steel corrode?

Only a tiny fraction of all steel beams in the World Trade Center were inspected. A few of them were very peculiar. A *New York Times* article in February, 2002 described them as:

> *Pieces of steel have also been found that were apparently melted and vaporized not solely because of the heat of fires, but also because of a corrosive contaminant that was somehow released in the conflagrations.*
>
> ...
>
> *Perhaps the deepest mystery uncovered in the investigation involves extremely thin bits of steel collected from the trade towers and from 7 World Trade Center, a 47-story high rise that also collapsed for unknown reasons. The steel apparently melted away, but no fire in any of the buildings was believed to be hot enough to melt steel outright.*

A brief article in *The Minerals, Metals & Materials Society* gives a technical analysis of a steel beam from Building 7. The most interesting paragraph:

> *Rapid deterioration of the steel was a result of heating with oxidation in combination with intergranular melting due to the presence of sulfur. The formation of the eutectic mixture of iron oxide and iron sulfide lowers the temperature at which liquid can form in this steel. This strongly suggests that the temperatures in this region of the steel beam approached ~1,000°C,*

The scientists who inspected the steel did not bother with any speculations on what could have caused the high temperatures.

The FEMA report describes these odd steel beams without technical details (Figure 7-13), and in such a vague manner that you have to carefully think about what this corrosion might mean. I say the *"hot corrosive environment approaching 1,000°C"* that FEMA refers to is evidence of explosives. The burning of office furniture, diesel fuel, or jet fuel will not create such high temperatures or such corrosive conditions. FEMA described the corrosion as *"an unusual event,"* but perhaps it is unusual only for fires; perhaps it is a common event with explosives.

Nothing happens without a reason; there is a reason the steel showed signs of high temperature corrosion. Why not look for the reason rather than terminate the issue? Or does FEMA know the reason, and are they simply avoiding it?

---

8. 2. 8 Appendix C: Limited Metallurgical Examination

Two structural steel samples from the WTC site were observed to have unusual erosion patterns. One sample is believed to be from WTC 7 and the other from either WTC 1 or WTC 2.

8. 2. 8. 1 Observations and Findings

a. The thinning of the steel occurred by high temperature corrosion due to a combination of oxidation and sulfidation.

b. Heating of the steel into a hot corrosive environment approaching 1,000 °C (1,800 °F) results in the formation of a eutectic mixture of iron, oxygen, and sulfur that liquefied the steel.

c. The sulfidation attack of steel grain boundaries accelerated the corrosion and erosion of the steel.

d. The high concentration of sulfides in the grain boundaries of the corroded regions of the steel occurred due to copper diffusing from the high-strength low-alloy (HSLA) steel combining with iron and sulfur, making both discrete and continuous sulfides in the steel grain boundaries.

8. 2. 8. 2 Recommendations

The severe corrosion and subsequent erosion of Samples 1 and 2 constitute an unusual event. No clear explanation for the source of the sulfur has been identified.

Figure 7-13   *A section of Appendix C of the FEMA WTC report*

Was the collapse beyond perpetual motion?

Perpetual motion requires using energy without wasting any of it so that the same energy can be used over and over. Even more absurd than perpetual motion is a process which uses more energy than is available to it, which requires it to create energy.

Cracking a concrete block into two pieces requires energy, and converting a concrete block into _powder_ requires even more energy. The smaller the particles, the more energy needed.

Perhaps 100,000 tons of concrete in each tower was pulverized to a powder. This required a lot of energy. The powder was ejected with a velocity so high that clouds of dust expanded to two or three times the diameter of the building. This also required energy. Thousands of steel beams in the building broke at their joints, and breaking those joints required energy. Energy was also needed to shred the corrugated steel sheets that were part of every floor. The high temperature of the rubble required energy as well. Where did all this energy come from?

I can think of only two ways to explain the powdering of the concrete without violating the laws of physics:

1) The buildings were incredibly defective.
   If the concrete was defective, not much energy would be needed to turn it into powder. Also, if the rivets, bolts, and welds that held the steel beams together were corroded and/or defective, not much energy would be needed to break the joints. Of course, if the towers were defective, it is amazing that they survived 30 years of storms.

2) Small packages of explosives were used.
   If small packages of explosives were placed at several locations on virtually every floor, they could provide the energy necessary to break the joints and shatter the concrete.

Both of these theories would explain why our government wanted the rubble destroyed so quickly. Are either of these theories correct? Before we try to answer that question, consider what the rubble would be like with each of those theories:

1) If the buildings were incredibly defective.
   No additional heat would be added to the rubble. The final temperature of the rubble would be due to whatever heat was remaining from the fire, and whatever heat was created as the pieces hit the ground (which converts the remaining potential energy into heat).

2) If small packages of explosives were used.
   The steel directly next to explosives would be exposed to a high temperature gas, although only briefly. This could melt small, thin portions of the steel, and it would add a bit of heat to the thicker pieces of steel.

   The explosives would shatter the concrete and the small particles would pick up a significant amount of heat. Those hot particles would raise the temperature of the rubble significantly.

   The steel in the basement was very thick, so the explosives had to be powerful, which would create a lot of heat. The combination of the basement walls and the falling rubble would trap a lot of the heat inside the basement.

My point is that if explosives were used, the rubble would end up with a significantly higher temperature than if the buildings had merely fallen down, and the temperature in the basement would be extremely high. Judging by the high temperature of the rubble five days after the collapse (Figure 6-5), it appears that explosives were used.

A Challenge for Physics Students

Can you estimate the amount of energy needed to pulverize the concrete in the towers? If you designed a building that shattered into dust, would you be able to figure out if your structure truly "fell down" or if it was blown up?

With the endless fighting between nations and religions, the world needs a way to determine when a building has been secretly destroyed with explosives. So, rather than practice physics with irrelevant problems, how about looking for a way to deal with _this_ problem?

Could it really be a scam?

The odd seating arrangements in Flight 11

The Boston Globe has a list of passengers and seat assignments for Flight 11. If their data is correct, the passengers were bunched up rather than scattered throughout the plane (Figure 8-1). Several rows were empty, while other rows were crowded with passengers. This is *not* the way seats are filled. Rather, airlines put a person in every row before they put strangers next to each other. The end result is that if a plane is half full of people, every row will have a person in it, and every person will have an empty seat next to him. There are two reasons the airlines do this. One is to distribute the weight evenly in the airplane. The other is that people are like birds that perch on telephone wires; we do not want to be touching strangers.

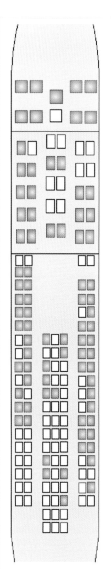

Figure 8-1

This diagram shows which seats in Flight 11 were vacant (white squares are vacant seats).

Passengers were not evenly spread throughout the plane. This shows that a large number of tickets were sold. The airline had to put passengers who purchased tickets later in time next to people who purchased tickets earlier in time. But on the day of the flight, many passengers did not show up. This created this strange seating arrangement in which strangers were clumped together.

Is this evidence that the people conducting this scam were trying to reduce the number of casualties by purchasing tickets to the deadly flights?

Why don't the airlines release the data for the other three flights? Why the secrecy?

A scam makes more sense

A summary of the main reasons why the 9-11 attack appears to be a scam:

- The **destruction of the rubble**. The destruction proceeded at frantic rate, and most importantly, it was a violation of our laws to destroy the rubble.

- An enormous amount of **concrete turned to powder** and flew out of the building with a very high velocity. All steel beams in the building broke, mainly at their joints and welds. I think this required an energy source, such as explosives.

- The steel beams from the towers **dropped at the rate objects fall in gravity**. This means they did not encounter any resistance along the way, which means they never hit any of the concrete floors. This means the concrete floors shattered into powder without being touched by those beams. I think the floors were shattered by explosives, not by falling debris.

- The **overhanging section of the South Tower never fell out of the clouds of dust**. I think explosives were destroying the floors as fast as that overhanging section fell down.

- The **temperature of the rubble was above the melting point of aluminum** in some areas, even after it was sprayed with water. I think the explosives added a lot of heat to the rubble.

- **Nobody wants to investigate.** President Bush and Cheney wanted to "limit" the investigation; investigators were hampered; and the FBI, FEMA, and other agencies either refused to investigate, or they did only a minimal, pathetic investigation. Furthermore, most members of our media, who boast that they are "watchdogs," have no interest in understanding what happened, nor do they care that our government violated our laws. Instead they encourage us to hate Al-Qaeda and support President Bush. This is not because these people never support investigations; after all, many of them demanded an investigation of the Clinton / Lewinsky affair. Why would these people *not* want an investigation of the 9-11 attack, which is the biggest crime the USA has ever experienced?

Explosives in Building 7 but not the towers?

Some people suspect that Building 7 was destroyed by explosives, but not the towers. There are also people who believe that the decision to blow up Building 7 was made *after* the towers were attacked. According to *that* theory, somebody decided to take advantage of the chaos that day by destroying Building 7.

However, anybody who suspects Building 7 was destroyed by explosives would have to come to the conclusion that explosives were used in the towers. To understand why, let's begin by considering the theory that somebody made the decision to blow up Building 7 *after* they saw the towers collapse.

This theory requires that several people get together and very quickly agree to a serious crime. At least one of them must have experience with demolitions in order figure out how many packages of explosives they needed. Then they would have to purchase the explosives, have them delivered, and install them in a 47-story building. All this would have to be accomplished within the span of a few hours. However, it was virtually impossible to drive a car into lower Manhattan after the planes hit, which means that it was virtually impossible for somebody to ask for a shipment of explosives to be delivered to the building by that afternoon. The only way they could acquire the explosives would be if there was a store within walking distance of Building 7 that sold packages of explosives for demolitions. Or, if a truck full of demolition explosives had been caught in the traffic jam near Building 7, they could break into the truck and steal the explosives.

As you can see, it is extremely unlikely that a group of people could have purchased (or stolen) enough explosives to bring down Building 7. If you respond that they could have used the diesel fuel that was already inside the building to manufacture their own bombs, that is even less likely. Making bombs with diesel fuel is not easy. More importantly, they could not use "bombs"; rather, they needed lots of small packages of explosives that could be *controlled precisely.*

So let's dismiss the possibility that somebody decided on September 11th to blow up Building 7. This leads us to the conclusion that they made this decision *before* September 11th. They purchased the explosives, wired them in the building while people were still working inside, and then waited for the attack.

This leads us to conclude that these people must have known that the attack was coming, although they may not have known which day. But how could they know the attack was coming? The only two groups of people who truly knew the attack was coming were the people involved in planning this attack, and the people who were spying on them. This leads us to the possibility that some agency, such as the CIA, discovered that this attack was coming but kept quiet about it rather than try to stop it.

This now leads us to the conclusion that whoever destroyed Building 7 was either part of the group that was planning the attack, or they had acquired information that the attack was coming and decided to take advantage of it. In either case they installed explosives in Building 7 in preparation for the attack. They then waited for the attack to occur. Their plan was to destroy the building and claim that the fire was the reason it fell down.

The question I have for you is: what would happen if the airplanes hit the towers but the towers did *not* fall down? Imagine the following scenario: The airplanes crash into towers; tremendous fires burn in the towers; after a few hours the fires are extinguished by the firemen and the towers remain standing; and then Building 7 collapses into a small pile of rubble.

Wouldn't it be suspicious if Building 7 crumbles from a fire if the towers survived much more severe fires? Remember, never in history has a fire caused a steel building to crumble. Therefore, if somebody blew up Building 7 with explosives and then claimed that a fire caused the collapse, the firemen would respond that *fires do not cause steel buildings to collapse.*

To better understand this issue, imagining yourself back in time to any year prior to 2001. Next imagine that a fire breaks out in Building 7, or some other steel building. Finally, imagine that after a few hours the small fires cause the entire building to crumble into a small pile of rubble. If such an event had occurred prior to 2001, it would have been the very first time a fire caused a steel-framed building to crumble. Such an unusual event would attract the attention of the entire world.

Scientists and engineers would want to analyze the steel beams to see how the fire did what no fire had done before. Universities would want information on the collapse so that they could use it in their engineering classes as an example of lousy engineering. Newspapers and television stations around the world would report it as the most bizarre fire anybody has ever seen. I also suspect that there would be thousands of lawsuits. Newspapers would be full of reports like those in Figure 8-2.

The point I am making is that it would not be safe to destroy Building 7 unless the towers collapse first. After the towers collapse, the collapse of Building 7 would appear to be just another weird event of that day's bizarre disasters. Therefore, whoever destroyed Building 7 would want to guarantee that the towers collapse first. This requires that they put explosives into the towers, also.

So now let's look at where we are with this scenario: A group of people have discovered that the attack is going to occur, so they put explosives in both towers and Building 7, and then they patiently wait for the attack.

This brings us to a dilemma. Putting explosives into Building 7 and both towers requires a lot of time, effort, and money. Furthermore, they would be risking *severe criminal charges*. What if somebody catches them installing the explosives? What if they get caught after they blow up the buildings? Would anybody be willing to go to all this trouble and take such a risk when they have no guarantee that the attacks will even take place? What if the hijackers are caught before they get on the plane? Or what if the hijackers decide that they are not competent as pilots and switch to a simpler attack, such as leaving a truck bomb in front of a government building? Or what if the hijackers decide to switch from hitting the World Trade Center to hitting the US Capitol? Or what if the hijackers turn out to be so incompetent as pilots that they crash on the way to the World Trade Center, or they miss the towers and hit some other buildings?

It is also possible that the hijackers would abandon the suicide mission simply because they decided they did not want to die yet. Certainly there have been people who were angry enough to join a suicide plot, but after a few months their anger diminished and they decided they would rather remain alive.

An even more likely problem is that the hijackers get control of the aircraft, change course towards Manhattan, and then the FAA realizes that something is seriously wrong. The FAA contacts the military, and the military sends up a plane to investigate. The military would eventually realize that the plane is heading towards Manhattan office buildings at an altitude so low that it will hit one of the buildings. Even if they do not shoot the first plane down, they would be likely to shoot the second plane down after they see the first one hit a building.

So now let's review where this scenario has taken us. If a group of people want to destroy Building 7, they must force the towers to collapse first, but they cannot collapse the towers unless the towers are hit by airplanes. Therefore, this plot to destroy Building 7 depends on some terrorists learning to fly commercial aircraft, getting control of those aircraft, and then flying into buildings without interference by the US military. This leads us to the conclusion that if somebody wants to destroy Building 7 they must also stop the FAA and military from interfering. This in turn requires at least some people in the military and FAA join this conspiracy.

So now this scenario has developed to the point at which a group of people are putting explosives into Building 7 and both towers, and some high ranking military and FAA personnel are involved. It also has the CIA and/or FBI observing the hijackers.

As you can see, a lot of people would have to be involved in this conspiracy simply to destroy Building 7. And this is just beginning. Whoever wants to blow up Building 7 and the towers must also be able to stop investigations. They must have the rubble destroyed immediately. However, it is

---

Skyscraper crumbles to dust!

Is your building safe? Yesterday in Manhattan, a 47 story tall, steel and concrete skyscraper collapsed into a small pile of rubble. What could cause such a total and complete destruction of a skyscraper? A nuclear bomb? An earthquake? An asteroid? No! According to experts, an ordinary **fire**! Diesel fuel used to power emergency generators caught on fire. Hospitals and many other buildings have backup generators and large tanks of diesel fuel. How many of these buildings will crumble if those tanks catch on fire? Is the building that **you** work in safe?

New World Record! 1 fire; 347,000 lawsuits!

Angry citizens are overwhelming the New York court system after a fire caused a steel building to crumble to dust! Most lawsuits have been filed against the designers of the building and the construction companies involved in the project, but the landlord has also been hit with thousands of lawsuits. The landlord is being accused of not properly maintaining the sprinkler system or the fireproofing.

Lawsuits have also been filed against the New York City government for allowing unsafe buildings.

Figure 8-2   *Headlines you would have seen in your newspapers if Building 7 collapsed before September 11, 2001*

a violation of our laws to destroy that rubble. This requires that these people have a lot of influence over our government.

By the time we have taken this scenario all the way to completion, we end up with a very large conspiracy. Also, it shows that if Building 7 was destroyed with explosives, then this entire 9-11 attack was a scam of unbelievable proportions. Why would anybody go to such trouble simply to destroy Building 7? For the amount of money this scam would require, they could purchase Building 7 and then tear it down.

You can't be half pregnant

The point of this section is that there are some people who believe that Building 7 was destroyed by explosives, but they do not believe the towers were destroyed by explosives. What I am trying to show you is that *if Building 7 was destroyed by explosives*, then the entire attack was a very large scam. You can't have *half a scam*! It was either all scam, or no scam.

Therefore, if you do not want to believe the entire attack was a scam, you need to find a sensible reason for the collapse of Building 7. However, keep in mind that never in history has a fire caused a steel building to crumble. Therefore, your mission, if you choose to accept it, is to find a sensible explanation for an event that never occurred before. Good luck!

Were terrorists really flying those planes?

The only way to guarantee that the hijackers are proficient pilots would be to replace them with suicide pilots who truly know how to fly those planes. Or it requires getting control of the aircraft

A few sites on the Internet claim those particular aircraft (the Boeing 767 and 757) are controlled by computer, and that it is possible for pilots on the ground to get control of those aircraft. Supposedly, the US government put this feature in some planes years ago to allow pilots on the ground to take control of hijacked aircraft (for the younger readers, years ago planes were hijacked on a frequent basis). This feature would also be of use during accidents, or when a pilot has a heart attack.

Thierry Meyssan believes a homing signal was broadcast from the World Trade Center a few hours before the planes hit, and that the airplanes had been modified so that they would follow the homing signal.

If the planes were being controlled by remote control, or if they were following a homing signal, then the hijackers could have been incompetent as pilots. Actually, the hijackers would not even have to be on the aircraft. Or, perhaps the hijackers had been provided with receivers that would pick up the homing signal.

"But the collapse didn't look like a demolition!"

When I first posted a document on the Internet in which I claimed that explosives were used to destroy the World Trade Center, a few people responded that the towers did not collapse in the manner that buildings are demolished, and therefore they could not have been destroyed by explosives. Rather than convince me that these buildings were not destroyed by explosives, they actually had the *opposite* effect. My reasoning was:

- The people making these remarks could not believe such a naive remark. Rather, they must be trying to divert attention away from explosives.

- Why would they want to divert our attention from explosives unless they knew that explosives were used?

- These people are more evidence that explosives were used.

Before I continue, let me explain why I consider the remark *"But the collapse didn't look like a demolition!"* to be a naive remark.

Let's assume Joe decides to rob a bank. Joe is aware that banks have security cameras that monitor the people in the bank, so he decides to wear a hairpiece and a fake beard. He also hides his gun in a small paper sack. Joe walks into the bank in his disguise, shows the paper bag to the teller, and demands money. I then post a document on the Internet in which I suggest that Joe probably robbed the bank with his pistol. What would your reaction be if someone posts the following response to me:

> *"Joe did not rob the bank! First of all, the person who robbed that bank had different hair than Joe. Second, Joe does not have a beard. Third, the person who robbed that bank did not have a gun; rather, he had a paper bag."*

Certainly your reaction would be:

- The person who posted that remark could not possibly believe it; rather, he must be trying to convince us that Joe did not rob the bank. But why would he try to convince us of Joe's innocence? If Joe is truly innocent he could offer evidence of his innocence.

- Joe must be guilty, and Joe or one of his friends must have posted that remark in an effort to divert our attention away from Joe.

Getting back to the complaint that the collapse of the towers did not look like a demolition, I was certain that the people making those remarks were part of the cover-up squad and were merely trying to mislead us. Why else would anybody post such remarks on the Internet and send such remarks to me? (President Bush refers to the people who attacked the World Trade Center as part of the *"Axis of Evil"* so, for lack of a better name, I will refer to the people who gave us the 9-11 scam as the *"Axis of Good."*)

I assumed the Axis of Good was putting out as much misinformation as possible in the hope of confusing the public. I had visions of hundreds of them spending hours at their computer, monitoring web sites and news groups. I imagined them spending hours each day posting a variety of idiotic messages in attempts to mislead and confuse us, as well as try to divert attention away from the issue of explosives.

There were a few times when I decided to respond to some of my critics. I explained to them in more detail why I believed explosives were used. I was shocked when a few of them eventually understood my reasoning and agreed with me that explosives were probably used.

I now realize that some of the idiotic remarks about the World Trade Center attack are coming from ordinary citizens. Most people are lacking accurate information about the collapse; most have not bothered to spend much time analyzing the collapse; and some are so patriotic that they are resisting the possibility that the attack was a scam. My point is that we must be careful about assuming the Axis of Good is making the dumb remarks.

Do the professors believe their theories?

Bazant submitted his theory to the *Journal of Engineering Mechanics* on September 13th, and posted his theory at three different universities at about the same time. This means that he spent no more than two days writing his theory. Why did he spend only *two days*? Or, if he wrote his report during the evenings in his spare time, why only two evenings? How could he believe that he had enough information about such a unique collapse when the only information available at that time were the images from the *Channel 4 Action Reporters*? How could he consider himself knowledgeable about a subject after watching TV for a few hours? I would think a real scientist would insist on spending more than two days just gathering information about the collapse.

Furthermore, Bazant did not mention Building 7. Was that because he was unaware that Building 7 collapsed? If so, that would prove that he did not even bother to read the most simplistic of news reports before publishing his brilliant theory. Or, did he avoid Building 7 because he did not know how to explain its collapse? If he is incapable of explaining the collapse of Building 7, why should we believe he can explain the collapse of the towers? I would think that a professor who knows enough to explain the collapse of the towers would also know enough to explain Building 7.

Do these professors believe their own theories? Or are they merely trying to find a less depressing explanation than the scam possibility? Or did somebody push or pay these professors to write about the collapse, and then provide the professors with false information?

Why hasn't Bazant bothered to correct the mistake about the towers falling like a stack of pancakes, or at least complete his theory so that we know what Figure 5-4C (page 42) would look like? Why did he rush to publish the theory but not bother to finish it at a later date?

I find it difficult to believe that a reputable professor would spend only a few days on a theory to explain something that nobody had ever seen before. I also find it difficult to believe that a professor would base his theory on a few television reports. Finally, I find it difficult to believe a professor would never bother to complete his theory when documents on the Internet are making fun of his Pancake Theory.

Perhaps the Pancake Theory had been prepared months before the attack. On September 11th somebody edited the document to fit the actual events and then looked for a professor to sign his name to it. This would explain why Bazant never finished his theory; i.e.; maybe it is not *his* theory.

University professors are regarded as experts simply because they are "professors." However, how can they be experts when they do not adequately explain the collapse of the towers or Building 7? How can these people be considered experts on fires when they fail to acknowledge the possibility that the soot and the lack of flames may be an indication that the fires were choking on their smoke?

There are many ways to destroy a building with explosives

In a conventional demolition, the explosives are timed so that the bottom of the building collapses first. The reason is to make the building drop vertically rather than tip to one side. Also, the people paying for the demolition want to use as few explosives as possible in order to save time and money. The small quantity of explosives results in large chunks of building remaining; i.e., the building does not turn into powder. Powder is a *side effect* of a demolition, not the purpose. Demolition companies try to minimize the production of powder because powder creates a mess that must be cleaned up. Also, if the powder travels to neighboring buildings there will be lots of angry people.

The towers did not resemble a conventional demolition because they were *not* a conventional demolition. The explosives in the towers were trying to simulate a collapse of a building due to a fire and airplane crash.

Extra explosives reduces side effects

Another reason the collapse of the towers did not resemble a conventional demolition is that the towers seemed to have a much larger quantity of explosives than a normal demolition. I suspect that extra explosives were used to pulverize the concrete into powder. There are two main advantages to pulverizing the concrete.

1) To eliminate the problem of giant chunks of the tower falling to the side.
    In a normal demolition the building is shattered when it is near the ground. The rubble does not fall through the air; rather, it simply collects at the ground. Since the Axis of Good was trying to simulate a building collapsing from an airplane crash, thousands of tons of rubble would be produced hundreds of feet in the air. This means that thousands of tons of rubble would have to fall hundreds of feet.

    If the explosives only broke the towers into pieces, large chunks of building would fall hundreds of feet. Chunks of the tower might collide with one another on the way down, which in turn could spread large pieces further out from the base of the towers. Some of those chunks might hit neighboring buildings and roads.

    By using enough explosives to pulverize the concrete and break every steel beam at its joint, there is no concern about large chunks of the tower falling to the ground. The concrete would fall as a powder, which would hit the ground so gently that nothing would be destroyed by it. And the steel would fall as short beams rather than as large assemblies.

    You might respond that the people destroying the towers would have no concern about the falling pieces of concrete, and therefore my reasoning is based on nonsensical assumptions. However, the purpose of this scam was not to kill people or destroy neighboring buildings. Rather, it appears that the Axis of Good went out of their way to reduce the number of casualties and destruction. They may be violent people, and some may suffer from serious mental problems, but they *are* human.

2) To simplify cleanup.
    Instead of having to deal with large pieces of concrete and twisted assemblies of steel, the crews only had to pick up short pieces of steel. This allows them to more rapidly destroy the rubble.

Normally a demolition company is responsible for cleaning up the powder, so they do not want to produce powder. However, this 9-11 demolition was going to be blamed on Osama, so taxpayers would cover all costs for the cleanup of powder. Therefore, the Axis of Good did not have to worry about how they would clean up the mess. Rather, they were more concerned about destroying all evidence as quickly as possible. The destruction of the rubble would occur at a significantly faster pace if the cleanup crews did not have to deal with large pieces of concrete or steel assemblies.

Building 7 was not hit by an airplane, so there was no need to fake a complex collapse that starts high up in the building. Furthermore, this building would be demolished late in the afternoon when not many people were around to watch it, so there was less concern about simulating a believable collapse. Building 7 was demolished in a conventional manner with a smaller amount of explosives. This is why large chunks of Building 7 survived.

Incidently, when a building is as tall as the World Trade Center towers, there are a lot of different ways in which to demolish it with explosives so that it does not appear to be a conventional demolition. For example, explosives could destroy the tower from both the very top and the very bottom at the same time, leaving the center to be the last section to be demolished. It would also be possible to start the explosions at three different locations in the building at once. For example, explosives at the 40th, 80th, and 110th floor could be detonated at the same time. The explosives could then work their way from those floors downward. This would not resemble a conventional demolition, either.

It would also be possible to set the explosives off in a horizontal manner rather than a vertical manner. In other words, one side of the building would start exploding, which would explode every window on that side of the building. The explosives would then work their way over to the other side of the building. My point is that there are a variety of ways to destroy a building with explosives so that it does not resemble a conventional demolition.

Why did the airplane almost miss the South Tower?

An airplane hit the North Tower almost directly in the center, but the plane hit the South Tower near the edge. The common assumption is that the pilot almost missed the building. Even the people who insist that these planes were flown by remote control are under the impression that the people flying the planes almost missed the building due to the fact that these planes were not very maneuverable.

My initial reaction was also that the pilot almost missed the South Tower. However, this attack seems to be so well-planned, and everything seems to have been executed so perfectly, that this may not have been a mistake.

The CoStar Group, Inc., a company that provides information on commercial real estate, put together a list of tenants of the World Trade Center to help with the identification of the missing people.[†] While they point out that they cannot be 100% certain of the tenants on that particular day, their report shows the North Tower had most of its vacant space above the 79th floor, and half of that was above the 90th floor. The 102nd floor was half empty. Therefore, hitting the North Tower above the 90th floor would reduce casualties at the crash zone. Is it a coincidence the hijackers hit the North Tower at floors 94 through 98? Or is this a sign the Axis of Good was trying to reduce casualties?

Hitting the tower at a high level also reduces casualties because most of the people would be below the crash zone, so they would be able to escape. Another advantage to hitting the tower at a high level is that if it severs the top section from the rest of the tower, only that small section should fall down; the entire tower should not topple.

The South Tower did not have any large areas of vacant space, except below the 30th floor, so there was no good location to hit it to reduce casualties. The best way to reduce casualties was to hit only a corner of the building. Finally, hitting a corner avoids the possibility that the airplane destroys so many core columns that the tower breaks into two pieces. Compare the orientation of the core columns in Figures 4-3 and 4-5; there was only 11 meters of flooring to protect the columns in the South Tower, not 20 meters.

Coincidental games and artwork

Ever since a truck bomb blew up at the base of the South Tower in 1993, millions of people have been wondering if somebody would attack the towers again. Therefore, the concept of attacking the towers could have popped up in the minds of artists when they wondered what to do for a new job. However, we should not dismiss such incidents as "coincidence" without investigating them. For example, a free game on the Internet called *Trade Center Defender* shows a photograph of the New York skyline as a background, with crude representations of the World Trade Center towers drawn on top (Figure 8-3). A jet flies across the screen towards the towers. The mouse is a cross hairs, and the object of the game is to click the cross hairs on the jet before it hits a tower. This game was supposedly available before September 11th, although by the time I discovered it

the background photograph had been changed to show the collapse.

Since I do not play computer games I am not a good judge of whether a game is "good" or "bad," but this game is so incredibly crude that I cannot believe that even a child would want to play it. Did somebody know this attack was coming and consider it amusing to create this game?

Almost all software, games, and documents on the Internet have a copyright notice, link to another site, or note that identifies the author. This game is one of the exceptions. This game doesn't even have identification embedded within its data. It appears that the person who created this game does not want to take credit for it. Is this just a coincidence?

The Houston Chronicle reported that a Houston rap group called *Inner City Hustlers* released an album in July, 2001 with the title *Time To Explode*. It showed the New York skyline and the World Trade Centers in flames. This would not have attracted my attention except the director of the company that created the artwork told the Chronicle that the musicians originally wanted to use the Houston skyline. So why did they switch to a New York City skyline? Was somebody influencing them?

July was also when artwork for an upcoming album by the group *Coup* was posted on the Internet, even though the album would not be released until November. Most people assume the similarity to the actual attack (Figures 8-4 and 8-5) was merely a coincidence, and that it was posted in July for promotional reasons. But the two members of this band live in Oakland, California, not New York, and the device the man is holding has "Covert Labs" written on it, suggesting a secret government agency. Would rap musicians who condemn businessmen and government select such symbolism without influence? And how often do music groups post artwork for their album many months before the album is ready to sell?

Figure 8-3 *"Trade Center Defender" may be the worst game ever made. Who made it? And why?*

[†] They also took those great photos of the small buildings of the World Trade Center in Chapter 1.

Did a few members of the Axis of Good think it would be amusing to convince music groups to put images of the upcoming attack on their album covers? If so, the Coup artwork was released in July because they were proud of themselves, not because they wanted to promote sales of a future album. Perhaps they passed the images and the Trade Center Defender game among themselves. (If it were possible to trace the flow of messages on the Internet, we might be able identify some members of the Axis of Good simply by looking at who received those images and games prior to September 11th.)

The Coup record label implies that the Axis of Good were so knowledgeable about physics that they could accurately predict the size and positions of the fireballs. They are obviously intelligent and educated. The only two mistakes they made are:

1) the fireballs are too dark.

2) There were no clouds in the sky that day.

Obviously, they are experts with explosives but no better at weather forecasts than TV newscasters.

Another interesting coincidence is that a television show called *The Lone Gunmen* was filmed in the year 2000 and shown in May 2001. The plot was about some government officials who use a laptop computer to take control of a passenger aircraft flying to Boston and crash it into the South Tower of the World Trade Center. The aircraft was going to hit the tower in almost the same location that Flight 175 hit it (Figure 8-6). Did a member of the Axis of Good write or influence the show?

Was John O'Neill's death a coincidence?

O'Neill was one of the Deputy Directors of the FBI until a few weeks before the World Trade Center attack. He quit his job at the FBI to work as security manager for the World Trade Center. Supposedly the main reason he quit the FBI was because he was angry at the Bush administration. O'Neill investigated terrorism for the FBI, and he accused the Bush administration of interfering with investigations and making deals with both the Taliban and Osama. He supposedly described it this way:

> *"The main obstacles to investigate Islamic terrorism were US oil corporate interests, and the role played by Saudi Arabia in it..."*

A magnification of the device the man is holding.

"Covert-Labs" is written on it.

Figure 8-4 *The actual attack*

Figure 8-5 *The July, 2001 artwork*

There were additional incentives to quit his job at the FBI, such as the job at the World Trade Center offered double his FBI salary (some reports say triple), and he had lost hope for getting significant promotions if he stayed with the FBI.

Late at night on September 10th, the day before O'Neill would start his new job, he met his friends Jerry Hauer and Robert Tucker to celebrate his new job. On September 11th he started working at his new job on the 34th floor of the North Tower. He was in the tower when the plane hit. He evacuated the tower like most other people, but he remained in the area. The last person to see O'Neill alive was an FBI agent, Wesley Wong. The two of them stopped to talk. At this time neither of the towers had collapsed. When O'Neill tried to make a call on his cell phone he had difficulty getting the phone to connect. He began walking away from Wong, towards one of the towers, perhaps to find a location with better reception. A few minutes later the South Tower collapsed. O'Neill's body was found about a week later. The fact that his body was discovered is a sign that he did not go back inside the tower, as some reports assume. Did he die from falling debris?

O'Neill accused the Bush administration of interfering with investigations on terrorism. He also accused the Bush administration of making deals with the Taliban and with Osama. Is it a coincidence that such a person would die? How about the coincidence that he quit his job for the FBI and had just started to work at the World Trade Center on September 11, 2001?

I find it difficult to believe that the people who offered O'Neill the job as security director of the World Trade Center did not realize that World Trade Center would be destroyed. The security department would have to know about the scam in order to allow the explosives in the building. I suspect their intention was to become O'Neill's employer only so they would have control over him, which in turn would make it easy for them to set him up to die in the attack. (I also wonder if the previous security director of the World Trade Center was offered the same high salary that O'Neill was offered, or if they deliberately offered O'Neill a very high salary to lure him out of the FBI.)

Jerry Hauer

O'Neill's death becomes more interesting when you consider who the person was who offered him the job at the World Trade Center. The *New Yorker* magazine implies that his friend, Jerry Hauer, was involved in his hiring.

Hauer was director of the World Trade Center in 1999. Hauer seems to be the main person who pushed for putting an "Emergency Command Center" in Building 7 to protect the mayor in case of a terrorist attack. A 50,000 square foot section of Building 7 between the 23rd and 25th floors was converted into a reinforced bunker.

During the 1990's there was paranoia that Saddam Hussein might attack America with anthrax, so this command center had the ability to resist biological attack, in addition to resisting attacks by conventional guns and bombs. It had its own air supply and 11,000 gallons of water. The windows and walls in this area were replaced and/or strengthened to be both bulletproof and bomb-resistant. CNN reports it was capable of resisting wind gusts of up to 160 miles per hour. It had three emergency generators and a 6,000 gallon diesel tank near the ground floor to power those generators. The bunker was finished in June of 1999 at a cost to taxpayers of about $13 million.

To get a better understanding of how ridiculous this bunker was, recall that the first five floors of Building 7 were almost completely taken up by transformers that were fed with 13,800 volts, and giant diesel tanks that held up to 42,000 gallons of fuel were placed near the transformers. The mayor puts a bunker above the transformers and the diesel fuel and considers himself safe from terrorist attack.

Despite what the FEMA report implies, Building 7 was *not* a conventional office building. Rather, Building 7 and this bunker belong in a *Three Stooges* movie. What were the people thinking when they designed this bunker? CNN quotes Hauer as saying:

> *"Particularly when it comes to biological terrorism, no city is where we're at."*

This bunker was able to resist biological attacks because it had its own air and water supply. If terrorists spread anthrax in the city, perhaps a dozen of the millions of people in New York City would be allowed to gather inside this bunker. They would be able to breathe clean air, drink clean water, and have plenty of diesel fuel for electricity. The bulletproof and bomb-resistant bunker would also protect them in case somebody tried to attack them with conventional weapons. Of course, since this bunker was not a hotel, it would be inconvenient to stay overnight, so the anthrax had to be cleaned up quickly.

Of all the buildings in New York City to put an Emergency Command Center in, this had to be the most ridiculous. It made more sense to put it in the basement of a conventional building. Perhaps this was the only building at the time that had enough vacant space for such a gigantic bunker. Or perhaps this was the only building that had a landlord who was gullible enough to allow all the risky activities that were going on inside.

There was more than one person (and more than one fireman) complaining that putting a reinforced bunker high up in such a dangerous office building was ridiculous. How could Jerry Hauer support such a dumb proposal? Is Hauer an idiot? And was Hauer really a friend of John O'Neill?

The WTC Attack Command Center

I think the 23rd floor of Building 7 was converted into a reinforced bunker in order to serve as the command center to destroy the World Trade Centers. Because it was 23 floors above ground, the Axis of Good would be able to observe the entire area and make a determination of how and when to set off the explosives. The bomb-resistant windows and walls would protect them from falling debris. The bunker had its own air supply so they would not have to breathe the asbestos and concrete powder. The bunker was designed to withstand winds of 160 mph so it would handle the brutal surge of powder and debris when the towers collapsed.

I doubt that the people who built that bunker were so stupid that they could not see the foolishness of what they did. The firemen had warned them about the fire hazard, and other people had complained also. Nobody could be stupid enough to believe the bunker made sense.

I doubt that the bunker was ever intended to be an "Emergency Command Center"; rather, it was a "WTC Fake Terrorist Attack Command Center" from the day it was proposed.

The reason photos of Building 7 show only tiny fires in only a few of the windows is because a few fires were set deliberately to create the impression that fires were burning. The Axis of Good never allowed those fires to spread to the rest of the building because they were going to spend most of the day on the 23rd floor.

The employees of Building 7 were evacuated between 9 and 10 in the morning, which was before either of the towers collapsed. The Axis of Good then had the entire building to themselves. This allowed them to do as they pleased without interruptions.

The towers were destroyed during the morning, and the dust was terrible for the rest of the day. The Axis of Good stayed inside the bunker drinking clean water, breathing clean air. (They may also have some spectacular photos of the attack.)

By 4 PM the dust had settled enough for them to leave Building 7. If you recall, CNN has a time line in which a fire was reported in Building 7 at 4:10 PM. Also recall somebody mentioned to Tom Franklin and other people between 4 and 5 PM that they should get away from Building 7 because

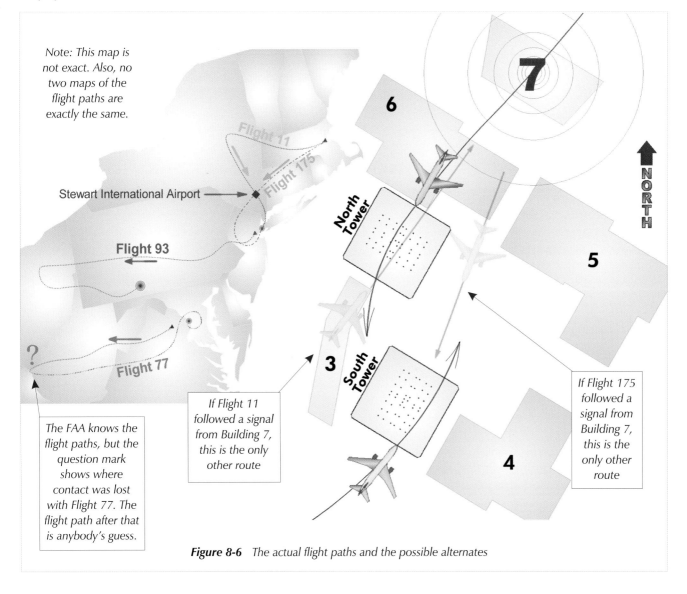

Figure 8-6 The actual flight paths and the possible alternates

it was going to collapse. My explanation of these events is that the Axis of Good left the bunker at about 4 PM. One of them made a phone call to the fire department to report the building on fire in order to create an official record that Building 7 was truly on fire. As they walked outside they made remarks to people in the area that they should stay away because the building was going to collapse.

Was Building 7 the source of a homing signal?

I doubt that real hijackers would care which direction they hit the towers. If I were a hijacker I would take the shortest route in order to minimize the time I was in the air. However, if the information Thierry Meyssan received is correct, a homing signal was used to control these aircraft. Meyssan believes that the homing signal was coming from "the World Trade Center" but it may have been coming from Building 7 rather than the towers. Also, the airplane's computers may have been following the homing signal rather than the hijackers following the signals.

If Building 7 was the source of the homing signal, and if the airplane's computers were flying the planes, both airplanes would try to get to Building 7 rather than the towers. This creates a problem. Specifically, if the destination is Building 7, the only way to make the planes hit the towers is to put them on a flight path in which the towers are directly in their way. Then, as the planes try to reach Building 7, they slam into the towers. However, this requirement severely restricts the possible flight paths. There is only one way to draw a line between the North Tower and Building 7, and there is only one line between the South Tower and Building 7. Each airplane must fly along those lines. The planes can fly the lines from either direction but, as shown by the faint airplanes (Figure 8-6), two of the directions are risky because it requires the planes pass very close to the other tower. The best flight paths are the ones that the hijackers coincidently decided to take.

The path of Flight 11 into the North Tower

Both planes started in Boston, which is north of New York City. Supposedly Flight 11 did not turn towards New York City until it was west of the city. In order to get on the path that would align it with both Building 7 and the North Tower it had to turn back towards the east, and then continue to fly east until it went past the city. Then it could turn towards the southwest. That would bring the plane directly over Building 7. As soon as it passed Building 7 the computer that was following the homing signal would notice the signal was getting weaker, so it would turn the plane around and head back towards Building 7, as shown by curve in the thin, black flight path in Figure 8-6. At 450 miles per hour, however, the plane would not have enough time

to turn. Instead, it would hit the tower just after its wings started to tip to make the turn.

It certainly is an interesting coincidence that the published path of Flight 11 shows the hijackers taking a path that lines it up with Building 7. Also, the hole created by the airplane shows the wings were tilted because the plane was in the process of turning when it hit the tower, just as if it was following a signal.

The path of Flight 175 into the South Tower

The only practical way to hit the South Tower if a plane from Boston is actually trying to get to Building 7 is to have the plane go south of New York City and then turn around and head northeast. It would then slam into the South Tower just before it reached Building 7. What a coincidence that the published flight path shows the hijackers doing exactly that. The hole created by the plane that hit the South Tower shows that it was in the process of making a sharp turn. If it could have continued the turn (if the South Tower had not been in the way), it appears that it would have ended up at Building 7.

Is it a coincidence that the hijackers selected the only flight paths possible if they were following a homing signal from Building 7? Maybe, but perhaps one of the reasons for the diesel fuel and backup generators in Building 7 was to ensure those homing signal transmitters had power, as well provide power to all of the other electronics used in this scam. The explosives in the tower may have been detonated with electricity that came from Building 7, also.

Stewart International Airport

On 13 September 2001 the *Telegraph*, a Nashua, New Hampshire newspaper, reported that a person who works at the Nashua air traffic control facility mentioned that Flights 11 and 175 came close to each other near Stewart International Airport, at New Windsor, New York (Figure 8-6). He also mentioned that the controller at his facility who handled Flights 11 and 175 also handled Egypt Air's Flight 990, which crashed for unknown reasons in the ocean off Massachusetts in 1999. (The official explanation for Flight 990 is that the pilot decided to commit suicide by crashing the airplane into the ocean.)

Is this New Hampshire newspaper reputable? Who is this unidentified FAA employee? The newspaper will only tell us that he *"spoke on the condition of anonymity."* If this mystery employee is correct, we have some more amazing coincidences to consider. We have the coincidence that the controller in charge of the mysterious Flight 990 was also in control of the mysterious flights that crashed into the World Trade Center. (Flight 990 brings up a subject this book will not get into, such as whether it was practice for the 9-11 scam). We also have the coincidence that the planes passed near each other over Stewart International Airport *at the same moment in time.*

What are the chances that two hijacked airplanes would cross each other's paths at the same moment in time? This could be an indication that there was a homing signal at Stewart International Airport.

The Air Force has a windowless, four story concrete building at this airport. It opened in 1958 to monitor the sky for Russian missiles. It was abandoned in the late 1960's when the technology became too obsolete to detect Russia's newer missiles. The building has been vacant ever since. The 120,000 square feet in this building would provide plenty of room for electronic equipment to control these aircraft, and the lack of windows would make it impossible for people to realize that something was going on inside.

The Bumble Planes theory

A speculation on the Internet (*The Bumble Planes*) suggests that the pilots of all four flights were tricked into landing at an Air Force base, such as by telling the pilots that America is under attack and they must turn off their transponders and land. The planes became unidentified blips on the radar screens when the transponders were turned off. The military then sent an unidentified military plane to cross the path of each plane. The blips merged on the radar screens, and when they separated the controller watching the blips had no idea which blip was which plane.

After getting the four planes to the Air Force base, all passengers were loaded onto Flight 93, which had plenty of extra seats. Empty airplanes under remote control hit the towers and the Pentagon, and Flight 93 was flown to an area where it could be shot down.

Although I don't see evidence that all four airplanes landed at the same location, the radar blips of Flight 11 and 175 may have merged over Stewart International Airport, and the planes may have landed there. Some variation of the Bumble Plane theory may explain what happened.

The seismic data from Building 7

If you recall, the graph of the seismic data for Building 7 (Figure 7-12) suggests that there were three phases to the collapse of this building. The third phase of the collapse is when the vibrations became larger, as if the building was collapsing for the second time. My explanation for that third phase is that the bunker had been loaded with explosives that were set to go off after the building had collapsed. This would guarantee that the bunker was completely destroyed. If a radio transmitter sent a homing signal to the airplanes, this second demolition would ensure the transmitter was destroyed, also.

Did the city want the towers destroyed?

Many reports claim that the World Trade Center was a financial burden on the city of New York. Some other people complained that the architecture of the World Trade Center was too bland and/or did not fit in with other buildings, and some landlords in the area complained that it had a negative effect on their income. This brings us to another area of mystery, secrecy, and rumors. Specifically, there are rumors that some New York City government officials wanted to demolish the World Trade Center many years ago.

The most affordable method to get rid of the World Trade Center is a conventional implosion in which small packages of explosives are used to shatter the building, which then drops vertically without hitting any other buildings. However, the insulation in the towers contained asbestos, and our environmental laws prohibit implosions of buildings that contain asbestos. Environmental laws require the asbestos to be removed before a building is imploded. The reason is that explosives pulverize a significant amount of the material in a building into a fine grained powder, but there are severe health risks involved with breathing powdered asbestos.

Many years ago some of the asbestos in the towers was encapsulated in plastic. In the early '80s much of the asbestos was supposedly removed. However, there was still asbestos in the building.

A couple of Internet sites claim that in September of 2000 the government asked for sealed bids on removing the remaining asbestos. It was referred to as:

> Contract WTC-115.310 - "Removal and Disposal of Vinyl Asbestos Floor Tiles and Other Incidental Asbestos-Containing Building Materials" at the WTC, with bids due Tuesday, October 17, 2000.

That request to remove the asbestos is supposedly at the Internet site of The Port Authority of New York and New Jersey, but I cannot get the link to work. Did the government delete the information because they considered it of no value to anybody? Or did they remove this information to reduce the chances that somebody would make a connection between their desire to destroy the towers and the subsequent destruction by a few terrorists? Or, am I misinterpreting the motives behind New York City's attempt to remove the asbestos from the World Trade Center?

Supposedly, when the government discovered that it would be very expensive to remove the asbestos, they gave up on their ideas of imploding the World Trade Center. However, we should consider the possibility that many people in the New York area decided to circumvent our "ridiculous" environmental laws by exploding the buildings and pretending that it was due to a terrorist attack.

The attack on September 11 involved more than the destruction of the World Trade Center. There was an attack on the Pentagon, and there was a plane that crashed in Pennsylvania. This leads us to conclude that the attack involved more than one group of people, and there was more than one motive. Some of the people in the New York area joined this scam to destroy the World Trade Center, while some military officials would have joined it in order to justify their budgets and wars. Since the attack would be blamed on Arabs, lots of Christians and Jews in different nations would have joined the scam simply to justify killing Arabs. Some people, including foreigners, may have joined the attack to remove the Taliban in an attempt to get oil pipelines to the Caspian Sea area. Other people may have joined this attack simply to profit from the sales of weapons.

What caused the holes in Building 5 and 6?

Christopher Bollyn of the *American Free Press* points out that the large hole in Building 6 (Figures 5-34 & 6-4) is so deep (below ground level) that it was not likely to be from falling debris. It is also a clean hole, not a ragged hole (Figures 8-7 & 8-8). Building 5 also has a peculiar hole.

The plane crashed into the North Tower at 8:46AM. Employees of Building 6 reacted to the crash by evacuating the building within a few minutes. Two police officers went to Building 6 to evacuate the building, but John Martuge of the US Customs insists that the employees decided to evacuate on their own, so the police were not needed. Let's assume Martuge is correct that the employees were frightened and decided to evacuate on their own; this leads us to wonder why the police wanted to evacuate Building 6 so quickly. At the time only the North Tower had been hit by an airplane; nothing had hit the South Tower. Furthermore, there was no reason to believe the tower would fall down. Meanwhile, the people in the South Tower heard a message over their public address system that they had nothing to worry about and could remain inside. Why the rush to evacuate Building 6 but not the South Tower and other nearby buildings?

Several photos (Figure 1-1 is an example) show a plume of dust coming from near Buildings 5 and 6 as each tower collapsed (all cameras were too far away to determine the exact source of the dust). These plumes shot upwards with

James R. Tourtellotte

Figure 8-7 *This photo was taken from inside Building 6. It shows the interior of the large hole in the center of the building (Figure 6-4 or 5-34). If this hole was caused by falling debris, why isn't it more jagged? The floors sheared off in a nearly perfectly vertical manner. One side of the Pentagon also had a perfectly vertical cut*

high velocity, while the rest of the dust spread outward. This implies the plumes of dust were under high pressure.

The collapse of the towers would have pushed dust and air into the underground passages, which would have increased the air pressure. Any explosives in the basement would have further increased the air pressure. The high pressure dust would have traveled underground, possibly causing damage to other buildings, utility lines, and subways. To minimize damage, a large vent to the underground area should be created. Is it just a coincidence that Building 6 shows a large hole that extends deep into the basement? Did the high pressure blow open that hole? Or did the Axis of Good put explosives in Building 6 to create a vent? If explosives created that hole, this could explain why the police rushed to evacuate Building 6.

Building 6 stood between the towers and Building 7, so if the Axis of Good was on the 23rd floor of Building 7, they might want to relieve the underground pressure before it reached Building 7.(Figure 3-1 gives a good view of the area) Perhaps the hole in Building 5 (Figure 6-4, page 69) was also a vent.

Was Ramsi Yousef responsible for the 1993 bomb?

The desire of the city to destroy the towers makes me wonder if the bomb that went off in 1993 at the bottom of the World Trade Center was a deliberate act to damage the World Trade Center so severely that the city would have justification to implode the towers. Did Ramsi Yousef really do that bombing? Or was he just a patsy?

Yousef supposedly wanted to topple one tower onto the other tower, but some reports mention that the bomb was not put in the correct location. Is this a coincidence? Was Yousef smart enough to make such a powerful bomb but too stupid to put it in the correct location? Furthermore, Salemeh was captured when he tried to get his deposit back on the van he rented to blow up the tower. How could he be both so stupid and so intelligent at the same time?

Perhaps the bomb was deliberately put in the wrong location because the Axis of Good did not truly want to topple the towers. Rather, they simply wanted to create such destruction that they had an excuse to get rid of the towers. And at the same time they would have an excuse to justify American involvement in the Mideast. However, just as the towers were so strong that they survived the airplane crashes in 2001, the towers were so strong that the 1993 bomb did not damage the tower enough to justify removing them.

Why did the attack occur on September 11th?

The military had been renovating a section of the Pentagon for years, and they wanted to hit that section in order to reduce casualties. However, by September of 2001 the renovation was almost complete. The military had only a few more weeks to do this scam.

September 11th was the day the residents of New York City were selecting candidates for a new mayor. Giuliani was going to be replaced. If Giuliani and/or his team were involved with this fake attack, the attack had to occur while they were in control of the city because the scam required control of the New York City police, fire, and other agencies in order to destroy the rubble.

After the attack Giuliani found reasons to extend his term as mayor during the period of emergency. He also struggled desperately to be important during this disaster, and for many months he was the center of attention. Time magazine gave him the honor of being "Person of the Year 2001" and "Mayor of the World." Some people suggested that he become president. He was considered to be a great leader.

At the other extreme, a book by Wayne Barrett ("Rudy!: An Investigative Biography of Rudolph Giuliani," July, 2000) has a lot of information that Giuliani would probably want to remain a secret, such as his father was caught in the act of armed robbery, and after getting out of jail worked for a loan shark. The book also discusses aspects of Giuliani's marriages and other relationships that a political candidate would prefer remain a secret.

Why were the casualties so low?

You do not need to know much about statistics to realize that something is unusual about the number of casualties. For example, the Pentagon is a very large building, and the portion that was being renovated was small. Therefore, the odds are that the terrorists would hit an area full of people, but they hit the section with the fewest people. Another example is that the terrorists hijacked four airplanes, and all four were extremely low on passengers, which is statistically unlikely. This implies that even the hijacking of the airplanes was a scam.

Only a couple thousand people died when the towers collapsed. Almost everybody in both towers evacuated. Hundreds–maybe thousands–of people had not arrived at work yet because some of the companies did not start work until after 8:45 in the morning. If the terrorists had decided to take a later flight, the buildings would have been full of people and tourists.

The low number of casualties is more evidence that the attack was a scam. The people who destroyed the towers deliberately waited until most of the people had evacuated. They knew when the buildings were evacuated because they were on the 23rd floor of Building 7. They could see the entire area, so they knew when people stopped coming out of the buildings. Sure, there were firemen inside the towers, but those firemen would be inside all day. They could not wait for the firemen to leave.

James R. Tourtellotte

Figure 8-8   *The interior of Building 6 and the rubble at the bottom of the hole.*

Why did the South Tower collapse first?

The North Tower was hit by an airplane first, and its fires were the most severe. So why did the South Tower collapse first? My guess is:

- The collapses were suppose to appear realistic. This required the towers to collapse while the fires were burning. However, the fires in the South Tower were so small and there were so many firemen rushing in that there was a risk the fires would soon become insignificant. It would look suspicious if the fires vanished and *then* the tower crumbled.

- The Axis of Good waited for the people to evacuate the towers, and the South Tower was evacuated much sooner. One reason the South Tower was evacuated so quickly is that many people left it as soon as the plane hit the North Tower. The elevators were still working at that time, so they got out quickly. The people who remained in the South Tower until after the plane hit had to walk down the stairs, but because some people had already evacuated by elevator, there were fewer people trying to get down the stairs. This made it easier for them to get out.

  By comparison, the stairways in the North Tower were so crowed with people that dozens or hundreds of people were still walking down the stairs when the South Tower collapsed.

Is our government too inept to be involved?

Some people complain to me the World Trade Center attack could not possibly be a scam because it would require *too many people* and *too much effort*. They point out that our government is so inept that they could not possibly have been involved with such a complex stunt.

Perhaps one of the best quotes to respond to these people comes from Mike Ruppert in interview on 19 April 2002:

> *"...the CIA, and FBI and all the intelligence agencies and the military are too incompetent to have pulled off this attack. But Osama bin Laden in a cave was capable of doing it?"*

Ruppert points out a bizarre aspect of the attack that most people overlook. First, consider how devastating this attack was:

- Three expensive buildings crumbled; there was lots of damage to nearby buildings; the subway under the World Trade Center was damaged; and the electric substation in Building 7 was destroyed.

- A portion of the Pentagon was destroyed.

- Four airplanes were hijacked and destroyed.

Now consider that all this destruction is blamed on 19 Arabs, none of which were experienced pilots, and the mastermind is living in a cave in Afghanistan, and some rumors claim he is suffering from serious health problems. This small group of Arabs has such talent that they can create destruction in America that almost defies description.

Millions of Americans insist that 19 terrorists did all this by themselves, and at the same time they insist the attack was *too complicated for Americans*. However, if 19 Arabs could do this, 19 CIA agents could do it, also.

I think this attack required a lot more than 19 people. If it is truly possible for 19 people to do this much destruction, 500 people could destroy a complete state; 4000 people could destroy all of America, 10,000 people could destroy the world. You should hope that this attack was a scam, and that it required thousands of people, years of effort, and millions of dollars.

A lesson for architects

Every photograph of New York was dominated by the two, rectangular towers of the World Trade Center. Unfortunately, many people considered the towers to be architectural oddballs among the smaller buildings of lower Manhattan, some of which were much more decorative.

I would describe the towers as having a serious, industrial aura, not an artistic, intimate, or playful appearance. I think they would have looked best around factories, power plants, and steel mills, as opposed to apartments, parks, or decorative office buildings (see photo on page 12).

If the towers had been half as tall, or if they had been designed with more artistic detail, they would have blended in much better. In such a case they might have been able to attract more tenants, which in turn would have caused the World Trade Center to be profitable. The city officials of New York would have been proud of the towers, rather than wishing they could destroy them. Also, the residents of New York would have been proud of the buildings.

The lesson to learn from this scam is that if you design a building that dominates all others, you better make sure it fits in with the neighboring buildings. Or at least don't put asbestos in it.

Flight 77 hits the Pentagon?

News reports about the crash of Flight 77 into the Pentagon that were written in September, 2001 informed us that there were no videos available of the crash. As a result, television viewers never saw the plane hit the Pentagon.

At the end of February, 2002 news about Thierry Meyssan, who wrote the book *The Frightening Fraud*, had reached the USA. His book was available only in French, but an English version of his Internet site pointed out that there is no evidence that Flight 77 hit the Pentagon. Thousands of people around the world looked through photographs and news reports of the crash of Flight 77, and many of us were agreeing with Meyssan. Accusations of a scam began appearing on the Internet.

On 7 March 2002 the military released five images from a video security camera that recorded Flight 77 hitting the pentagon. When the military released this video they proved they were *lying* about not having any video. Obviously they had been keeping this video a secret. I suspect they released the five images in an attempt to counteract Meyssan by showing us that Flight 77 actually did hit the Pentagon, and that it hit very low to the ground. Figures 9-1 and 9-2 are the first two of those five frames. (The military labeled the images "Plane" and "Impact," and they inserted the incorrect time and date in the images.)

There are three important aspects to these two frames.

1) **The White Smoke.** The red arrow in Figure 9-1 points to the white smoke from Flight 77. This resembles the exhaust of a missile. A Boeing 757 does *not* leave a trail of white smoke.

    Whatever is producing the white smoke is hidden behind the rectangular object in the foreground. It would be more useful to see the frames before and after this. What a coincidence that the military decided to release the frame in which a large 757 is hidden behind a small object!

2) **The Bright Fireball.** In Figure 9-2 the white smoke has dissipated slightly, and whatever produced the white smoke has exploded. The fireball from an airplane crash (or an automobile crash) will be dark orange and full of soot (Figures 4-6 & 4-7), but the fireball at the Pentagon was bright and clean. This implies plenty of oxygen was available; i.e., explosives.

    The Pentagon is 23 meters (77 feet) tall. The fireball in Figure 9-2 is perhaps 50% taller than the Pentagon. Since the fireball is a bright yellow at this large size, it must have been even brighter when it was half this size. Why not release *all* of the video frames? So that we can watch the fireball grow?

    I suppose the frames preceding Figure 9-2 showed the fireball glowing such a bright white that it looked like 10,000 people were arc welding at the same time!

3) **The video is low quality.** Several news magazines printed these video images, and their copies are just as lousy; i.e.; nobody has good quality video. Why did the US military compress the images so severely when they knew people were going to print them? Was it to hide the details?

Figure 9-1 *Frame 1 from security video*

Figure 9-2 *Frame 2 from security video*

I put Figure 9-3 together to supplement Meyssan's photos.[†] The giant spools of cable on the grass are useful aids in helping identify which part of the building you are looking at. These spools are in front of the section that collapsed. By the way, somehow the airplane flew past them without hitting them.

The uppermost image (Figure 9-3A) shows the Pentagon only minutes after the crash. Firemen are spraying foam along the ground floor because that is where most of the fire was. (There are five floors in the building).

In Figure 9-3B the fire trucks are empty. The ground floor shows signs of severe damage, but no large holes. The dotted circle underneath the outline of the airplane shows what could be a large hole in the building. In figure 9-3A, however, this area does not appear to be a hole, and compared to Figure 4-1 this does not appear to be a hole from an airplane.

The other dotted circle shows what appears to be a dent in the building. The outer walls on the Pentagon are thick and strong because they were designed to resist attack. Therefore, only something with considerable mass, such as an engine, would be able to create such a dent. Since the object did not penetrate, it must have fallen to the ground. Since the only objects on the ground underneath this dent are small, if an engine made that dent, it shattered into small pieces.

In Figure 9-3C the upper three floors separated along a perfectly straight line, and that caused those upper three floors to tilt downward. The right side remained attached to the building.

Figure 9-3D shows the building after all of the broken material had been removed. The important aspect of this photograph is that the rear portion of the first and second floors are still intact. Only the upper three floors were completely destroyed. This makes is appear as if the airplane hit the building between the 3rd and 5th floor. (The yellow outline of the airplane in Figure 9-3B is at the 3rd and 4th floors.)

The airplane was larger than one floor

The US Military insists that the plane hit the ground floor. The yellow outline of a Boeing 757 in Figure 9-3C show that this is impossible. That outline shows a 757 with the engines touching the grass. The fuselage alone is more than 4 meters

(13 ft) tall, and the section where the wings join the fuselage is even larger. From the bottom of the engines to the top of the fuselage is more than 5½ meters (18 ft). Each engine was 2¾ meters (9 ft) tall. The two human shaped objects in yellow next to the engines show an average sized man and woman. (The firemen appear to be larger than those yellow figures because they are in the foreground.)

The plane would hit two floors even if the plane was perfectly horizontal and even if the engines were sliding along the grass because the cabin and engines were taller than one floor of the building.

Airplanes are not normally horizontal while flying; rather, the nose is usually tilted upward. Figure 9-3A shows a side view with the airplane tilted 5°. This tilting would cause the nose of the plane to hit the 2nd floor, even if the tail was dragging in the grass. The airplane would have to be several feet deep in the dirt in order to hit *only* the ground floor, but photos do not show evidence that the airplane even touched the ground.

Figures 9-6, 9-7, and 9-8 were taken by a passing motorist before the firemen arrived. He focused on an area in front of the helicopter landing pad. (The helicopter pad would be to the left edge in Figure 9-3. The spools of cable at the extreme right edge in his photographs show how to align this photograph with Figure 9-3.)

Fires are everywhere. If the airplane crashed into the section that collapsed, how did all these other areas end up with so many large fires?

Where is the airplane debris?

An empty 757 contains about 60 tons of metal, plastic, and glass. People and luggage added many tons more. Where did all of that debris end up? Although I cropped most of the grass out of these images, there is nothing on the grass that resembles airplane parts, luggage, or human bodies. This implies the entire plane penetrated the building.

Figures 9-3D show that the first two floors are intact at the rear. Therefore, the plane somehow penetrated the Pentagon at the 1st and 2nd floors without destroying the rear of this section of building. Did the plane crumple like an accordion? Or it was shredded into pieces, and by the time the pieces reached at the rear of the building they were too small to destroy it? In either case, Figure 9-11 should show some of the pieces.

The airplane is 155 feet long, which is *much* longer than this section of the building. Look at Figure 9-10 and try to find a way to fit the airplane into the collapsed area. Compare the width of a ring in the Pentagon to the size of the World Trade Center towers (Figure 3-2). The Pentagon had a lot of office space because it had five sets of rings, but each ring was narrow.

[†] I combined two photographs to make Figure 9-3C because one photograph did not show the grass, while another photograph did not show as much of the building. There is a slight mismatch in these two photos, which is why a horizontal line is running across the bottom and why there is a different color to the building along the right side.

A

Boeing 757 Specs
47m long (155 ft)
38m wingspan (125 ft)
4m fuselage diam (13ft)
2¾m engine diam (9 ft)
60 tons when empty

Pentagon Specs
5 floors
23m tall (77 ft) at
  peak of roof
No steel frame; it is a
  concrete structure.

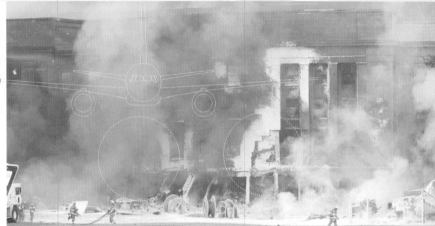

B

A composite of five Photos from US Military sites

C

D

Figure 9-3

*There is no sign
of an airplane*

Two pieces of the airplane were discovered!

I am aware of two objects that the military believes are the only pieces of the 757 that were recovered from the rubble. Actually, the military does not even claim the small piece in Figure 9-4 is a part of the 757; rather, they *believe* it is a piece.

The larger scrap of airplane in Figure 9-5 is in the area to the left of the helicopter pad. (The white arrows marked with **1** in Figures 9-6 to 9-8 are pointing to the helicopter pad. The automobile burning in the background of Figure 9-5 is on the helicopter pad.) The scrap in Figure 9-5 is beyond the left edge of Figure 9-8. This implies that the aircraft hit the portion of the building that collapsed, and somehow this scrap was thrown over the helicopter pad.

This scrap is painted in at least three different colors, which implies it was visible to people, such as the outer skin of an airplane. However, it does not look much thicker than aluminum foil, so could it be a part of the exterior aluminum sheeting of a 757? Or did it come from the *interior* of the airplane? That would require the aircraft break apart in such a strange manner that a thin scrap of aluminum from the *inside* was thrown out of the aircraft while every other portion of the aircraft vanished. Is it a coincidence that this piece of 757 resembles the skin on a small drone or missile?

Where are the *thick* pieces of metal from this airplane? How did only two of the most fragile pieces survive? An engine, landing gear, and part of the fuselage survived the crashes at the World Trade Center; why did all parts of the plane vanish at the Pentagon?

Figure 9-5 also shows flames inside the second floor of the Pentagon, but there is no fire below or above that area. How did fires get set in such a strange manner? Lastly, there is a lot of paper debris on the grass behind this aircraft part. Did the blast from the airplane crash cause papers to fly out of the Pentagon? Or did a bomb explode inside the Pentagon?

US military

Figure 9-4   *The caption at the military Internet site that has this photo:*

"A Pentagon worker holds what is believed to be a piece of the aircraft that crashed into the Pentagon on Sept. 11, 2001"

US military

Figure 9-5   *This is a piece of a Boeing 757? Notice how large the blades of grass are next to this thin piece of metal.*

Courtesy of Steve Riskus

Figure 9-6   *1: helicopter pad   2: area that later collapsed   3: spools of cable*

Courtesy of Steve Riskus

Figure 9-7   *The white arrows correspond to the same areas as in Figure 9-6 and 9-8.*

How did the area by the helicopter pad end up with such serious fires if the plane hit near the spools of cable? If fuel sprayed over there, why didn't the grass get roasted?

Courtesy of Steve Riskus

Figure 9-8 *At least two vehicles are burning on the helicopter pad. The plane crashed in the area behind the tree. How did the objects on the helicopter pad catch on fire?*

Where is the aircraft debris?

The caption given to the photo in Figure 9-9 by the Navy:

"A fireman stands in front of the exit hole where American Airlines Flight 77 finally stopped after penetrating the Pentagon."

The fuselage of a Boeing 757 is more than 4 meters (13 feet) in diameter, so it did not pass through this small hole. The engines were 2¾ meters (9 feet) in diameter, so *each* of the two engines were larger than this hole. Also, this hole is along the ground. Did a small piece of the plane slide along the ground and then punch this hole in the wall? If so, where are the pieces of the plane that made this hole?

The red rectangle in Figure 9-10 shows the area of the first and second floors that were destroyed. This area can be seen in Figures 9-3D and 9-11. Since Figure 9-9 shows that none of the plane passed through the hole, the entire plane and 64 passengers must have squeezed inside the red area of Figure 9-10.

The terrorists were the World's Best Pilots

The Pentagon is a large building, but it is low to the ground. A 757 is more than half the height of the building if the tail is included in the measurement. The easiest way for the terrorists to hit the building would be while diving down at an angle (Figure 2-6). However, the terrorists decided to hit the building while flying horizontal. More amazing, instead of hitting at the 3rd or 4th floor, which would have been relatively easy, they risked crashing by flying only millimeters above the ground to hit the first floor.

Figures 9-6 to 9-8 show the railings, automobiles, and other objects that the pilot had to fly over. The military expects us to believe the terrorists flew only slightly above the cars along the highway. After passing over the highway the terrorists had only a fraction of a second of flight time remaining, and in that brief time they dropped the plane to a few microns above the grass.

Airplanes do not normally fly horizontal. Rather, the nose is normally tilted up, which means the tail (which the pilot cannot see) would be near the ground while the nose was higher up. For the airplane to hit only the ground floor would require holding the plane perfectly horizontal while skimming the surface of the ground. This can be difficult because airplanes tend to roll and tilt. Also, the aerodynamic properties of the wings change slightly when an airplane is skimming the surface of the land, which makes flying close to ground even more difficult. For the terrorists to fly so low was a tremendous achievement, especially when traveling at 555 km/hour (345 mph), which is the speed the flight data recorder supposedly shows. (The military claims to have

US Navy

Figure 9-9   *The US military claims this hole in the Pentagon was caused by Flight 77*

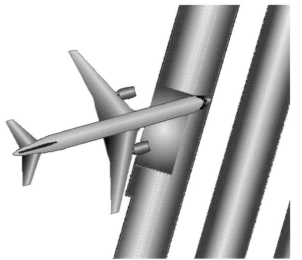

Figure 9-10   *The Pentagon consists of 5 rings of buildings, separated by a gap for light and air.*

*A 757 is **much** longer than the width of a ring. The red area shows the portion of the first and second floor that collapsed (see Figure 9-11) How did the airplane hit the ground floor while destroying **only the red area?***

found the flight data recorder, but the engines, fuselage, and dead passengers are still missing.).

Some witnesses claim that Flight 77 knocked down a lightpost along the highway. However, a broken lightpost does not prove that Flight 77 crashed into the Pentagon; a missile can also hit lightposts. It is possible a person driving by hit the lightpost with his car when he was startled by the explosion.

The pilot's view of the ground from a 757 is not very good, so flying millimeters above the ground would be a tremendous achievement. Actually, I would say it is *absurd* to believe an inexperienced pilot could fly such a plane a few millimeters above the ground. The flight path of this plane is enough to convince me that no human was in control of it. I think only a computer is capable of flying an airplane in such a tricky manner. If terrorists flew that plane, they would qualify as the World's Greatest Pilots since they did tricks with a commercial aircraft that I doubt the best Air Force pilots could do. (Look closely at Figure 2-9, page 20)

Of course, I could be mistaken, so why not put this to a test and settle this issue? Let's ask the Air Force to fly a Boeing 757 as close to the cars and grass as the terrorists flew. And top military leaders should be inside the plane to show us that they truly believe it is possible.

Figure 9-11 *The rear portion of the first and second floor are still intact, which means the entire plane should be in the rubble the workers are scooping up. That rubble should contain two giant engines, 3,500 kilograms of human body parts, 200 airline seats, hundreds of suitcases, and **57,000 kilograms** of aircraft pieces. Teeth usually survive fires so – with about 2000 teeth in that rubble – certainly some teeth should have been discovered. The military goes to extremes to recover dead soldiers, but did they make any effort to recover Flight 77?*

The CIA drones

The CIA has unmanned aircraft, referred to as "Predator drones," which are capable of firing missiles (Figure 9-12). This came out in the news on February 10, 2002 after the CIA sent one of these drones towards a group of suspected terrorists in Afghanistan and the drone fired a missile at them (it turned out that the missile killed only ordinary Afghans). Figures 9-13 to 9-15 are a few other drones the USA has developed

The CIA is *not* a military organization, so why does the CIA have such weapons? The US military has drones, also, but as of September 11, 2001, they were *not* capable of firing missiles. Rather, they were used for surveillance. This means the CIA had more advanced weapons than the US Military.

The CIA has a secret budget, and obviously they have been spending some of their secret money on advanced military weapons. Is it possible that the CIA is out of control? Is it possible they have other weapons we do not yet know about?

Is it a coincidence that the terrorists were flying a giant passenger plane in the same manner that a small Predator flew in Afghanistan? Is it a coincidence that the Pentagon security camera (Figure 9-1) shows the 757 producing white smoke, just like a missile, and exploding, just like a bomb, thereby resembling the Predator that fired a missile at people in Afghanistan?

On September 12 the *Washington Post* reported:

> *But just as the plane seemed to be on a suicide mission into the White House, the unidentified pilot executed a pivot so tight that it reminded observers of a fighter jet maneuver. The plane circled 270 degrees to the right to approach the Pentagon from the west, whereupon Flight 77 fell below radar level, vanishing from controllers' screens, the sources said.*

If the *Washington Post* is correct:

1) The airplane made a turn so sharp that it would be difficult in such a large, unmaneuverable airplane.

2) The plane was headed towards the White House. I did not realize the significance of that until Steve Koeppel (the former Air Force pilot mentioned in Chapter 2) pointed out that if the plane had flown anywhere near the White House it would have been seen by thousands of tourists with cameras. Certainly one of them would have taken a photo of a commercial airplane flying low and making tricky maneuvers. I am not aware of any photographs of this airplane. Flight 77 was invisible from Ohio to the Pentagon (Figure 8-6).

The terrorists hit an empty part of the Pentagon

Supposedly the terrorists made a 270° turn around the Pentagon before hitting it. By coincidence, the terrorists decided to hit a section that did not have many people in it so casualties were much lower than if they had hit elsewhere. They crashed into a section that was being renovated, so the people who normally worked there had been sent to other offices.

The Pentagon is supposedly the largest office building in the world, so there could have been thousands of deaths. What a coincidence that the terrorists did not hit a section of the building that was full of people. What a coincidence the terrorists did not hit Rumsfeld's office.

How rapidly did the fireball expand?

The date and time is displayed in the lower left corner of the five frames of video that the Pentagon decided to let us see, although the time is incorrect by about 32 hours (Figures 9-1 and 9-2). The time is shown only to the nearest second, but I suspect the real video has IRIG time code recorded on an audio track, in which case the military could precisely identify each frame.

The first and second frames have identical times. The first frame shows the building before the plane hit. The second frame shows a fireball that is at least 50 percent taller than the pentagon. This means that within 1 second the plane crashed and a fireball grew to a height of at least 30 meters (100 feet).

If we could see the frames between those two we could estimate the rate at which the fireball expands. This would let us determine whether the fireball was from jet fuel or an explosive. Jet fuel fireballs, as with automobile fireballs, do not expand very quickly. By comparison, the fireball from an explosive can expand at an enormous rate.

Why does the Pentagon restrict us to only five frames of video? Why not allow us to see the entire video? Television news channels showed the video of the planes hitting the World Trade Centers at least 2 million times during September. Why not broadcast the video of this plane crashing into the Pentagon at least *once*?

I think the Pentagon refuses to release the entire video because it would show a small object flying close to the ground, with white smoke pouring out the rear of it, and then it would show the fireball expanding so quickly that even "ordinary" Americans would realize that it was from an explosive.

If the video proves that a 757 hit the building then the Pentagon officials are *idiots* for keeping the video a secret. Their secrecy is allowing conspiracy rumors to run wild.

The suspicious behavior of the US Military officials is evidence that they are involved in this scam. Besides, they lied about not having video of the crash, so why should I trust

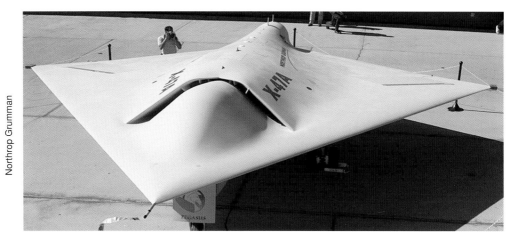

Figure 9-12   *A Predator drone*

Figure 9-13   *A Northrop Grumman X-47A*

Figure 9-14   *A Boeing X-45A*

Figure 9-15   *A Global Hawk*

them on other issues? How many times does a person have to lie to *you* before you question his other remarks?

If it looks and acts like a drone...

When an airplane has all the characteristics of a drone, it probably was a drone. America has a variety of drones that could have been used to hit the Pentagon. Some of these drones look similar to commercial aircraft, while others look like they belong in a science-fiction movie. If the Global Hawk (Figure 9-15) were painted to look like an American Airlines plane, it would certainly fool some people when it flew by at 350 miles per hour.

Which witness do we believe?

Witnesses always offer different details to an event, but the people who saw Flight 77 hit the Pentagon seem to disagree with each other more than "normal." Some of the witnesses who saw Flight 77 may be involved with the scam, while others may have been fooled by a drone. An example of the confusing testimony is this from the *Australian Broadcasting Corp.*:

> *"I saw this large American Airlines passenger jet coming in fast and low," said Army Captain Lincoln Liebner. Captain Liebner says the aircraft struck a helicopter on the helipad, setting fire to a fire truck.*

He saw Flight 77 but, unfortunately, he saw it hit a helicopter on the helicopter pad, not the section of the building that collapsed. (Figure 9-8 shows the helipad.)

An example from the *Washington Post*:

> *Steve Patterson, who lives in Pentagon City, said it appeared to him that a commuter jet swooped over Arlington National Cemetery and headed for the Pentagon ...*
>
> *He said the plane, which sounded like the high-pitched squeal of a fighter jet...*
>
> *The plane, which appeared to hold about eight to 12 people...*

He supports the theory that a small drone hit the Pentagon. That same article has another person suggesting a drone or missile:

> *"We heard what sounded like a missile, then we heard a loud boom," said Tom Seibert, 33, of Woodbridge, Va., a network engineer at the Pentagon.*

Tim Timmerman, in this *CNN* interview, also supports the drone possibility:

> *...it didn't appear to crash into the building; most of the energy was dissipated in hitting the ground, but I saw the nose break up, I saw the wings fly forward, and then the conflagration engulfed everything in flames.*
>
> *...I saw the airplane just disintegrate and blow up into a huge ball of flames.*

There is no evidence that the plane hit the ground; the grass is in perfect condition. Timmerman may have seen a missile that exploded before it hit the Pentagon, creating the illusion that it hit the ground. Figure 9-2 also suggests the missile exploded before it hit the Pentagon.

From Joel Sucherman, an editor for *USA Today*:

> *"It was coming in at a high rate of speed, but not at a steep angle--almost like a heat-seeking missile was locked onto its target and staying dead on course."*

He points out that the airplane was flying very fast but was not diving towards the Pentagon. The behavior of the airplane reminded him of a heat-seeking missile that had perfect control of the aircraft and knew exactly where it was going, not a human pilot who had his hands on a steering wheel and was looking out the window to figure out where to crash the airplane.

Two explosions at the Pentagon?

Some witnesses reported hearing two explosions:

> *"I heard two loud booms - one large, one small," said Lisa Burgess, a reporter for Stars and Stripes newspaper.*

And from the *Washington Post*:

> *"I heard a plane. I saw it. I saw debris flying. I guess it was hitting light poles," said Milburn. "It was like a WHOOOSH whoosh, then there was fire and smoke, then I heard a second explosion."*

The first explosion was the missile, so perhaps the second was a bomb inside the Pentagon. Something caused a portion of the Pentagon to collapse, and since it does not appear to be due to an airplane crash, it must have been due to explosives that were placed inside the building.

The Phone Calls

10

The phone calls are used as evidence that the hijacks were authentic, so the phone calls had better be real.

Flight 11, to the North Tower

According to the *Boston Globe*, the terrorists in Flight 11 were so naive about cockpits that they accidently broadcast messages over the radio instead of to the speakers in the cabin. At 8:24AM a controller heard such remarks as, *"We have some planes. Just stay quiet and you will be OK. We are returning to the airport. Nobody move."*

This means the FAA knew Flight 11 was hijacked 22 minutes before it hit the towers. That would give them time to call the military. Well, not necessarily. The controller who heard those messages was even more naive; he responded with, *"Who's trying to call me?"* rather than announce a hijacking had taken place. This controller didn't even notice the plane was off course. (I suppose this is the same controller mentioned on page 91, in regards to Stewart International Airport. I would not be surprised if he was also watching TWA Flight 800, another mysterious accident. Or was Flight 800 practice for Flight 93?)

The *Los Angeles Times* reported that Madeline Sweeney, a flight attendant on Flight 11, made a phone call to Boston's Logan Airport. She told a manager that her plane has been hijacked, two flight attendants had been stabbed, and one passenger appears dead. Therefore, the airlines knew Flight 11 was hijacked before any airplane hit the World Trade Center, even if that suspicious controller was pretending everything was fine with the flight. But the FAA did nothing.

Flight 175, to the South Tower

Who called from Flight 175? I cannot find any reports of any callers. This plane was in the air for 16 minutes after Flight 11 crashed, and when the plane approached New York City the passengers would have seen the smoke from the North Tower. So why no phone calls from worried passengers? Why didn't any flight attendant call?

Flight 77, to the Pentagon

Flight 77 was flying normally near Indianapolis when Flight 11 crashed into North Tower at 8:46. An air traffic controller contacted the pilot of Flight 77 about a minute later for a routine course correction. Their conversation ended at 8:50:51. About 6 minutes later a controller

contacted the pilot again, but this time the pilot didn't answer. The controller realized there was a potential problem with Flight 77, so he tried over and over to contact the pilot, and called for help *in less than two minutes.* Nobody could help, of course, but compare his rapid call for help to the controller watching Flights 11 and 175 who did nothing.

At 8:57 AM Flight 11 had crashed and Flight 77 had vanished. A few minutes later, at 9:03, Flight 175 crashed into the South Tower. Transcripts show that at 9:09 the controllers were discussing *both* crashes, so the information was traveling fast. Flight 93 was flying normally at this time, so controllers had no reason to worry about it, but the moment it changed course the controllers should have suspected a serious problem. However, the response to the hijacking of Flight 93 was as sluggish as it was with Flights 11 and 175. Who was watching Flight 93?

Barbara Olson calls from Flight 77

Barbara Olson's phone call is used as proof that Flight 77 crashed into the Pentagon, so her call is very important. She made two phone calls to her husband, who was at work at the Justice Department. Both calls were brief because her phone connection was cut off. As her husband described it:

> *"She had had trouble getting through, because she wasn't using her cellphone, she was using the phone in the passengers' seats,"* says Olson. *"I guess she didn't have her purse, because she was calling collect, and she was trying to get through to the Department of Justice, which is never very easy."*

She told her husband that the hijackers forced the passengers and the pilot towards the rear of the airplane. The strange aspect of her phone calls is that in *both* phone calls she wanted to know what she should tell the pilot:

> *Moments later, his wife called again. And again, she wanted to know, "What should I tell the pilot?"*

Why would she call her husband to find out what she should tell the pilot? Is her husband an expert on what to tell pilots during highjackings? Actually, why would *any* passenger call *anybody* for such information? Why not let the pilot make his own phone call?

Why was Flight 77 so quiet?

Barbara Olson's flight was in the air a long time. It traveled all the way from Washington D.C. to Ohio before turning around to fly hundreds of miles to the Pentagon (Figure 8-6). Why didn't any passengers worry about their lives? Why didn't they call their friends and family? Why didn't any of the men try to fight the hijackers?

Flight 77 had 64 people whereas Flight 93 had only 45. This is 42% more people. Therefore, there should have been 42% more phone calls from Flight 77. However, Flight 77 was amazingly quiet. Why was Olson the only caller? What were the other passengers and crew members doing between Ohio and the Pentagon? The passengers were as quiet as *dead bodies*.

Contact with Flight 77 was lost near Ohio. The military wants us to believe that the hijackers turned off the transponder and flew hundreds of miles without the FAA noticing an unidentified blip on their radar screens. Some reports suggest that perhaps the plane was flying below radar, but how can a 757 fly along the ground without somebody noticing? And wouldn't at least one of the passengers have called their family to mention they were cruising at the tops of trees?

If Flight 77 and its dead passengers had been recovered from the rubble at the Pentagon then we could conclude that Flight 77 did indeed make that long journey to the Pentagon. However, the US military has photos of only two suspicious pieces of metal (Figure 9-4 and 9-5), both of which appear to be from a small aircraft, and I cannot find any news reports of dozens of dead bodies in the rubble.

The most likely explanation for Flight 77 is that it was shot down near Ohio. Barbara Olson's call seems to be a fake to add some realism to the flight. I think her odd conversation was because a female CIA agent made the phone call, and it did not occur to her that Olson should be making a sad call to say goodbye. Instead she made the mistake of selecting a topic of conversation that none of the other callers had selected.

Barbara Olson called from an airline phone, not her cellphone.† Her husband assumes she did not have her purse, but a CIA agent needed a lousy phone connection to hide her voice. The agent had to call Ted's office, and Ted's secretary would answer. The agent had to add noise to the line, and the best excuse for a terrible phone connection is that it is an airline phone. The calls were also brief to minimize the time people could listen to her voice.

Barbara Olson's death

Olson was originally scheduled to fly on September 10, but she changed her flight to the morning of the 11th so she could be with her husband for a few minutes that morning because that day was his birthday. It was a tragic decision.

At a trial in the Supreme Court in March, 2002, Ted Olson defended the CIA and the US government. One of his remarks:

> *It's easy to imagine an infinite number of situations where the government might legitimately give out false information. It's an unfortunate reality that the issuance of incomplete information and even misinformation by government may sometimes be perceived as necessary to protect vital interests.*

Did Ted Olson provide false information to us about his wife's phone calls in order to *"protect vital interests"*?

Were the terrorists just pawns in this attack?

Flight 93 had lots of phone calls, but not Flights 11 or 175 (which hit the two towers). There were 92 people on Flight 11 and 65 people on Flight 175. That is 349% more people than Flight 93. Madeline Sweeney called from Flight 11, and she was describing a depressing situation (two flight attendants stabbed, one passenger dead). Why didn't any of the other passengers make phone calls? Why did the people on Flight 93 make almost all of the phone calls?

What if the terrorists were pawns? What if computers flew the airplanes into the towers? In such a case the terrorists would be dangerous to the scam because the airplane might be damaged if a fight breaks out. Worst of all, if the hijackers failed to get control, the pilot would send a message that the plane was flying itself. The scam would have a higher chance of success if everybody on the plane was killed *before* the hijacking took place, such as by releasing nerve gas via a radio signal, or by replacing the planes with drones.

The odd flight paths (Fig. 8-6 on page 90) could mean that both planes landed at Stewart International Airport, and drones could have replaced them.

Sweeney called Boston Airport, not a close friend, and provided information about the hijacking, as if she was a reporter. This could be interpreted as a fake call to provide a public record of the hijacking to give it some realism.

Why was Flight 93 delayed?

The *Boston Globe* reported that Flight 93 pushed back from its gate at 8:01, but was "delayed" from taking off by nearly 40 minutes. United Airlines would not explain the delay. Flights are delayed so often that this report may be irrelevant. However, since this attack appears to be a scam the delay may have been deliberate. But why would the Axis of Good want to delay it?

---

† Experiments by scientists at www.physics911.ca show that cell phones did not work in airplanes as of 2001.

Flight 93 was sitting at an airport only a few miles from the towers, and it was ready to take off. If something happened to either Flight 11 or 175, Flight 93 could take off and crash into the towers within minutes. Flight 93 finally took off when Flight 11 was only 4 minutes away from hitting the North Tower; Flight 77 was about 15 minutes away from vanishing; and Flight 175 was about 20 minutes from hitting the South Tower. Perhaps Flight 93 was released to take its part in the scam when it appeared as if the attack on the World Trade Center was on schedule.

Did a missile hit Flight 93?

Flight 93 supposedly crashed when a few passengers attacked the hijackers. However, some reports support the theory that the military shot the plane with a missile, such as an article in *The Telegraph* (page 91, Stewart International Airport) that reported air traffic controllers in Nashua heard from other controllers that an F-16 fighter was closely following Flight 93.

An *Associated Press* report tells of a frantic passenger on Flight 93 who called the emergency number 911 from the bathroom to report the plane was "going down" and that he heard an explosion and saw white smoke. He called at 9:58, and was the last call from the plane. The more interesting aspect of that phone call was reported by the *Washington Post*:

> *FBI agents quickly took possession of the tape of that 911 call, which constitutes the only public evidence so far of what went on during the doomed plane's last moments. The FBI declined to provide any information about the tape's contents or the identity of the caller.*

Reports also mention that Glenn Cramer, the operator who received the phone call, has been told by the FBI not to discuss that phone call.

How could keeping that phone call a secret possibly – as Ted Olson would say – *protect vital interests*? How would the USA be in danger if we knew who that passenger was and what he was saying (or screaming, as some reports claim)? Why are we allowed to know about other phone calls but not *that* particular call? Why is there so much secrecy if nobody has anything to hide?

Which airplane landed in Cleveland?

To futher confuse the issue, WCPO television in Cincinnati reported at 11:43AM that Flight 93, from Boston, landed in Cleveland due to a bomb threat. Since Flight 93 was from New Jersey, and since it supposedly crashed, which plane landed in Cincinnati? Why does nobody care that nothing makes sense about the 9-11 attack?

Todd Beamer

Beamer's call is used not only to prove Arabs were behind the attack, but also to imply that America is full of "heros." However, there are a few odd aspects of Beamer's phone call that not only suggests the US government was involved in the attack, but also that America is full of liars:

A) Beamer talked to a stranger

Almost everybody made a phone call to their husband, wife, or mother. All calls were brief, and everybody was worried. For example, Jeffery Glick called his wife, who was with her parents at the time. The first time he called he was told that his wife was asleep, but the second time he was more certain that he was going to die, so he *demanded* to talk to her.

Todd Beamer was the oddball in the group. Some reports say he dialed his wife but the call didn't go through, and some reports claim he dialed the operator. Regardless of how it happened, he ended up talking to a telephone operator (Lisa Jefferson). Beamer could have asked Jefferson to connect him to his wife, but instead he talked to Jefferson. Why would he spend the last moments of his life talking to a stranger? There were strangers on the airplane; why not talk to *them*? Why suffer the *low quality of an airplane phone?*

B) Beamer talked "forever"

Beamer talked longer than anybody. I can understand Beamer talking to Jefferson for a minute or two as he explained that he was in a hijacked airplane and *trying to call his wife*, but after a while I would expect him to ask why the call did not go through. I would expect him to ask Jefferson to *fix the problem* and connect him to his wife before he dies. However, he spent 13 minutes talking to Jefferson.

Furthermore, he never actually terminated the phone conversation with her; it was a "forever" phone call. When a couple of the other passengers decided to fight the hijackers, he decided to join them. So he put the phone down and went to fight the hijackers. Jefferson remained on the line waiting for him to come back, even though the phone soon became silent. Other Verizon employees told her that the plane must have crashed. Jefferson started to cry. After 15 minutes she hung up the phone with tears in her eyes, but Beamer never hung up; his call never ended. Isn't this romantic? No; it is suspicious.

If Beamer and the other men had been successful in their fight with the hijackers, he would have gone back to the phone and resumed his conversation with Jefferson. He then would have talked for... What? Another 13 minutes? An hour? At what point would he want to talk to somebody he knows? If he wanted to talk to strangers, weren't there enough of them in the airplane?

D) Beamer's audio recording is a secret

Since the telephone company (Verizon) recorded the entire conversation, they *could* give a copy of the audio tape to his wife. Instead, they *faxed a summary* of the phone call to her. Am I the only person who considers this to be weird? How would you feel if a telephone company sent a fax to *you* to let you know that your friend, spouse, or child had just died? And what if they had an audio recording of his last conversation but would not let you listen to it?

If the tape has nothing on it except such remarks as *"tell my wife I love her,"* as well as a few descriptions of the passengers on the plane, why does Verizon keep it a secret from his wife? Two possible reasons are:

1) Maybe Beamer is an embarrassment

Jefferson claims Beamer asked her to pray with him. Why didn't Beamer ask to pray with his pregnant wife? Why not pray with the other passengers on the plane? Perhaps because they were *not praying*.

Perhaps Beamer and/or Jefferson was such an embarrassment that the phone company decided it would add more pain to the tragedy to let people know what they were really talking about.

2) Maybe it was *not* Todd Beamer

Unless several family members and friends of Beamer listen to the tape and identify the voice, there is no evidence that the call was actually from Beamer.

C) Beamer behaved like a news reporter

Just like Madeline Sweeney, Beamer calmly described the passengers, the hijackers, and the situation. Both of their conversations are as suspicious as a person trapped inside a burning building making a call to a stranger to describe the fire. Why would Beamer provide such information to a telephone operator? Was he trying to help the FBI solve the case? If so, why not ask to be transferred to the FBI?

Was Beamer one of the heroes on Flight 93?

Tom Burnett called his wife four times. In his fourth call some reports quote him as saying:

> *I know we're all going to die. There's three of us who are going to do something about it. I love you, honey.*

If those reports are correct, *three* men decided to attack the hijackers. If Tom was one of them, who were the other two? I would guess Jeremy Glick, a judo champion, and Mark Bingham, a 6-foot-5, former college rugby player, because they were both large and had experience in violent sports. Beamer preferred baseball, and in an NBC interview his wife said September 11th, 2001 was the day he was going to start a *diet and fitness program*:

> *Since college, you know, he had spent a lot of time behind a desk, and he really wanted to get that body back.*

Beamer's call seems to be a fake

Beamer's strange phone call makes the most sense if it was made by a CIA agent. The CIA would want to provide information to somebody who would pass it to the TV news in order to convince us that the hijackings were real.

Incidently, Beamer was scheduled to fly on September 10th but switched to the 11th. Another tragic decision; another weird phone call from a person who made a tragic decision. Or was September 10th the originally scheduled date for this attack?

"Let's Roll!"

Beamer's expression is used as proof the call was from *him*. If his phone call was a fake, that means the Axis of Good knew Beamer. This would be easy because Beamer was a salesman who traveled frequently. (The Axis of Good may have even arranged for him to travel that day) Or, Beamer may have lived near some members. Beamer lived a few miles from Trenton, New Jersey, where the anthrax letters were mailed. Is this a coincidence? Or was he living among the Axis of Good, and were the anthrax attacks coming from the same group of people?

Will we ever settle these issues?

Why not demand the FBI release all phone calls and information so that we can settle these issues?

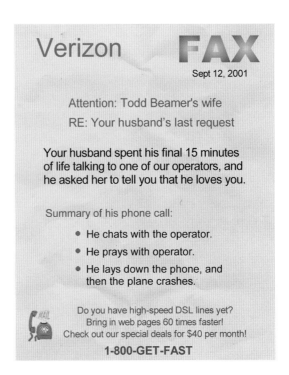

Figure 10-1   My wild guess at what the Fax looked like

Is our Government Inept, or Corrupt?

11

While I was writing this book, many people complained to me that our government merely *appears* to be involved in the September 11th attack because they are *incompetent*. So I decided to include information about the assassination of President Kennedy to show that our government was just as "incompetent" in 1963. Or, did our government kill Kennedy? Can you figure it out by looking at the Warren Report? Furthermore, if our government *is* incompetent, how is an incompetent government any better than a government of criminals? Either way, *we have a serious problem*.

The Warren Report

The "Warren Report" is the US government's official investigation of the assassination of President Kennedy. It is analogous to the FEMA report about the World Trade Center collapse, but the Warren Report has much more detail. It contains the testimony of 552 witnesses, and it contains our government's analysis of that testimony. A lot of people put a lot of time and effort into the Warren Report.

As is typical of crimes, the testimony in the Warren Report is full of contradictions. The government had to pass judgement on which testimony was the most accurate, and which testimony should be ignored. They ended up concluding that Oswald killed Kennedy. However, some people looked at the same conflicting testimony, decided to ignore different bits, and ended up concluding the FBI killed Kennedy. Other people ignored still other bits and found a military or CIA killing. Some people found a Soviet killing. How do we determine whose theory is more accurate?

This chapter will discuss the testimony of the doctors who treated Kennedy at the hospital. (Unless specified otherwise, the quoted material is from the Warren Report.)

Who was on duty at the Parkland Hospital?

The hospital was only a few miles from the location Kennedy was shot, so he arrived within a few minutes. The Warren Report does not provide details about what was happening at the hospital at the moment Kennedy arrived, but we can assume that most experienced doctors were busy with patients. Some doctors may have been in surgery and could not stop what they were doing. Who were the first

doctors to see Kennedy? Were they the best doctors the hospital had? Or were the trainees the first to see him?

In case some of you are unaware of what goes on in hospitals, after a medical student gets out of school he often gets on-the-job training at a hospital. These students are often referred to as "interns," and sometimes as "doctors," but they could be referred to as "trainees" or "students." Also, in 1963 there were fewer concerns about malpractice because Americans did not file nearly as many lawsuits in that era, and monetary awards were much smaller. One of the reasons malpractice cases have since become so numerous is that there were occasional abuses in that era, such as when nurses, interns, and medical equipment salesmen assisted with medical treatments when the doctors were busy. Today hospitals are careful not to allow anybody to do something they were not specifically trained for.

As you read about the treatment Kennedy received, try to figure out if the first few doctors to help him were experienced doctors or just students. It is also interesting to speculate on how many lawsuits would be filed if a hospital behaved in the same manner today.

The potential danger in letting a student or a salesman treat Kennedy is that he may be familiar with only a few treatments, so he could easily give Kennedy an inappropriate treatment simply because it is the only treatment he has learned. And a salesman may be familiar only with the equipment he sells.

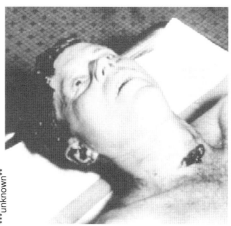

Figure 11-1

A low quality photo of Kennedy taken by autopsy personnel.

The bullet hole in his neck was widened to give him oxygen.

***unknown**

Doctor Carrico was the first to arrive

As the Warren Report explains, Doctor Carrico noted that Kennedy had some serious medical problems:

> *Dr. Carrico noted two wounds: a small bullet wound in the front lower neck, and an extensive wound in the President's head where a sizable portion of the skull was missing. He observed shredded brain tissue and "considerable slow oozing" from the latter wound, ...*

In Appendix 8 we find more details:

> *Dr. Carrico noted the President to have slow, agonal respiratory efforts. He could hear a heartbeat but found no pulse or blood pressure to be present.*

People such as myself, who lack medical training, would assume the lack of pulse and blood pressure means that Kennedy's heart was not beating, which in turn means there was only a few minutes before irreversible brain damage occurs. Since I don't know how to start a heart beating, if I had to deal with Kennedy I would have given up and announced that Kennedy was dead. But Dr. Carrico did not consider him dead yet:

> *He noted that the President was blue-white or ashen in color; had slow, spasmodic, agonal respiration without any coordination; made no voluntary movements; had his eyes open with the pupils dilated without any reaction to light; evidenced no palpable pulse; and had a few chest sounds which were thought to be heart beats. On the basis of these findings, Dr. Carrico concluded that President Kennedy was still alive.*

Doctor Carrico had a plan to treat Kennedy and bring him back to good health. He decided to use the bullet hole in his neck to help him breathe. The plan was to widen the bullet hole, insert a tube in the hole, and connect it to a machine that forces oxygen into Kennedy's lungs. This procedure is known as a "tracheotomy."

Doctor Carrico started this tracheotomy almost immediately after seeing Kennedy. Soon afterwards Doctor Perry arrived and took over the tracheotomy while Carrico started other treatments.

I never had any medical training, so perhaps that is why I don't understand the purpose of the tracheotomy. Specifically, why put oxygen into his lungs when his heart is not circulating the blood? Was it because these doctors had no idea what to do about a failed heart, so they did what they knew and hoped that soon a heart specialist would arrive?

And why did these two doctors ignore the bullet wound in Kennedy's head? Was it because brain problems are even more complex than heart problems, and neither of these doctors had a clue as to what to do with the head wounds?

Even with my lack of medical training I can figure out how to force air into a person's lungs, but I don't know how to start a heart beating, and I have no idea how to deal with head injuries. Maybe these two doctors were *as inept as me.* Maybe they were not real doctors; maybe they were salesmen for tracheotomy equipment, or maybe they were students. Maybe the oxygen tank was the only device they knew how to use!

The doctors told the Warren commission that the tracheotomy required 3 to 5 minutes. This is plenty of time for the doctors to ask themselves why they bother to force oxygen into his stagnant blood.

Doctor Jones soon arrived to help with the medical treatment:

> *While Dr. Perry was performing the tracheotomy, Drs. Carrico and Ronald Jones made cuts down on the President's right leg and left arm, respectively, to infuse blood and fluids into the circulatory system. Dr. Carrico treated the President's known adrenal insufficiency by administering hydrocortisone.*

So, just in case a heart specialist arrives in time to start his heart beating, the oxygen, hydrocortisone, and other fluids these doctors were forcing into his stagnant blood would begin to circulate. However their testimony never indicates that they called for a heart specialist. Furthermore, with a "sizeable portion" of his skull missing, if his heart started beating again, wouldn't his blood just pour out of his head and onto the floor? Shouldn't the doctors close the hole soon? Or did they not know how to do *that*, either?

A fourth doctor soon arrived:

> *Dr. Robert N. McClelland entered at that point and assisted Dr. Perry with the tracheotomy*

So now we discover that three Dallas doctors are needed to give a dead man a tracheotomy. Is this typical for a tracheotomy? Or were these doctors incompetent? As I was reading the Warren Report, I was visualizing college students who were anxious to help:

> *"Come on, you guys! It's my turn to do something! Move over! I just got here; you've already done a lot of stuff! I wanna help!"*

Anyway, Kennedy now has four doctors giving him injections and oxygen. Unfortunately, Doctor Perry told the Warren Commission that air and blood got into Kennedy's chest, and he suspects it was because they goofed on the tracheotomy!

How difficult is a tracheotomy? Then ask yourself, if they cannot perform a tracheotomy, how could they do something complicated, such as getting his heart to beat?

Doctor Perry decided to correct the problems they caused with their lousy tracheotomy by putting a few more holes and tubes into Kennedy:

> *When Dr. Perry noted free air and blood in the President's chest cavity, he asked that chest tubes be inserted to allow for drainage of blood and air. Drs. Paul C. Peters and Charles R. Baxter initiated these procedures*

So these other two doctors had to insert drainage tubes to undo the damage caused by the tracheotomy. It seems to me that these doctors were *incompetent*. Was this the first tracheotomy these doctors had performed? As I read this section of the Warren Report, I was getting visions of students who had never performed such work:

Carrico:	*"Oh, hi doc Perry! Look what I'm doing! I'm giving the President a trakyotemy… um, trikatomy..uh.."*
Perry:	*"A tracheotomy?"*
Carrico:	*"Yeah! You wanna finish it?"*
Perry:	*"Sure! I always wanted to try that!"*
McClelland:	*"Hi guys. Hey! Let me help! What are you doing?"*
Perry:	*"It's called a tracheotomy. You can take that knife and cut this hole a bit bigger so I can cram this tube down his throat."*
	(A few moments later...)
McClelland:	*"Oops! When I turned on the oxygen, it went into his chest cavity instead of his lungs!"*
Peters:	*"Hey! I'll take care of that! Move over!"*
Baxter:	*"No, that aint how to fix it! Look, just insert a drainage tube by his ribs, over here!"*

While those incompetent doctors were making Kennedy's situation worse, Doctor Clark arrived and gave Kennedy a "closed chest cardiac massage" in order to start his heart beating. He was the first doctor to work on Kennedy's heart. Maybe the *real* doctors were finally starting to arrive!

Unfortunately, Doctor Clark discovered that his life-saving procedure had an unfortunate side effect, as Doctor Jenkins told the Warren Commission:

> *.. with each compression of the chest, there was a great rush of blood from the skull wound.*

Well, golly! I guess the bullet holes and missing skull portions should be sealed off *before* somebody starts pumping blood. Did any of the doctors complain to Doctor Clark about the "great rush of blood"? Once again I found myself with visions of immature students:

Clark:	*"Hey, guys! Check this out! I'll get his heart to beat!"*
	(He starts pumping Kennedy's chest)
Jenkins:	*"You idiot! Blood is squirting all over! Quit it!"*
Clark:	*"Hey, don't criticize! I don't tell you how to… uh, whatever you're doing with that stupid, plastic tube."*

Soon more doctors arrived, and more treatments were given. Kennedy was surrounded by doctors; they must have resembled ants around a drop of honey. But would you say these doctors were *helping* Kennedy, or making his situation worse? Furthermore, if the Parkland Hospital treats the *President* in this manner, what would they do to you or me? The doctors obviously didn't worry about malpractice in 1963. The doctors gave Kennedy what could be described as:

> *The Medical Treatment From Hell;*
> *If You Live Thru It, You'll Be Sorry!*

Actually, it seems the doctors were following a script from a Hollywood horror movie. What was going on at this hospital?

Stress can cause idiotic behavior

Jackie Kennedy climbed on the trunk of the car and started crawling towards the back of the car after the bullet hit her husband in the head. The car was moving at the time, and starting to accelerate, so she risked falling off. To make the situation more bizarre, she insisted that she didn't remember doing it (photos prove she did), which means the event was never recorded in her memory! She can be considered proof that a person can behave in a strange manner under stress, and then not have any memory of it! She is a good example of how unreliable the human mind is under stress.

Therefore, maybe all of the doctors "flipped out" when they saw their dead President. Rather than face the fact that Kennedy was dead, perhaps these doctors went into some sort of "medical denial" mode in which they assured themselves that their patient will be OK despite evidence to the contrary. Maybe the doctors were in a "temporary state of medical insanity."

Or were the doctors so accustomed to performing unnecessary surgery in order to boost their income that they just couldn't stop themselves?

Alive for a "medical purpose"?

The Warren Commission asked the doctors about their treatments and the condition of Kennedy. Doctor Perry testified that when he first saw Kennedy:

> *He was, therefore alive for medical purposes*

A cadaver has a medical purpose. For example, we can give a cadaver a tracheotomy and a shot of hydrocortisone, and in so doing we can learn how to perform those operations. But we cannot get the heart of a cadaver to beat, nor can we fix the brain of a cadaver, so students cannot practice those techniques on cadavers. Perhaps the first doctors to see Kennedy were students, and perhaps they gave Kennedy the only treatments they had practiced on cadavers. This would explain why, when the real doctors finally arrived, Kennedy was full of holes, hydrocortisone, and bubbles of oxygen.

Or does being alive for a "medical purpose" mean that *money* can be made from the patient? Did those doctors get paid for their treatment of Kennedy? Maybe they knew Kennedy was dead, so they decided to take advantage of the situation by performing quick and simple procedures that would bring them a lot of profit in a short period of time.

So...were they students? Or doctors?

Doctor Perry was asked by the Warren Commission whether he had any experience treating gunshot wounds. I was wondering the same thing as I read the Warren Report! Also, I was wondering about his age. I was visualizing a college kid. I was expecting Perry to respond to the question with something like:

> *"Well, I got a B+ on my last quiz about treating deep wounds!"*

I was shocked to read that Doctor Perry estimated that he had already treated 150 to 200 gunshot wounds. Some of the other doctors claimed to have treated even more gunshot victims than Perry.†

Apparently the hospital sent only highly experienced doctors to treat Kennedy. But if all of the doctors were experienced, how do we explain their idiotic treatments?

---

† How could a society have so many gunshot victims that a doctor can treat *hundreds* of victims during a few years? Is America a *nation* or a *war zone*?

Did the doctors even want to help Kennedy?

Doctor Perry's testimony suggests that the doctors had *no interest* in helping Kennedy. Here is just one of his remarks:

> Mr. Specter: *Why was it, Dr. Perry, that there was no effort made to examine the clothing of President Kennedy and no effort to turn him over and examine the back of the President?*
>
> Dr. Perry: *At the termination of the procedure and after we had determined that Mr. Kennedy had expired, I cannot speak for the others but as for myself, my work was done. I fought a losing battle, and I actually obviously, having seen a lot of wounds, had no morbid curiosity, and actually was rather anxious to leave the room. I had nothing further to offer.*

Perry rushed in the room, assisted a sloppy tracheotomy, and was *"rather anxious"* to leave. Was this just another boring, gunshot victim? Was the doctor concerned about missing his golf appointment?

Whereas Perry was *anxious* to get out of the room, Doctor Jenkins described the attitude of the doctors as:

> *...those in attendance who were there just sort of melted away, well, I guess "melted" is the wrong word, but we felt like we were intruders and left.*

The doctors were treating Kennedy in *their* hospital. Why would doctors feel like *intruders* while trying to save their President's life in their own hospital? Who were they intruding on? Was somebody in the room with them to make them uncomfortable? Was the FBI or CIA bothering them?

The doctors also ignored (or avoided) Jackie Kennedy. Here is a remark from Doctor Perry when he was asked about her:

> *I was informed subsequently that Mrs. Kennedy left the room several times to just outside the door but returned although as I say, I saw her several times in the room. I did not speak to her nor she to me so I do not have any knowledge as to exactly what she was doing.*

Later in the interview he was asked for more details:

> Mr. Specter: *Where was Mrs. Kennedy, if you know, during the course of the treatment which you have described that you performed?*
>
> Dr. Perry: *I had the initial impression she was in the room most of the time although I have been corrected on this. When I entered the room she was standing by the door, rather kneeling by the door, and someone*

was standing there beside her. I saw her several times during the course of the resuscitative measures, when I would look up from the operative field to secure an instrument from the nearby tray.

Is it common for a doctor to ignore the president's wife during such a tragedy? Did any of the doctors even say "Hello" to her? Or did all the doctors behave like Perry; i.e., rush in, perform a few sloppy medical procedures of no value, and then rush out? Is this standard hospital treatment in Texas? Is this what is referred to as *"Southern Hospitality"*? Furthermore, if this is how Southern Doctors treat the President, how do they treat people of other races?

How serious was the head wound?

Kennedy had a wound in his head, but it was not visible from certain directions. Also, Kennedy had a lot of hair, and the hair partially covered the wound. His hair was full of blood, but the doctors did not consider it serious enough to bother looking closely at his head. Nor did they turn Kennedy over to see the back of his head or the back of his body.

Is it really possible that experienced doctors would ignore bloody hair? Would a real doctor give a patient a tracheotomy and injections of hydrocortisone without first looking at his bloody head? Don't real doctors examine a patient *before* making a decision on the treatment? Or was the head wound just a tiny scratch that could be ignored?

The autopsy report has fancy medical terminology that makes it difficult to understand exactly what the head wound looked like:

> *There is a large irregular defect of the scalp and skull on the right involving chiefly the parietal bone but extending somewhat into the temporal and occipital regions. In this region there is an actual absence of scalp and bone producing a defect which measures approximately 13 cm. in greatest diameter.*

A more understandable description of the wound comes from Clinton Hill, a Secret Service agent. He climbed into Kennedy's car after the shooting and rode to the hospital with them. His description of Kennedy's head wound:

Mr. Specter: *What did you observe as to President Kennedy's condition on arrival at the hospital?*

Mr. Hill: *The right rear portion of his head was missing. It was lying in the rear seat of the car. His brain was exposed. There was blood and bits of brain all over the entire rear portion of the car. Mrs. Kennedy was completely covered with blood. There was so much blood you could not tell if*

there had been any other wound or not, except for the one large gaping wound in the right rear portion of the head.

How obvious does the JFK scam have to be?

When I first began reading the Warren Report, I was visualizing immature college students who were trying to behave as doctors. I was shocked by their behavior. But when I discovered the doctors were adults with many years of experience, I realized that the only way to explain the insane medical treatment is that the doctors were removing bullets and/or converting bullet holes to "treatment holes." The hole in Kennedy's neck was *not* to help him breathe.

The testimony from the doctors is enough to convince me that our government, hospitals, police, and media were involved in the Kennedy killing. The rest of Warren Report makes the conspiracy even more obvious.

Even the world's most incompetent medical student who failed every medical course would have immediately realized that Kennedy was hopelessly dead when he saw brains "oozing" out of a hole that was *13 cm wide*.

Actually, I suspect that some of the more intelligent doctors would have deduced that Kennedy was dead when they realized – as Clinton Hill described it:

> *"There was blood and bits of brain all over the entire rear portion of the car."*

Or how about his remark:

> *"The right rear portion of his head was missing. It was lying in the rear seat of the car."*

While some people might insist that the goofy behavior of the doctors was due to stress, these doctors had seen hundreds of gunshot victims and other medical problems. Certainly every doctor knew that Kennedy was dead the moment they saw what the Warren Report described as *"shredded brain tissue."* Their idiotic treatment of Kennedy was merely to cover the signs that there was more than one sniper.

The doctors never turned Kennedy over or looked closely at his head because the rear of his head was *in the car*. A portion was also in the road (a piece of skull was found the next day). Note that Figure 11-1 does not show the left, rear of his head. I cannot find any photo that shows the hole. Also, the photo is abnormally low quality, as if somebody wanted to hide the details and holes.

How could people in 1963 not realize the killing was a scam? Was the information suppressed so well that most people never knew what actually happened? Did the media in 1963 lie about the killing as much as they lie about the 9-11 attack? Were there millions of "patriots" who demanded blind obedience to President Johnson, just as there are millions today who demand we obey Bush? Were people ridiculed as "conspiracy nuts" for suggesting the killing was a scam, just as people today are ridiculed for pointing out that the 9-11 attack was a scam?

How obvious does the Kennedy scam have to be before the American patriots stop calling us "conspiracy nuts" and face the fact that America is incredibly corrupt? What if the doctors had asked Clinton Hill to scoop up the bits of brain in the car so they could stuff it back into Kennedy's head? Or what if the doctors asked Jackie Kennedy to scrape the brains off her dress so they could put it back in his head? How about if the doctors were laughing as they asked for the bits of brains? How absurd would the medical treatment have to be in order for our society to correct the lies in our history books and admit that the killing was a scam?

"Partial death" murders (or "late-term" murders)

What would have happened if the bullets had only *wounded* Kennedy. A wounded Kennedy would create the same problem that occurs with "partial birth abortions." Would the government allow Kennedy to live after going to this much trouble to kill him? I doubt it. Rather, the doctors would kill Kennedy and pretend that he died despite their best efforts.

Maybe the doctors were relieved when they saw the hole in Kennedy's head because maybe they didn't want to kill him. However, it is also possible that the doctors were hoping he would come in alive so that they could kill him. This would explain their lack of enthusiasm. Their behavior suggests boredom and disappointment. Since Kennedy was dead by the time the doctors arrived, the doctors had nothing to do except the boring work of removing bullets.

Is the Dallas hospital a CIA testing center?

Years ago I heard rumors that the CIA developed killing techniques that make it difficult to determine the cause of death. How would the CIA know if their killing techniques were difficult to detect unless some doctors inspected the victims and gave the CIA a report? Wouldn't the CIA have to kill people and then let doctors inspect the bodies?

Maybe some of the doctors who "treated" Kennedy were the doctors who would send reports to the CIA about their LSD and other experiments.

Doctor Perry was one of the doctors who "treated" Oswald after Jack Ruby shot him. The Warren Report claims that Oswald died from that little bullet. Doctor Perry told the commission that when Oswald arrived at the hospital he was unconscious and blue from lack of oxygen. He said the bullet tore some of Oswald's major arteries. However, since the doctors lied about Kennedy, why should we believe their reports about Oswald? For all we know, the doctors tore Oswald's arteries, and during the ride to the hospital an FBI

agent may have choked him until he was blue and unconscious.

The Southwest hate capital of Dixie

An interesting paragraph from the Warren Report about the people in Dallas:

> *Increased concern about the President's visit was aroused by the incident involving the US Ambassador to the United Nations, Adlai E. Stevenson. On the evening of October 24, 1963, after addressing a meeting in Dallas, Stevenson was jeered, jostled, and spat upon by hostile demonstrators outside the Dallas Memorial Auditorium Theater. The local, national, and international reaction to this incident evoked from Dallas officials and newspapers strong condemnations of the demonstrators. Mayor Earle Cabell called on the city to redeem itself during President Kennedy's visit. He asserted that Dallas had shed its reputation of the twenties as the "Southwest hate capital of Dixie."*

After reading about the doctors who "treated" Kennedy, I think Dallas was premature in shedding its reputation as "Southwest hate capital of Dixie." Incidentally, why doesn't the USA have any "Love Capitals" or "Honesty Capitals"?

Why do people believe Oswald acted alone?

The killing occurred 40 years ago, and it is *painfully obvious* that the killing was a scam, so why do millions of Americans insist that Oswald acted alone?

Furthermore, the killing is a significant scandal in American history, but our schools do not teach us about this scandal. Why not? Does our government influence school textbooks, as we condemn the Russian government for doing?

The *World Book Encyclopedia* that I grew up with, published in 1965, lies about the killing. For just one example:

> *Doctors worked desperately to save the President, but he died at 1pm.*

In reality, Kennedy was shot in the head at about 12:30, and he died instantly. The doctors did indeed work desperately, but only to remove evidence of the snipers.

The article was written by Eric Sevareid, a news reporter. His article should be used as evidence that reporters should not be allowed to write encyclopedia articles.

I checked the Internet for the latest version of the *World Book Encyclopedia* to see if the lies have been corrected, but that section of the article is still the same. Sean Wilentz, a history teacher at Princeton University, updated the article but did not remove the lies. Obviously, Princeton's history teachers should not be allowed to write encyclopedia articles, either.

I think the main reasons millions of people believe Oswald acted alone are:

1) Our government is so incompetent and the American people fight with each other so often that many of us find it difficult to believe that the government nitwits can get together for such a killing.

2) America's "free press" has been corrupted by money, political pressure, and who knows what else. This results in school textbooks and news reports that are full of lies about the killing, and information is suppressed. Our media keeps us ignorant and misinformed. Incidentally, Dan Rather (the TV news reporter) was a young reporter at the Kennedy killing. He was such a special person that he was supposedly the only news reporter allowed to view Zapruder's 8 millimeter film of the killing. But he lied in his news reports about what he saw in that film. Nobody noticed the lie because the film was hidden from the public until 1975 when Geraldo Rivera somehow got a copy and broadcast it on television. However, by 1975 nobody remembered or cared about Rather's 1963 report.

Dan Rather was given a promotion shortly after the killing, and soon he became rich and famous. Coincidence?

3) Admitting the Kennedy killing was a scam is admitting America is a hypocritical, corrupt nation.

I did not realize the Kennedy killing was a scam until a few years ago. I suppose I picked up the "Oswald Acted Alone" theory from encyclopedias, school textbooks, and magazines. Somehow the issue of the Kennedy killing came up in a discussion I was having with an older relative who was an adult in 1963, and he mentioned that J. Edgar Hoover and other government officials killed Kennedy. I was surprised to hear him say this, and I defended the FBI. I could not believe top officials in the FBI were *that* corrupt.

He continued to talk about how dishonest Lyndon Johnson was, and how Earl Warren was a gullible fool who had been taken advantage of. He complained about other officials, as well, and mentioned that the CIA had ties to organized crime and Jimmy Hoffa.

I already knew that the Kennedy family was not one of America's best behaved families, but if I were to believe my relative, practically every high ranking member of the American government should be arrested for at least one serious crime. Furthermore, he implied some people on the Supreme Court are easily manipulated, and some of our unions and corporations are corrupt. I knew America had problems, but I could not believe America was as crummy as he was making it appear. I essentially told him: *"Give me a break!"*

I did to him what millions of Americans are doing to me today; namely, I resisted the possibility that America is incredibly corrupt. I preferred my fantasy in which the FBI was honest, just as most Americans are trying to live in a fantasy in which Americans are the Greatest People In The World and Osama is the source of our problems.

I discovered the Warren Report on the Internet a few months after I defended the FBI. As I read through it I realized that our government killed Kennedy. Actually, the killing is so obviously a scam that I felt like a fool for defending the FBI. From now on I will consider the FBI guilty until proven innocent.

What is "free" about our press?

The Kennedy and the 9-11 scams show that America's "free press" is a joke. The only thing "free" about our press is that government officials can *freely manipulate it*. Or perhaps wealthy people are free to manipulate journalists, as this man suggests:

> *The business of the journalist is to destroy the truth, to lie outright, to pervert, to vilify, to fawn at the feet of Mammon and to sell his country and his race for his daily bread. ... We are the tools and vassals of rich men behind the scenes. We are the jumping jacks, they pull the strings and we dance. ... . We are intellectual prostitutes.*

Those remarks are attributed to John Swinton, a New York journalist, in 1880. Did he really make those remarks? If so, was he serious? Do most journalists care more about money and/or fame than performing a useful service to society? Can the articles in the *New York Times* be controlled by money? If so, is the CIA using any of their secret budget to control the "intellectual prostitutes" today?

If the Kennedy killing was a scam, what else was?

After I published the first edition of this book, I was informed of the reports by such people as General Benton Partin. Partin calculated the pressure that would have resulted from Tim McVeigh's bomb (which supposedly destroyed the Murrah Building in Oklahoma City in 1995), and his calculations prove that a bomb of fuel oil and fertilizer exploding in the street could *not* do such extensive damage to the Murrah building. Unless somebody can show that Partin's calculations are incorrect, there is no need to investigate further – *that attack was a scam also!*

The FBI did *not* investigate the Oklahoma City bombing. Rather, the building was demolished and the rubble was quickly destroyed, just as with the 9-11 attack.

When I first heard of the arrest of McVeigh in 1995 I wondered why he was caught driving away in a rundown car that was missing its license plate. How could he be intelligent enough to create a powerful bomb but so stupid that he would drive away in a car that would attract the attention of the police? It seemed that somebody wanted the police to notice McVeigh. Partin and others explain why; namely, *the attack was a scam,* and McVeigh was a *patsy.*

Why do so few people know about Partin's report? Because our news reporters suppressed his report. The news reporters also gave us false information about McVeigh and the attack.

How obvious does the 9-11 scam have to be?

Only a small percentage of Americans believe the 9-11 attack was a scam. I think the main reasons most Americans believe Osama was behind the attack are:

1) It is difficult to believe that a group of people could be so violent and destructive as to fill the buildings with explosives. This is far beyond "normal" crimes. And they did this while thousands of people were working inside.

2) Such a scam would be so complex and expensive that only a government would have the resources to do it, but the American government seems too incompetent to succeed at such a complex scam, and not many Americans can handle the possibility that foreign governments are involved in these scams.

3) Our "free press" is corrupt. The news reporters are suppressing information and lying to us. The *American Free Press* is a national newspaper that discusses the 9-11 attack, and a few Internet sites (for example, *public-action.com,* and *Serendipity*.com) have been discussing it for months, but those people are never interviewed on television or put on the cover of *Time* magazine. The end result is that most Americans have been kept ignorant about the attack.

4) Most people are too ignorant about explosives, concrete, the demolition of buildings, and steel

beams to be able to carry on an intelligent discussion about how the buildings collapsed. For an amusing example, when I pointed out that Building 7 should not have collapsed from a small fire, a few people responded to me that they heard the fire *created stress in the building.* In other words, these people give human qualities to the building. I suppose those people would have sent psychiatrists to the buildings instead of firemen.

5) The people who promote the scam theory are individuals that nobody knows. We appear to be a group of oddballs, whereas the TV news reporters appear to be "official."

6) Admitting the attack was a scam is admitting America is an incredibly corrupt nation, possibly beyond anything the world has ever seen. I think this is the primary reason most Americans refuse to consider that the attack was a scam.

Most Americans are in denial

How obvious would the explosions in the World Trade Center have to be in order for the majority of Americans to face the possibility that the attack was a scam? What if *colored* explosives had been used, as in fireworks? Would that be obvious enough? Or would *Scientific American* and university professors publish idiotic theories about the cobalt, barium, and other exotic elements in the aircraft engines reacting with the magnetic strips on credit cards to create colored sparkles?

Before you can accept the possibility that the 9-11 attack belongs in the Guinness Book of World Records as **The World's Most Incredible Scam,** you must be willing to accept the possibility that America's government, universities, and media are corrupt beyond your wildest dreams. The people who insist that Americans are "The Greatest People In The World" will find it difficult to accept such a possibility.

How can we be the greatest people in the world when we consistently elect corrupt government officials? How can we boast about our honesty and our high morals when we allow one incredible scam after the next? How can we boast about our "Free Press" when it covers up colossal scams and lies to us to an extent that not even *Pravda* has been accused of? How can we boast about our universities when some professors are promoting false theories to deceive us, and other universities ignore the issue?

More on JFK

(According to the Warren Report)

Oswald's childhood

Oswald's father died two months after he was born, and his mother apparently struggled to support herself and her children. When Lee was three years old she put him in an orphanage where his older brother and half-brother were already living. A year later she took him back, presumably because she could now afford him, but they were always poor. He ended up with a couple of different step fathers, and he and his mother moved from one city to another every couple of years. He was a misfit throughout his life, and moving to new homes every few years made it even more difficult for him to form friendships.

He was living in New York City when he was 12 years old. This was the age he began to resist going to school and show such serious emotional problems that his teachers were complaining about him. He was sent for psychiatric treatment, which created a temporary improvement in his behavior, but his teachers soon resumed complaining.

He and his mother moved to New Orleans when he was 14 years old. He was not as much trouble at this age, but he was still a misfit who did not want to be in school. Just before he turned 16 years old he dropped out of school to join the Marine Corps. They told him he was too young, so he ended up working at various low paying jobs. At about this age he became attracted to Marxism. I suspect that he was escaping his misery by withdrawing into fantasies. Marxism promises a society in which everybody loves each other, and the wealthy people share their food and material goods.

A few months later he and his mother moved to Fort Worth, Texas. He reentered high school but dropped out a few days after his 17th birthday to join the Marine Corps. He obviously believed that he would be happier as a Marine, perhaps because of the advertisements that show Marines having fun and seeing the world. As you might expect, he was a misfit in the Marine Corps, but he did not cause much trouble.

Oswald as an adult

Just before he turned twenty years old he asked to leave the Marine Corps a few months before his scheduled release on the grounds that he wanted to help his mother, who was ill. However, after getting out of the Marines he stayed with her for only three days and then bought a ticket on a ship to Europe. From there he went to Moscow. He had obtained a passport while still in the Marines, so apparently he had planned this trip while in the Marines.

He arrived in Moscow a couple days before he was 20 years old. He asked to become a Russian citizen but, for reasons the Warren Report never specified, the Russians told him to get out of Russia by that same evening. Perhaps they could see that he was mentally unstable and did not even want him to remain overnight.

He had probably been fantasizing for years that he would be happy in a Marxist nation, but the Russians shattered his fantasy after he spent a significant amount of his money to enter the Marxist paradise. By the afternoon he had become so depressed that he cut his wrist in a suicide attempt. He was taken to a hospital for treatment. Apparently the suicide attempt caused the Russians to feel sorry for him because they decided to allow him remain in Russia for one year. They gave him a job as an unskilled laborer.

Initially his life in Russia was exciting because many Russians wanted to meet the newly arrived American, but that excitement did not last long. The Russians quickly realized that he was a loser. Oswald then resumed his lonely life.

Oswald learned the Russian language and somehow socialized enough to meet and marry a Russian woman named Marina. What kind of woman would marry a loser like Oswald? The information her American friends provided to the Warren Commission suggests she was from a poor family and saw Oswald as her ticket out of Russia.

Oswald became disillusioned with Russia but he continued to believe that Marxism would create a happy society if some nation would implement it correctly. When his one year period was up, he asked to remain in Russia for another year. The Russians granted his request. However, Marina was convinced that she would be happier if she could move to the USA. Apparently she convinced him to leave because in June, 1962, when he was 22 years old, he and Marina left Russia and settled in a poor section of Fort Worth, Texas.

Since his wife was Russian, some of the other Russians in the area wanted to meet them. A few became friends with her, to a certain extent. Nobody became friends with Lee Oswald, however.

I doubt that there was even one period of Oswald's life when he was happy. Rather, his life appears to have been wasted wondering where happiness could be. He thought happiness was in the Marine Corps, but it wasn't. He thought it was in Marxism, but he discovered that Russia was not implementing Marxism in the manner he fantasized. Marina, likewise, was looking for happiness.

The world is full of people like Oswald who have miserable lives for various reasons, and who waste their lives in a futile search for happiness. The most common fantasy is that large sums of money will bring happiness, but some people have fantasies of fame, and some fantasize of Marxism. It never occurs to these people that happiness is not an item that can be acquired.

Oswald never had a driver's license or a car, and he never learned any useful skills. He had difficultly holding a job for more than a few months. Marina never learned English while Oswald was alive. According to the people who knew him, he did not want her to learn English. Was he was worried that if she knew English she would be able to socialize with other people and meet other men? Did he want her to be completely dependent on him? We will never know, but once an American woman named Ruth Paine tried to show him how to drive a car. Paine knew enough Russian for ordinary conversations, but she could not explain how to drive a car in Russian. She spoke to Oswald in English, but he would respond to her in Russian. Oswald tended to speak Russian whenever possible, even when it annoyed other people. This implies his insistence on speaking Russian was because he was trying to withdraw into a Marxist fantasy.

Most men in 1962 supported their families financially, but this was not easy for him because he had such difficulty holding a job that he could not adequately support himself. His situation became worse when Marina gave birth to a baby girl in 1962. Jeanne De Mohrenschildt, a Russian immigrant who had been in the USA for many years, was perhaps Marina's best friend. Her remark about their situation:

> *"Well, I wouldn't say they were completely starving, but they were quite miserable, quite, quite miserable..."*

Some of the Russians in the area felt sorry for Marina and occasionally gave her clothes and other gifts. Nobody seemed to give Lee Oswald any gifts, however.

De Mohrenschildt mentioned there were often fights between the two of them, so it was not likely to be a happy marriage. In fact, once Marina complained that she was not sexually satisfied with Oswald. This surprised De Mohrenschildt because American women in 1963 did not normally complain about such issues. This could be a sign that Oswald's sexual behavior was so awful that his wife could not refrain from complaining about it.

After one particular fight in which Marina got a black eye, the De Mohrenschildts drove over to their house and took Marina, her baby, and their possessions to somebody else's house. However, as is typical in cases of abuse, Marina soon went back to Oswald to resume her pathetic relationship.

In case you are visualizing Marina as Miss Russia of 1963 who was abused by a terrible man, the description provided by Jeanne De Mohrenschildt suggests she and Lee Oswald were losers who somehow found each other in the crowd of normal people. Consider these three remarks:

> *She is lazy... She was not a woman to arrange the home or make a home.... She had no idea how to feed that baby.*

De Mohrenschildt was friends with Marina, but she was not impressed with her. I think De Mohrenschildt felt a bond to Marina only because they were both immigrants from Russia, not because she truly wanted Marina as a friend.

Ruth Paine feels sorry for the Oswalds

Lee Oswald could not hold a job. In April, 1963 Lee and Marina decided that he should move to New Orleans to look for a job while Marina and the baby waited in Texas. When he found a job they would take a bus to New Orleans to join him.

A 31 year old woman named Ruth Paine, who they met in February, 1963, visited Marina on April 24th, the day Lee Oswald was leaving for New Orleans. Paine lived in a house in Irving, Texas with her two small children. She felt sorry for Marina and offered to let her stay at her house while Lee looked for a job. Paine did not like the idea of a pregnant woman and young child taking a 12 hour bus trip to New Orleans, so she offered to drive Marina and her daughter to New Orleans when Lee found a job. Paine was very generous.

Ruth Paine was an American, not a Russian, and she belonged to the Quaker church, not the communist party, but she lived in a neighborhood with many Russian immigrants. More importantly, she had learned enough of the Russian language to be able to talk to Marina.

Paine's husband, Michael, had moved into his own apartment many months earlier, so perhaps she was happy to have companionship. Since she and Marina had young children, perhaps they helped each other with childcare. The Paines had not yet been divorced; in fact, they would get together each week for dinner and movies.

Oswald found a job in New Orleans within two weeks. On May 11th Paine drove Marina and her baby daughter to New Orleans so they could start a new life in a new city. Unfortunately, Oswald was fired from his job after about two months. His family had to survive on the small unemployment income he received.

While in New Orleans he spent some time with Communist organizations that supported Fidel Castro. By August of 1963 Oswald was so involved in communist activities to help Castro that he was briefly mentioned by, and interviewed by, local television, radio, and newspapers. He was arrested once at a demonstration and taken to a New Orleans jail for a very brief period. In jail he requested a meeting with the FBI. The FBI sent John Quigley to talk to him. Why would Oswald want to talk to the FBI? Quigley's speculation was that Oswald *"was probably making a self-serving statement."* However, if Oswald wanted to make a statement, why would he do so to the FBI rather than a newspaper reporter or lawyer? I suspect that Oswald had a more important reason to talk to the FBI, but what could that reason be?†

By September of 1963 Oswald was almost 24 years old, and Marina was pregnant with their second child. Soon this unskilled misfit would have to support a wife and two children. As is typical of humans, Oswald refused to admit that he was the source of his troubles. Rather, he was convinced that somebody was picking on him or treating him unfairly. For example, he claimed that he sometimes failed to get a job because the employer had heard of his communist activities. To some extent Oswald was correct because many Americans in that era were paranoid of communists. However, discrimination could explain only a small portion of his troubles. His two main problems were that he was lacking useful skills and his personality was unpleasant.

Unlike Marxism, which provides jobs to all people regardless of whether they can do anything useful, Capitalism is cruel to unskilled, incompetent, and unwanted people. The unemployable people often end up as criminals, welfare recipients, or government employees. Oswald never seemed to consider a government job, however, aside from the Marine Corps. Perhaps he was too angry at the USA.

In September Oswald decided to look for a job in Dallas. Ruth Paine once again felt sorry for Marina and offered to let Marina stay at her house. On the 23rd of September she drove Marina from New Orleans to her home in Irving, Texas. On October 7th Lee Oswald rented a room in a house in Dallas. His plan was to look for a job during the week and take a bus to Paine's home on the weekends to be with his family.

On October 10th the CIA told the FBI that Oswald was contacting the Soviet Embassy in Mexico, so the FBI told Quigley to find him and investigate. How would the CIA know that Oswald was contacting the Soviet Embassy? Does the Soviet Embassy tell the CIA who is contacting them? Or does the CIA spy on the Soviet Embassy?

Mary Bledsoe, the lady who owned the house in Dallas that Oswald rented a room from, told him to leave after five days. Oswald was still in the process of looking for a job, so he had to find another place to live in addition to a job. Nobody wanted Oswald for a friend, employee, or a renter.

Never feel sorry for Underdogs

If I was in Ruth Paine's position, I would be worried that Oswald would never hold a job for more than a few months, with the result that Marina and her children would be needing assistance forever, and that they would always be short of money. Also, I would be concerned that Lee Oswald would become increasingly frustrated and angry, which would make him increasingly unpleasant when he visited on the weekends. Paine may have been regretting her decision to help the "Underdogs."

When somebody feels sorry for an adult who cannot take care of himself, the end result is usually a parasitic relationship. However, feeling sorry for "Underdogs" is the American tradition, so Paine probably reminded herself that she was a good American for helping the "Downtrodden" and the "Less Fortunate."

Americans do not differentiate between a healthy person who needs assistance for a brief time due to an unexpected problem, such as an earthquake or illness, and a person who needs support during his entire life due to mental defects. Rather, both types of people are referred to as "underdogs."

Ruth Paine helps Oswald get a job

Paine and some other women in the neighborhood got together in the morning on a regular basis to socialize.‡ Paine mentioned to the other women that Lee Oswald was looking for a job. One of the women replied that her 19 year old brother, Wesley Frazier, had just been hired at the Texas School Book Depository in Dallas, so perhaps the Depository has more jobs. Marina could not speak English so she asked Paine to find out if the Texas School Book Depository had more job openings. On October 14th Paine made a phone call and was connected to Roy Truly, the superintendent:

---

† According to Michael Piper's book *Final Judgement,* Oswald was told to join the Castro movement to make it appear as if Oswald had Castro and communist connections. This could explain Oswald's request to talk to the FBI; ie, Oswald may have complained to Quigley: "I went to the demonstration – for you – and now I am in jail! **Get me out of here!**"

‡ For the younger readers who rarely see their mother: in 1963 most women had only part-time jobs or remained home. They took care of the house, arranged dinners and other social events, and did things with their children and neighbors.

Mr. Truly: I received a phone call from a lady in Irving who said her name was Mrs. Paine.

Mr. Belin: All right. What did Mrs. Paine say, and what did you say?

Mr. Truly: She said, "Mr. Truly," – words to this effect – you understand – "Mr. Truly, you don't know who I am but I have a neighbor whose brother works for you. I don't know what his name is. But he tells his sister that you are very busy. And I am just wondering if you can use another man," or words to that effect.

And I told Mrs. – she said, "I have a fine young man living here with his wife and baby, and his wife is expecting a baby – another baby, in a few days, and he needs work desperately."

Now, this is not absolutely – this is as near as I can remember the conversation over the telephone.

And I told Mrs. Paine that … to send him down, and I would talk to him … that I didn't have anything in mind for him of a permanent nature, but if he was suited, we could possibly use him for a brief time.

That was the only time Paine and Truly talked to each other. When Oswald made a routine call to his wife, she told him to contact Roy Truly about a possible job. Oswald was hired for unskilled labor, undoubtedly because of the wonderful recommendation from Paine.

Oswald tries to hide from the FBI

Oswald found another room to rent in Dallas. He rented the room under a phony name. His wife was upset with him for using a phony name and told him to stop it, but he continued. He justified his fake name on the grounds that he didn't want the lady who owned the house to know his real name in case the newspapers mention his communist connections. More interesting, he said he wanted to hide from the FBI because his meetings with them were unpleasant. How many meetings did he have with the FBI? What occurred at the meetings? In New Orleans he *requested* a meeting; a few months later he was *hiding* from the FBI. What was going on between the FBI and Oswald? Not surprisingly, the Warren Report never explains.

Oswald was so afraid of the FBI and so convinced that they were trying to hurt him that he even told his wife to remove his name and phone number from Paine's phone book. He wanted to become invisible to the entire world. He also told his wife that he suspected the reason he gets fired from jobs is because the FBI tells his employers to fire him. He was not willing to believe that he gets fired because

he is annoying, incompetent, and lacking in skills. He was certain that his problems were due to other people.

"I live in Irving, also! What a coincidence!"

One of Oswald's co-workers was Wesley Frazier, the 19 year-old teenager from Ruth Paine's neighborhood. Although Oswald was not very sociable, he obviously talked to Frazier at least once. Both Oswald and Frazier were surprised to discover their connection to Ruth Paine. Obviously, Paine never told her neighbors that she helped Oswald get a job at the book depository. Why did she keep this information a secret? Why not tell her neighbors the good news that Oswald will be working with one of them? It appears as if during Oswald's entire life everybody ignored and avoided him.

When Frazier discovered that Oswald's wife was living with Paine, he offered to let Oswald commute with him so that he could go home each night to be with his family. Fortunately for Paine, Oswald decided to remain in Dallas during the week and ride home with Frazier only on Fridays. Oswald would stay with his family over the weekend and ride back to work with Frazier on Monday morning.

The FBI locates Oswald

FBI agent Quigley located Oswald on November 1, 1963, despite Oswald's phony name. You can run from the FBI, but you can't hide![†] How did the FBI find Oswald so quickly? Oswald's photo was *not* printed in the newspapers or shown on television; there was *no* nation-wide hunt for Oswald. If the FBI is truly capable of quickly finding people who hide from them, why is there is so much crime?

Quigley said he didn't yet know that Kennedy would be in a motorcade, nor did he realize that Oswald wanted to shoot somebody famous, so he did not see any potential danger to Kennedy. Quigley also points out that Oswald was just one of many people he had to investigate.

Quigley's remarks are understandable. America probably has more people with guns than the entire rest of the world put together. And our nation has lots of angry, unhappy people who fantasize about killing somebody. The FBI cannot be expected to closely watch every mentally unstable American and accurately predict which of them will commit a crime.

For all we know, several angry guys showed up at various Kennedy motorcades with a fantasy of killing Kennedy. It is also possible that several of these Assassin Wannabes were watching the Dallas motorcade, but that none of them tried to shoot Kennedy. They may have been jealous when Oswald was accused of killing Kennedy.

[†] Organized crime hid from Quigley and other FBI agents for decades, but I won't discuss that embarrassing scandal.

The few people who have been caught shooting at famous people don't seem to care which famous person they kill, and they rarely try to kill the first time they see a famous person. Rather, the Assassin Wannabe carries his gun to meetings just in case the opportunity arises, but rarely do they use it. Only once in a while does one of them get the opportunity to shoot. Most of the time they are merely in the audience, quietly hiding their gun. When famous people look out over their audience, they might like to wonder how many people brought along a gun just in case they get the chance to use it.

Did Oswald try to kill General Walker?

Somebody (the police never figured out who) fired a rifle at the retired General Walker months before the Kennedy killing while Walker was sitting at his desk at his home. However, the bullet missed. Marina Oswald's testimony makes it appear that Lee Oswald was the person who shot at Walker. Oswald purchased an inexpensive rifle about one month before, and Marina said that his behavior on that particular day gave her the impression that he was worried he may not come back home. For example, he deliberately left his wedding ring and wallet at home, along with a note on what to do if he does not come home. She also implies that Oswald fantasized about killing Richard Nixon. Her testimony can make you wonder if Oswald had a few other failed murder attempts, also.

Oswald appears to have been an unhappy, angry person looking for somebody famous to kill. He did not seem to care who he killed; rather, he just wanted to kill somebody famous. If the FBI realized that he wanted to kill somebody, they would have known that he would make a great patsy for the Kennedy killing. Unfortunately, since Oswald could not hit General Walker at close range while Walker was sitting at a desk, it would be unlikely that he could hit a moving target at a longer distance. Furthermore, Oswald had an inexpensive rifle that was not very accurate. The FBI would have to provide a higher quality rifle.

Kennedy is shot on November 22, 1963

The plan was to kill Kennedy on Friday, November 23. In order to make Oswald a patsy for this killing, he had to bring his rifle to work and leave it at the crime scene. However, his rifle was hidden in a blanket in Paine's garage, where his other personal possessions were stored. So he rode to Irving with Frazier on Thursday after work to get his rifle. This was the first time Oswald traveled home with Frazier during the week. He spent Thursday night at Paine's house and left early Friday morning with Frazier to go to his job. Oswald had a package with him. He told Frazier the package contained curtain rods. Supposedly nobody knew

he owned a rifle, so nobody suspected the package might contain a rifle.

At 12:30 on Friday afternoon Kennedy was shot. The FBI wants us to believe that Oswald fired three shots over a time span of 5 to 8 seconds from the sixth floor of a building. Oswald was shooting downward and towards his right. Kennedy was about 55 meters (180 feet) from Oswald when the first shot was fired and 80 meters (260 feet) when the final shot blew his brains out. The Warren Report says that an analysis of an 8mm film of the shooting shows that the car was moving at 18 km per hour (11.2 mph) at the time of the shootings, which meant that Kennedy was moving at 5 meters (16.4 feet) per second. Most of Kennedy's body was protected by the car; his head was the only target. Hitting Kennedy's head while it was moving at those speeds is equivalent to hitting a large bird in flight. Did Oswald have to be an expert to hit a target that was moving so fast? No; the FBI claims the shots were easy because the bullets Oswald had chosen had a high velocity, and he had a telescopic sight on the rifle. The FBI's conclusion was that anybody "proficient" with a rifle could make those shots.

Oswald had a bolt-action rifle, so he had to push and pull a lever back and forth to load the next bullet. The Warren Report claims that some "expert riflemen" tried making three shots with his rifle to see if anybody could be so accurate while shooting so fast with such a lousy rifle, and the experts were averaging 5 to 9 seconds for three accurate shots. The FBI concluded that the shots were easy. Why do hunters use *shotguns* rather than rifles if hitting moving targets is so easy?

To people like me, who have only almost no experience with guns, the shots appear to be very difficult. I shot a BB gun dozens of times, and I shot a .22 rifle at a rifle range a couple of times, but I found it difficult to accurately hit a *stationary* target that was close to me. Hitting a stationary target is difficult because it requires an understanding of how to compensate for gravity and wind; hitting a human head that is 50 meters away and moving at 5 meters per second is even *more difficult*, with or without a telescopic sight and high speed bullets. If the wind was strong that day, the shots would be even more difficult. Was there any wind?

According to Lieutenant Baker, one of the motorcycle cops riding along the cars, the wind *was* strong:

> *As we approached the corner there of Main and Houston we were making a right turn, and as I came out behind that building there, which is the county courthouse, the sheriff building, well, there was a strong wind hit me and I almost lost my balance.*

The FBI expects us to believe that Oswald was shooting downward and towards his right, which is an awkward position for a right-handed person, such as Oswald. I think even left handed people would consider the shots difficult. And the strong wind would have made it even more difficult.

Oswald was using large bullets, so the recoil of the rifle would have been substantial, especially for a man as slim as Oswald. As soon as he pulled the trigger, the recoil would cause Kennedy to disappear from the telescopic sight. The Warren Report says Oswald's rifle *"had less recoil than the average military rifle,"* but that remark is as stupid as: *"Oswald's rifle had less recoil than a cannon."* The Warren Report was probably trying to trivialize the recoil.

Nobody can hold a rifle steady while firing such powerful bullets. Furthermore, Oswald had to push and pull a lever to load the next bullet, and that motion could easily change the position of the gun, which would cause Kennedy to vanish from the telescopic sight.

The FBI expects us to believe that this unskilled laborer who did not know how to drive a car was capable of making such incredible shots that he could have been the 1964 Olympic Rifle Champion. Or am I a fool? Were the shots easy?

Why not test the FBI theory?

On the anniversary of Kennedy's murder we should block off the streets in Dealy Plaza and spend the day pulling a mannequin down the street at the speed Kennedy was moving. Tourists can then try to duplicate Oswald's easy shots from that 6th floor window. Each person gets an

inexpensive, bolt-action rifle, three bullets, and eight seconds. Although Oswald didn't practice the shots, we could give the "Government Supporter Nuts" a slight advantage by letting them practice.

If it turns out that lots of people can hit the mannequin, then it is possible that Oswald made all those shots. If, on the other hand, not even the experts can hit the mannequin, we would have lots of entertainment watching the Government Supporter Nuts struggle to devise some idiotic explanation for how Oswald did what nobody else can do. So, why don't we put the FBI theory to a test and settle this issue once and for all? The event could be advertised as the *"The Conspiracy Nuts vs. The Government Supporter Nuts."*

Three shots are fired, or four shots, or five...

One of the interesting aspects of the Kennedy killing is that the witnesses disagree on the number of shots. The FBI expects us to believe that humans are incapable of counting three gunshots that are spaced a minimum of 2.3 seconds apart. The first shot would have occurred when nobody expected it, so it is understandable that the first shot would cause a lot of people to blurt out, *"What was that?"* But if 2.3 seconds later there was a second shot, and then 2.3 seconds later a third shot, wouldn't the witnesses be able to remember a total of three shots? Is counting three loud gunshots beyond our abilities?

Figure 12-1   James Altgens took this photo just after Kennedy was hit in the neck. Both motorcycle cops realize
Kennedy has been hit, although both may have been expecting this would happen.

*Connally is not easy to see because he is twisted backwards towards his right to look at Kennedy. The
rear view mirror is in front of Kennedy's eyes, but we can see one of his hands near his throat.*

*In the car behind Kennedy is a man who is smiling; is he happy that Kennedy was hit?
The motorcycle cop along the right edge may be smiling, also.*

Figure 12-2 *This was Oswald's view. It is assumed that he rested his gun on the box. Could* ***you*** *hit a passenger in those cars?*

Figure 12-3 *The large, grassy areas are Dealy Plaza. The two circles on Elm street are approximately where Kennedy was hit by bullets. The first shot was in the neck, and the second in his head.*

Figure 12-4

The arrows show the path of the motorcade. Most of the people were along Main and Houston. The grassy area where Mary Moorman and Jean Hill were standing did not have many people. Neither did the Grassy Knoll area.

Oswald's best opportunity to shoot Kennedy was as Kennedy traveled down Houston street towards Oswald. This was an easier shot and the large crowds of people would have made it more appealing to a nutty guy who wanted to kill somebody famous.

Traffic on Commerce Street stopped when the motorcade came by. James Tague and others got out of their car to watch the motorcade.

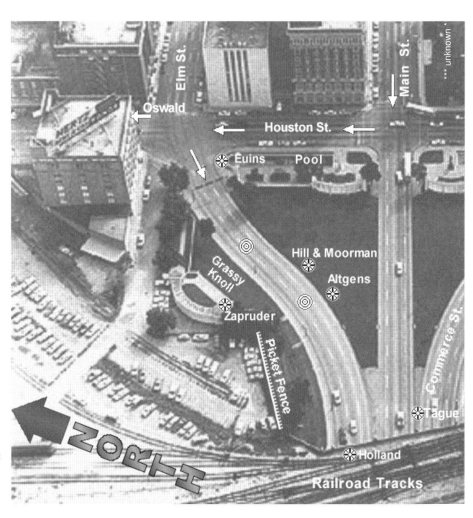

Kennedy's car had three rows of seats (Figure 12-5). Kellerman was a Secret Service agent sitting in the front seat next to the driver. John Connally, the Governor of Texas, was directly behind Kellerman and directly in front of Kennedy. Next to Connally was his wife.

Behind Kennedy's car was a car of Secret Service agents. This car would follow as close to Kennedy's car as practical. At low speeds a couple of agents would walk along the side their car, and at higher speeds they would stand on its running board. At the time Kennedy was shot the agents were standing on the running board (Figure 12-1). Kellerman, one of the agents, believed the first bullet hit Kennedy:

> *Roy Kellerman, in the right front seat of the limousine, heard a report like a firecracker pop. Turning to his right in the direction of the noise, Kellerman heard the President say "My God, I am hit," and saw both of the President's hands move up toward his neck. As he told the driver, "Let's get out of here; we are hit," Kellerman grabbed his microphone and radioed ahead to the lead car, "We are hit. Get us to the hospital immediately."*

Connally also supports the theory that the first shot hit Kennedy:

> *Governor Connally testified that he recognized the first noise as a rifle shot and the thought immediately crossed his mind that it was an assassination attempt. From his position in the right jump seat immediately in front of the President, he instinctively turned to his right because the shot appeared to come from over his right shoulder. Unable to see the President as he turned to the right, the Governor started to look back over his left shoulder, but he never completed the turn because he felt something strike him in the back. In his testimony before the Commission, Governor Connally was certain that he was hit by the second shot, which he stated he did not hear.*

The angle the bullet made as it passed through Connally's chest requires Connally be twisting around to look at Kennedy. The photos verify that Connally was in this twisted position. Therefore, he twisted around after hearing the first shot, and *then* he was hit by a bullet while in that twisted position. This means Connally was hit by the second shot, not the first shot. Furthermore, if we can believe the description of the bullet's path through Connally's body, he was hit by a bullet from Oswald's direction, not from a sniper in front of Kennedy.

Mrs Connally also implies the first shot hit Kennedy:

> *Mrs. Connally, too, heard a frightening noise from her right. Looking over her right shoulder, she saw that the President had both hands at his neck but she observed no blood and heard nothing. She watched as he slumped down with an empty expression on his face.*

Further in the report we find an interesting remark:

> *Mrs. Connally heard a second shot fired and pulled her husband down into her lap. Observing his blood-covered chest as he was pulled into his wife's lap, Governor Connally believed himself mortally wounded. He cried out, "Oh, no, no, no. My God, they are going to kill us all."*

Connally's remark could be a sign that he was involved in this scam. Specifically, when he realized he had been shot he assumed that *"they"* had turned against him and decided to kill everybody. Only two shots had been fired at this time; who would have assumed two shots were coming from a "they" except for a person who knew that a group of people were behind this killing? Unfortunately, we frequently use words in imprecise and incorrect manners, so it risky to consider his choice of words as anything more than interesting.

Figure 12-5 *In the first row of seats was Greer (the driver) and Kellerman (Secret Service). Governor Connally and his wife were in the second seat.*

Roy Kellerman was in the seat in front of Connally. His description of the shots:

...Kellerman said, "Get out of here fast." As he issued his instructions to Greer and to the lead car, Kellerman heard a "flurry of shots" within 5 seconds of the first noise.

On the witness stand, Kellerman clarified the "flurry of shots" as sounding like two shots very close together. The analogy he gave to Representative Ford:

Rep. Ford: *You don't recall precisely a second shot and a third shot such as you did in the case of the first?*

Kellerman: *Let me give you an illustration, sir, before I can give you an answer. You have heard the sound barrier, of a plane breaking the sound barrier, bang, bang? That is it.*

Kellerman started his law enforcement career as a Michigan State Trooper, and he told the Warren Commission that he has "heard all types of guns fired." I would expect him to be able to identify gunshots, in which case his description of a double sound could be a sign that two shots were fired almost simultaneously.

Jean Hill was standing along the road almost directly next to Kennedy when he was hit. She had no experience with guns, but she thought there were 4 to 6 shots, and the final shots sounded "automatic." She also said it seemed as if the shots were coming from different guns, and that the shots were coming from the area across the street from her, not from the building Oswald was in.

Roger Craig, a deputy sheriff on duty in the area but far away from Kennedy at the time he was shot, testified that the final two shots were very close together in time. Craig also mentioned that the shots had echoes. An echo should not cause a problem if each shot was 3 seconds apart, but most witnesses were certain there were several shots close together, which would cause the echoes and shots to overlap in time, possibly confusing people.

Rufus Youngblood, a Secret Service agent in Lyndon Johnson's car (which was near the corner of Elm and Houston at the time of the shots), said there were three shots over a total of about 5 seconds. He also mentioned that there seemed to be a subtle difference in the sounds of the final two shots.

A 16 year old boy, Amos Euins, was sitting directly in front of the building that Oswald was in. He said he looked up at the 6th floor window after the first shot, saw a man with an object that looked like a pipe, and then he heard the second shot, which he says came from the pipe. He said he heard four shots. He could see only the top of the killer's head, but he says the killer seemed to have a white spot on his head (i.e., a bald spot), but he wasn't sure of the man's race.

To summarize this, the witnesses heard two to six shots; they disagreed on the time intervals between the shots; and some said that the shots sounded different from each other. How could the witness disagree to such an extreme over three gunshots? The FBI wants us to believe that the cops and spectators were idiots. However, I suspect that the extreme confusion over the shots was most likely because there were at least two snipers, and at least one was in front of Kennedy.

Was the driver of Kennedy's car involved?

William Greer, the driver of the car, told the commission that he accelerated at the second shot, which was "about simultaneously" when Kellerman gave the order to accelerate. At the other extreme, Jean Hill said the motorcade "came to almost a halt" once the shots began.

You might wonder why Greer would slow down if he was part of the conspiracy because if he slowed down it would be the same as admitting he was helping the snipers. However, the killing occurred at the end of the motorcade. There were not many spectators in that area, and there should not have been any spectators with motion picture cameras at that part of the motorcade. By having the murder at the end of the motorcade rather than where the crowds of people were, neither the murder nor the slowing down of the car should have been documented on film or seen by many people. Unfortunately for the FBI, a man named Abraham Zapruder decided to film the end of the motorcade because the other areas were too crowded. Zapruder's film did not record sound, but it allows us to determine the speed of the car during the shooting. In Appendix 12 of the Warren Report we find the remark:

Motion pictures of the scene show that the car slowed down momentarily after the shot that struck the President in the head and then speeded up rapidly.

Appendix 12 shows that Jean Hill was correct that the car slowed down, but her mind exaggerated the situation. It also implies that Greer deliberately slowed down during the shooting in order to help the snipers make their shots.

As you might expect, the Warren Commission never asked Greer why he slowed down. Actually, the issue was never even brought up. Greer, and other people who appear involved in this killing, was given special treatment, or at least it appears to me that we can determine who was involved simply by the questions they were asked.

Greer told the commission that he assumed the gunshots were a motorcycle backfiring, so he wasn't concerned when he heard the first shot. A great Secret Service agent he was;

Jean Hill could recognize gunshots better than he could, and she didn't seem to know anything about guns!

Jean Hill also claimed to have noticed a man on the other side of the street run away during the shooting. She said the man was the only person moving; everyone else was in shock over the shooting. Her first reaction was to catch the man, so she ran across the street after him. She claims that she ran in front of the moving motorcycles and cars that were following Kennedy's car. But the man quickly disappeared, and she gave up as soon as she had crossed the street.

How could a woman with no experience with guns recognize gunshots better than Greer? And why would she, rather than the cops, chase after possible suspects? Or did she just imagine herself chasing the man, just as she imagined that the car "came to almost a halt"? Was she crazy?

Most people said they either recognized the first noise as a gunshot, or they were frightened by the noise and began to look around at what caused it. The driver of Kennedy's car, most of the police, and most Secret Service agents were the exceptions. Greer wasn't the least bit concerned or curious about what the noises were. Jean Hill should have shouted to him:

"Hey, driver! Somebody is shooting at Kennedy! Don't slow down! Step on the gas pedal while I chase after suspects! And toss me your gun! You certainly wont need it, you dumb jerk!"

Secret Service agent Clinton Hill

Clinton Hill (no relation to Jean Hill) was one of the agents who would routinely jump off the running board of his car in order to provide protection to Kennedy's car. His description of the shots:

Mr. Hill:	*Well, as we came out of the curve, and began to straighten up, I was viewing the area which looked to be a park. There were people scattered throughout the entire park. And I heard a noise from my right rear, which to me seemed to be a firecracker. I immediately looked to my right and, in so doing, my eyes had to cross the Presidential limousine and I saw President Kennedy grab at himself and lurch forward and to the left.*
Mr. Specter:	*Why don't you just proceed, in narrative form, to tell us?*
Rep. Boggs:	*This was the first shot?*
Mr. Hill:	*This is the first sound that I heard; yes, sir. I jumped from the car, realizing that something was wrong, ran to the Presidential limousine. Just about as I*

reached it, there was another sound, which was different than the first sound. I think I described it in my statement as though someone was shooting a revolver into a hard object—it seemed to have some type of an echo. I put my right foot, I believe it was, on the left rear step of the automobile, and I had a hold of the handgrip with my hand, when the car lurched forward. I lost my footing and I had to run about three or four more steps before I could get back up in the car.

Between the time I originally grabbed the handhold and until I was up on the car, Mrs. Kennedy—the second noise that I heard had removed a portion of the President's head, and he had slumped noticeably to his left. Mrs. Kennedy had jumped up from the seat and was, it appeared to me, reaching for something coming off the right rear bumper of the car, the right rear tail, when she noticed that I was trying to climb on the car. She turned toward me and I grabbed her and put her back in the back seat, crawled up on top of the back seat and lay there.

Hill's testimony verifies Zapruder's video that the car did not accelerate until *after* all of the gunshots. Hill would be the person most likely to be correct about when the car accelerated because if the car had accelerated *between* shots, he would have spent more time running to catch up to it, and he may never have caught it. The car was moving more than 11 mph when he started chasing after it, so if the car accelerated quickly, he never would have caught up to it. Obviously, the car never went faster than a man can run, and a man who is wearing a suit and tie.

Furthermore, according to Hill, the acceleration was brief. Perhaps Greer accelerated briefly to give the impression that he was trying to help Kennedy, and then he resumed a steady pace just in case the snipers were still shooting.

Clinton Hill was another of the many witnesses who said the second gunshot sounded different from the first. Later in his interview Hill described the second shot in more detail:

Mr. Specter:	*And did you have a reaction or impression as to the source of point of origin of the second shot that you described?*
Mr. Hill:	*It was right, but I cannot say for sure that it was rear, because when I mounted the car it was—it had a different sound, first of all, than the first sound that I heard. The second one had almost a double sound—as though you were standing against something metal and firing into it,*

*and you hear both the sound of a gun
going off and the sound of the cartridge
hitting the metal place, which could have
been caused probably by the hard surface
of the head. But I am not sure that that is
what caused it.*

His description of a "double sound" resembles the
description given by Kellerman.

What was happening to Jackie Kennedy's mind?

One of the interesting aspects of the murder from a
human behavior point of view is that after the bullet hit John
Kennedy in the head, Jackie gets out of her seat and starts
climbing onto the trunk of the car. In Zapruder's film it
appears as if she is trying to crawl off the car. If she had
continued crawling she would have fallen on the road, but
by the time she gets near the end of the car Clinton Hill had
climbed onto the car and pushed her back to her seat.

Why was she crawling toward the back of the car? She
claimed she cannot remember doing it. Was her behavior
due to panic? Was her first reaction to run from the area?
Her odd behavior and her inability to remember it makes me
wonder how reliable the human brain is under stress.

Clinton Hill says that Jackie appeared to be reaching for
something, and he says he thought he saw something fall off
the back of the car, also. Zapruder's film shows that after
Kennedy's head is hit by a bullet, something with a pinkish
color falls off the rear of the car. The next day somebody
found a piece of Kennedy's skull in the street. This could
mean that when the bullet hit Kennedy's head, a piece of his
skull flew off the back of the car. Jackie's behavior could then
be explained as an attempt to fetch the object she saw come
off her husband's head.

Actually, Jackie's behavior could help explain this
murder. The reason is that Oswald was shooting Kennedy
from the rear, so his bullet should have entered the rear of
Kennedy's head and exited at the front. I haven't shot
anybody in the head yet so I don't know what a high
powered, copper coated bullet does when it hits the rear of a
human head, but judging by what BB's do to glass windows,
I suspect the exit hole would be larger than the entrance
hole, and the skull fragments and brains would spray towards
the front rather than the rear. In other words, I would expect
the *front* of Kennedy's skull to fly towards the *front of the car*,
rather than the back of his skull fly towards the rear of the
car.

Zapruder's video shows a puff of blood at Kennedy's
face, which could mean a shot came from the rear, but the
way Kennedy's head jerks backwards from the shot it
appears that the bullet entered at that puff of blood.

What was going on at the railroad bridge?

James Altgens, a news photograher, arrived early to find
a good location for photos. He decided to go to the top of a
railroad bridge that Kennedy would pass under at the end of
the motorcade. By standing on top of this bridge he would
be able to see the entire area and get a photo of Kennedy
and all other cars as they drove under the bridge. However,
there were cops on top of the bridge, and they told him that
only railroad employees were allowed in that area.

It would make sense for the police to keep everybody
away from this bridge because Kennedy would pass
underneath, and somebody could drop rocks on Kennedy,
or shoot at him. The police had good reason to keep people
away. So Altgens decided to go to the corner of Houston and
Main streets. About 12:15 he saw the red lights of the lead
car of the motorcade far in the distance on Main Street.
While he waited for the cars to get closer he glanced behind
him and he noticed about a dozen people on top of the
bridge. A cop was nearby, so he told the Warren
Commission that he complained to the cop:

*I wonder what the heck all those people are
doing up there when they wouldn't let me up
there to make pictures?*

The cop replied that they were probably railroad
employees. According to S. M. Holland, a supervisor of the
railroad, there were 14 to 18 people on the bridge at the
time Kennedy drove by. Some were railroad employees,
some were cops, and some he did not recognize. Did the
railroad coincidently decided to send a crew on that
particular day to work on that particular section of the track
at that particular time of the day? And if so, why didn't the
cops chase them away and tell them to come back in 30
minutes when the motorcade was finished? Why send only
photographers away? It reminds me of the World Trade
Center after the collapse in which anybody with an acetylene
torch was welcomed into the area but anybody with a
camera was threatened with arrest.

After Altgens took photos of the motorcade along Main
and Houston streets, he ran across the grass to take pictures
as the cars passed down Elm street (Figure 12-1). He was
only a short distance from Kennedy when the bullet blew
some of Kennedy's brains out. His description of that shot
makes it appear as if the bullet blew a hole in the *left* side of
Kennedy's head, not his *right* side:

*"... There was flesh particles that flew out of
the side of his head in my direction from where
I was standing, so much so that it indicated to
me that the shot came out of the left side of his
head. Also, the fact that his head was covered
with blood, the hairline included, on the left
side all the way down, with no blood on his
forehead or face—"*

That would put the sniper near the railroad bridge or near the picket fence (Figure 12-4). Also, note his remark about the lack of blood on his face. This implies the bullet did not exit from the *front* of his head. Note that there is no hole or damage to the front of Kennedy's face in Figure 11-1. The Warren Report wants us to believe that Kennedy's head was tilted down, which caused the bullet to enter near the base of his head and exit at top of his head. However, that does not explain why the blood and hole was on the left, rear of his head, and why no blood sprayed forward in the car.

The Peek-A-Boo Bullet

Kennedy and Connally were taken to the hospital, and luck was with the FBI:

> *A nearly whole bullet was found on Governor Connally's stretcher at Parkland Hospital after the assassination. After his arrival at the hospital the Governor was brought into trauma room No. 2 on a stretcher, removed from the room on that stretcher a short time later, and taken on an elevator to the second-floor operating room. On the second floor he was transferred from the stretcher to an operating table which was then moved into the operating room, and a hospital attendant wheeled the empty stretcher into an elevator. Shortly afterward, Darrell C. Tomlinson, the hospital's senior engineer, removed this stretcher from the elevator and placed it in the corridor on the ground floor, alongside another stretcher wholly unconnected with the care of Governor Connally. A few minutes later, he bumped one of the stretchers against the wall and a bullet rolled out.*

No other bullet was recovered. A few "bullet fragments" were found, but of the three shots Oswald supposedly fired, only this nearly perfect bullet was found (Figure 12-6). The tip of the bullet was mashed slightly, but the rest of it was in such excellent shape that it was easily traceable to Oswald's

gun. What a lucky coincidence it was found, and that it was in such good condition.

The FBI claims that this bullet hit Kennedy in the back, traveled through his neck, and popped out of his neck. Then it hit Connally in the back, passed through Connally's chest and broke a rib. The bullet then popped out of his chest, penetrated his wrist, hit a bone in his right wrist, popped out of his wrist, and then hit his leg. By the time it hit Connally's leg it was traveling too slowly to penetrate into his leg, so it just left a bruise. Then it got stuck in his clothing. And it did all this without much damage to itself.

When Connally arrived at the hospital he was put on a stretcher and taken into one of the rooms. The FBI claims the bullet fell out of his clothing and rolled into the part of the stretcher where bullets hide from view. His stretcher was then put into an elevator and sent back to the storage area. Down in the storage area somebody pushed the stretcher up against a wall and the bullet appeared.

Oswald's bullets had a copper jacket (which causes bullets to hold their shape better than ordinary bullets). This could explain why the Peek-A-Boo Bullet was so well preserved after traveling through two people and hitting bones. However, if the Peek-A-Boo Bullet could survive, why did the other two bullets disappear? Why were only tiny "bullet fragments" found of the other bullets?

Considering that Oswald was shooting downward from a height of about 20 meters, and considering that Kennedy was on the right side of the car, I would expect all of the bullets to continue towards the center of the car, where they would be located, rather than in the grass where they might be lost. Apparently Oswald was using a mixture of "Peek-A-Boo" bullets and "Disappearing Bullets."

The car was given a major renovation a few months after the murder. Was the FBI hiding the bullet holes?

"Does that refresh your memory, you jerk?"

A hospital employee, Darrell Tomlinson, found the Peek-A-Boo Bullet. He said he moved Connally's stretcher off the elevator and pushed it against the wall. There was already another stretcher in the room, so now there were two.

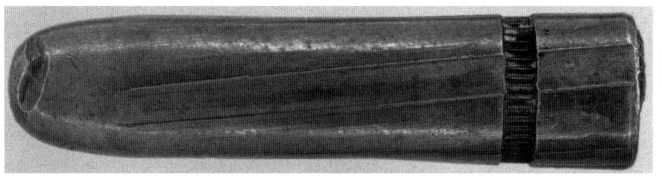

CORBIS

Figure 12-6   The Peek-A-Boo bullet

Tomlinson said somebody later came into the room to use the bathroom, and pushed the *other* stretcher away from the wall on his way to the bathroom. Some time later Tomlinson pushed that stretcher back against the wall and noticed a bullet roll off. But that was *not* Connally's stretcher! Or did Tomlinson forget which stretcher was Connally's? All stretchers look the same, so how could he be sure which was Connally's stretcher?

Mr. Specter reminds him that the Secret Service talked with him about which stretcher the bullet was found on:

> Mr. Specter: Now, after I tell you that, does that have any effect on refreshing your recollection of what you told the Secret Service man?
>
> Tomlinson: No it really doesn't – it really doesn't.

Tomlinson found the bullet on the wrong stretcher, so an FBI and Secret Service agent had a special talk with him before his interview with the Warren Commission to convince him that he actually found the bullet on Connally's stretcher. Tomlinson apparently agreed that it was Connally's stretcher at this special meeting, but in court Tomlinson reverted to his original statement. Mr. Specter tried several times to convince Tomlinson to give the "correct" testimony, but Tomlinson refused. Two of Tomlinson's remarks:

> *"I would be going against the oath which I took a while ago"*
>
> *"I'm not going to tell you something I can't lay down and sleep at night with."*

Obviously, Tomlinson believed the trial was an honest attempt to understand the events, and therefore he wanted to be as accurate as possible. He did not want to give incorrect information to such an important trial.

Specter's treatment of all witnesses is similar; i.e., he attempts to push the witnesses into saying what they are supposed to say rather ask them what they saw.

Since Tomlinson would not cooperate, the FBI had no choice but to ignore Tomlinson and write in the final report that the Peek-A-Boo Bullet was found on Connally's stretcher, even though the witness who found the bullet said otherwise. Witnesses are often wrong, so the FBI is doing us a favor by correcting their mistakes.

If Tomlinson had been an unskilled, illiterate laborer who could barely support himself or satisfy his wife, like Oswald, I would be willing to accept the possibility that he was making a mistake, but he was the hospital's "senior engineer." He was in charge of the power, heating, and air-conditioning equipment for the hospital.

Next time you are at a hospital notice that some hallways are full of carts and stretchers pushed up against the walls. Who would push one *away* from the wall into the cramped area where people walk? The guy who pushed the stretcher away from the wall as he went to the bathroom did

something that no normal person would do. Rather than walk around the stretcher, he pretended that it was in his way. I suppose he had the bullet in his hand and he placed it on the stretcher as he pushed it away from the wall.

Lieutenant Baker

Lieutenant Baker was a Dallas police officer who was riding a motorcycle in the motorcade. As the Warren report tells us, when the first shot was fired, Baker…

> *…was certain the gunshot came from a high-powered rifle. He looked up and saw pigeons scattering in the air from their perches on the Texas School Book Depository Building. He raced his motorcycle to the building, dismounted, scanned the area to the west and pushed his way through the spectators toward the entrance. There he encountered Roy Truly, the building superintendent, who offered Baker his help. They entered the building, and ran toward the two elevators in the rear. Finding that both elevators were on an upper floor, they dashed up the stairs. Not more than 2 minutes had elapsed since the shooting.*

I never went to medical school, so a few people have suggested my ignorance is the reason I considered the treatment given to Kennedy at the hospital was absurd (some people insist the doctors really were trying to help). I never went to a police academy either, so I suppose some people will complain that my ignorance is the reason I consider Baker's response to the killer to be absurd. I would have reacted very differently if I had been in Baker's situation. First, somewhere inside the building was at least one killer with a very powerful rifle. He may have other guns, and he may not be alone. I would have naively told everybody outside to get away from the building, and I would have told the other cops to surround the building. The building was standing by itself; it was not connected to other buildings. This made it easy for the cops to trap the killer(s) inside. Also the building was virtually empty because almost every employee was outside, so there were not many people inside to consider as suspects.

Second, I would have been scared to run into that building with the unarmed Roy Truly and a little revolver. I would have stayed outside until other cops arrived with rifles, and I would have told Roy Truly:

> *"Yes, you can help. You can remain outside with your employees, and keep them calm and away from the building."*

If Baker's response to the killer was correct, then I do not know proper police procedures when dealing with snipers in a building. According to Baker, the proper procedure is to run into the building with a revolver while following an unarmed civilian.

Truly testified that he was certain the shots did *not* come from this building, so that explains why he was willing to run into the building ahead of the cop, but how do we explain Baker's desire to follow an unarmed civilian?

The unarmed Roy Truly started running up the stairs, with Baker following behind with his little revolver in his hand, ready to protect the two of them. If they encountered the killer(s), Baker could hide behind Truly and take a few shots at the killers. Is this what they teach at the Dallas Police Academy?

It is also important to note that the two of them were *running* up the stairs, rather than *quietly sneaking* up the stairs. Apparently the proper police procedure when looking for sniper(s) in a building is to let them hear you running up the stairs so that you don't surprise them; a good cop gives snipers time to re-load their weapons and get into position.

Truly quickly reached the second floor landing and started running up the next flight of stairs towards the third floor. He climbed a few steps and then realized that Baker was no longer following him. Truly assumed the cop stopped on the second floor without bothering to say anything. What would *you* do if you were in Truly's position? Keeping in mind that Baker believes a killer is inside the building with a powerful rifle, would you:

A) Continue running up the stairs by yourself to look for the killer.

B) Look for Lt. Baker.

C) Go back outside.

Truly decided to go back to the second floor and look for the cop. His explanation of what happened next:

> Mr. Truly: I heard some voices, or a voice, coming from the area of the lunchroom, or the inside vestibule…

Truly goes inside the vestibule to look, and there he sees Baker in the lunch-room doorway, with his gun pointing at Oswald. Perhaps Baker is a better cop than I thought; after all, he just found the killer!

Baker told the commission that he got a glimpse of somebody through the windows in the door, and he decided to chase after him. Was Baker planning to arrest Oswald for the killing, or at least hold Oswald for questioning? Here is Truly's testimony about what happened when he entered the room and saw Baker and Oswald:

> Mr. Truly: When I reached there, the officer had his gun pointing at Oswald. The officer turned this way and said, "This man work here?" And I said, "Yes."
>
> Mr. Belin: And then what happened?

> Mr. Truly: Then we left Lee Harvey Oswald immediately and continued to run up the stairways until we reached the fifth floor.
>
> Mr. Belin: All right. Let me ask you this now. How far was the officer's gun from Lee Harvey Oswald when he asked the question?
>
> Mr. Truly: It would be hard for me to say, but it seemed to me like it was almost touching him.
>
> Mr. Belin: What portion of his body?
>
> Mr. Truly: Towards the middle portion of his body.

> *Later in his testimony:*

> Mr. Belin: Could you see whether or not Lee Harvey Oswald had anything in either hand?
>
> Mr. Truly: I noticed nothing in either hand.
>
> Mr. Belin: Did you see both of his hands?
>
> Mr. Truly: I am sure I did. I could be wrong, but I am almost sure. I did.
>
> Mr. Belin: About how long did Officer Baker stand there with Lee Harvey Oswald after you saw them?
>
> Mr. Truly: He left him immediately after I told him—after he asked me, does this man work here. I said, yes. The officer left him immediately.
>
> Mr. Belin: Did you hear Lee Harvey Oswald say anything?
>
> Mr. Truly: Not a thing.
>
> Mr. Belin: Did you see any expression on his face? Or weren't you paying attention?
>
> Mr. Truly: He didn't seem to be excited or overly afraid or anything. He might have been a bit startled, like I might have been if somebody confronted me. But I cannot recall any change in expression of any kind on his face.

Baker and Oswald were so close together that the gun was almost touching Oswald's stomach. How did the two of them get so close together? According to the Warren Report:

> With his revolver drawn, Baker opened the vestibule door and ran into the vestibule. He saw a man walking away from him in the lunchroom. Baker stopped at the door of the lunchroom and commanded, "Come here." The man turned and walked back toward Baker. He had been proceeding toward the rear of the lunchroom.

Baker demanded that Oswald turn around and come over to him. So Oswald started walking towards Baker. Obviously Oswald continued walking towards Baker until he came within _kissing distance_. Is it standard police procedure to have suspected murderers get that close to you? What if Oswald had pushed the gun away with one of his hands and punched Baker in the face with the other hand? Furthermore, Truly heard voices; what were Baker and Oswald talking about? Or were they _whispering_?

Neither Baker nor Truly said that Oswald seemed nervous, frightened, or out of breath, even though he supposedly just killed Kennedy and ran down four flights of stairs. How would _you_ feel if a cop put his gun in your stomach?

Oswald's wife testified that he left his wedding ring and wallet at home that morning, as if he knew he may never come home again Therefore, Oswald may have been expecting to be arrested, which would explain his relaxed behavior.

After Truly interrupted Baker and Oswald, Baker's response was to ask whether Oswald was an employee. Baker then _immediately_ let Oswald go; there were _no further questions_. Apparently the American police have been told that employees never commit crimes at their place of employment.

After discovering that Oswald was an employee, and therefore could not possibly be involved in the killing, Baker and Truly continued to run up the stairs. They soon arrived on 5th floor. This is where an elevator car was sitting (this was the primitive type of elevator that required a human operator). There were three employees on the 5th floor who were watching the motorcade from the windows. One of them (Bonnie Williams) saw Baker:

> Mr. Williams: Well, at the time I was up there I saw a motorcycle policeman. He came up. And the only thing I saw of him was his white helmet.

He saw only the top of Baker's helmet, and he saw Baker go into the elevator. This means Baker did not bother to look around the 5th floor. Obviously Baker was not interested in _searching_ the building for the killer; rather, he was _going somewhere_. Where was he going? Why wasn't he searching for the sniper?

Baker and Truly went into the elevator on the 5th floor and started up. Should they stop at the 6th floor and look around? Of course not! The 6th floor was where Oswald's gun and bullet shells were laying. Baker and Truly skipped the 6th floor and continued up to the 7th floor, which was the top floor of the building. After getting out of the elevator on the 7th floor they ran up the stairs to the roof rather than search the 7th floor. Why did Baker want to go to the roof? Did he really believe the sniper was hiding on the roof? As I read this section of the Warren Report, my imagination gave me a vision of Baker singing _"Up On The Roof"_ (emphasize the "po" in "police" to make it fit the tune):

> When po-lice work starts getting me down,
> And murders are just too much for me to take...
> I follow Roy Truly to the top of the stairs,
> And all my cares just drift right into space...

In reality, Baker didn't sing any songs, but he did look around the roof a while, and he peered over the edge of building to... to what? To see if the killer had jumped off the building? I thought the doctors were strange, but Lt. Baker makes the doctors seem rational! Am I the only person who wonders if the script the police were following for this Kennedy killing had come from a _Keystone Cops_ movie?

After a few minutes on the roof, Baker relaxed. His concern about finding the killer was over. Baker and Truly then walked down to the 7th floor. Truly made an interesting remark about the walk down the stairs from the roof:

> Mr. Truly: I believe the officer told me as we walked down into the seventh floor, "Be careful, this man will blow your head off."

What sort of advice is "be careful"? What exactly should Truly do to protect his head? More interesting, Baker was implying the killer was _still in the building_! Would Baker search for the dangerous killer on their way down to the ground floor?

When they got back down to the 7th floor Baker glanced in a small room very briefly, and then they walked into the elevator. Baker had no interest in searching the entire 7th floor.

Truly operated the elevator on the ride down. Truly stopped the elevator at the 6th floor, apparently without being asked by Baker, on the assumption that Baker might want to look around. However, Baker did not bother to get out of the elevator, so Truly continued down. Baker believed there was a dangerous killer somewhere inside, and Truly had to _"be careful,"_ but Baker did not want to waste his precious time searching the entire building for the killer. So they went down to the ground floor and then walked out of the building. The other cops soon entered the building to search for guns and bullet shells. The police _never conducted a search for the killer!_

Was Baker told to meet Oswald in the lunchroom?

The only sensible explanation for Baker's idiotic behavior is that he was told to meet Oswald and the sniper in the lunch room and give them an update on the situation:

> OK, nobody is outside yet. Joe, you can run out the back door. And Oswald... **idiot**! Get over here so I don't have to yell!

> Now go out the front door, and let people see you walk out. Jack will pick you up in 15 minutes on Elm Street in front of this building...

(the lunch room door opens)

Uhhh,... Hi Roy Truly! Uhhhh,.... I was wondering... is this guy an employee? He is? Oh! Gosh, I'm sorry for putting my gun in your stomach! I thought you were a traveling salesman. Well, Roy, let's continue running up the stairs to look for the killer. And be careful, Roy! We don't want to get our heads blown off!

What were the other cops doing?

While Baker and Truly risked their lives running up to the roof in pursuit of the killer, most of the other cops were standing around doing virtually nothing, at least according to James Tague:

> *Mr. Tague:* "The only thing that I saw that I thought was wrong was that there was about 5 or 6 or 7 minutes in there before anybody done anything about anything."

When asked to clarify that remark, Tague said only one motorcycle cop (i.e., Baker) stopped and went over to the building. According to Tague, the other cops just waited outside doing nothing.

> *Mr. Liebeler:* You didn't see any other policemen around in the area?
>
> *Mr. Tague:* Not for 4 or 5 minutes. If Oswald was in that building, he had all the time in the world to calmly walk out of there.
>
> *Mr. Liebeler:* Apparently that is just what he did do.

My guess is that the cops were waiting to see Baker's head at the edge of the roof. That was the signal to enter the building and start the search for the murder weapon. What a clever script! If the FBI plots my death I hope I get an equally impressive script! However, I would prefer a musical rather than a drama.

Was the building ever surrounded by police?

It was several minutes after the shooting before the cops bothered to guard the entrances of the building to stop people from going in or out. Furthermore, they sealed only the *front* entrance. A secret service agent, Forrest Sorrels, who was in the car ahead of Kennedy, rode to the hospital with the motorcade, and then decided to get a ride back to the murder site to talk to witnesses. He arrived at the parking lot at the rear of the building 20 to 25 minutes after the killing. He told the Warren Commission that he simply walked in the rear door. He said the building was open at the rear, and people were wandering around back there.

Actually, even after the cops sealed off the front entrance people could easily get in or out. Victoria Adams worked in the building, and she was outside when the police sealed off the front entrance. As she described the situation:

> *Mr. Belin:* Now at this time when you went back into the building, were there any policemen standing in front of the building keeping people out?
>
> *Miss Adams:* There was an officer on the stairs itself, and he was prohibiting people from entering the building, that is correct. But I told him I worked there.
>
> *Mr. Belin:* Did he let you come back in?
>
> *Miss Adams:* Yes, sir.

The front entrance of the building was sealed, except to everybody who said they were employees. The police were turning away only... who? The homeless? The guy who refills the vending machines? The police action is so absurd that somebody could use it as script for slapstick comedy without any editing!

The teenage boy, Amos Euins, who said the killer had a white spot on his head, testified that he overheard a man tell a policeman that a construction man with a bald spot just ran out the back of the building. The sixth floor of that building was undergoing construction at the time, so it would have been a good disguise for a sniper.

None of the cops cared who went into or out of the building. Certainly the reason was because if the cops had surrounded the building neither Oswald nor the sniper could get out. Baker had to get in there quickly, check if everything was OK, tell Oswald what to do next, and chase away any employees who might interfere with the exiting of the sniper. Baker's lack of concern for his life and Truly's life was because he knew there weren't any killers inside the building. Truly didn't have to "be careful;" nobody was going to blow his head off.

I doubt if Oswald was even allowed to shoot at Kennedy. The FBI was certainly concerned that Oswald was such a crummy shot that he might hit the wrong person, so if the FBI had any concern for human life... well, I suppose Oswald was allowed a few shots, which would explain the shots that missed Kennedy.

Got Bullets, FBI?

There was one missing detail the FBI needed to complete this murder; a bullet from Oswald's gun. Oswald didn't have his gun until that morning; somehow the FBI had to get a bullet from it and then take it to the hospital. So on the sixth floor Oswald waited with his loaded rifle. The FBI sniper had his own, higher quality rifle. Oswald spent some of his time putting his finger and hand prints on various objects.

The sniper told Oswald to fire his gun into a bucket of sand at the same time he hears the sniper make his second shot. This shot was inside the room, so this was the shot that rattled the room so severely that it knocked debris onto Bonnie Williams's head on the floor below (this is mentioned in the next section). This is why the Peek-A-Boo bullet was in perfect condition, except for its tip. Also, this shot would have sounded different to the witnesses because it was inside the building.

The sniper gave the Peek-A-Boo bullet to somebody who rushed it to the hospital. The lack of blood on the bullet would never be noticed because the bullet would be given to the FBI for a careful analysis. The FBI operates a world famous laboratory that excels in analyzing evidence and making it fit whatever particular scam they are engaged in at the time.

It is interesting to review the way Clinton Hill describes one of the gunshots:

> *... as though you were standing against something metal and firing into it, and you hear both the sound of a gun going off and the sound of the cartridge hitting the metal place...*

The metallic sound that Clinton Hill heard might be because the Peek-A-Boo bullet was fired into a metal bucket of sand. Are the dents at the tip of the bullet from sand particles? (Figure 12-6) Or is that what a bullet looks like after passing through Kennedy's neck and Connally's body?

The employees on the floor under Oswald

Bonnie Williams was one of three employees watching the motorcade together from a window on the 5th floor, directly under Oswald's window. Two of his remarks:

> *And then the thing that happened then was a loud shot—first I thought they were saluting the President, somebody even maybe a motorcycle backfire. The first shot—there was two shots rather close together. The second and the third shot was closer together than the first shot and the second shot, as I remember.*

> *Well, the first shot-I really did not pay any attention to it, because I did not know what was happening. The second shot, it sounded like it was right in the building, the second and third shot. And it sounded-it even shook the building, the side we were on cement fell on my head.*

After all the shots had been fired, the three men ran down to the window at other end of the 5th floor. When asked why he ran that direction when he assumed the shots were directly above his head:

> *We saw the policemen and people running, scared, running—there are some tracks on the west side of the building, railroad tracks. They were running towards that way. And we thought maybe—well, to ourself, we know the shots practically came from over our head. But since everybody was running, you know, to the west side of the building, towards the railroad tracks, we assumed maybe somebody was down there. And so we all ran that way, the way that the people was running, and we was looking out the window.*

In case you missed the significance of his remarks, most of the crowd assumed the shots were coming from the railroad tracks or picket fence area, not the building with Oswald. Williams followed the crowd to the other end of the building to see what was happening in that direction.

The FBI wants us to believe that the people who thought the shots came from the picket fence were morons, but considering how many morons that would be, it is more likely that they were correct about hearing shots near the railroad tracks.

My guess as to what happened is that the first shot came from a sniper in front of Kennedy, and it hit Kennedy in the neck. The sound of his gun caused the people to look towards the railroad tracks. Bonnie Williams and the other two men on the fifth floor were far away from this sniper, so they did not realize it was a gun shot, but they saw the people looking towards the railroad tracks. After a couple seconds, the sniper with Oswald made a shot, which was the second shot, and this bullet hit Connally, probably by mistake. This shot was from the sixth floor, and Bonnie Williams realized it came from directly above his head. But by the time the second shot was fired, the crowd had already noticed that the first shot came from the railroad area, so the crowd assumed this second shot also came from that same area. Apparently, nobody suspected more than one sniper. Then Oswald shoots into the bucket of sand, creating such a vibration of the sixth floor that some cement fell down on Williams's head. Finally, a sniper (maybe two of them) in front of Kennedy fire a shot, at least one of which hits Kennedy in the head.

The FBI says a bullet hit the curb on Main Street, and a piece of concrete hit James Tague in the face, causing a small amount of bleeding. Figure 12-4 shows Tague almost in a line with Kennedy and Oswald. I suppose the sniper with Oswald fired a second shot just to make it appear as if the shots were coming from the building, and to cover Oswald's shot into the bucket of sand. He knew he could not be successful with this shot, so he aimed towards the grass, but he accidently hit the curb, which caused a piece of concrete to hit James Tague in the face. Another bullet hit the curb near Jean Hill and Mary Moorman; this could have come from either the snipers at the picket fence or the sniper with Oswald, but I suppose it came from a sniper near the fence.

My guess is there were at least five shots; two from the sniper pretending to be Oswald, one into a bucket of sand, and at least two from snipers in front of Kennedy.

Oswald rides a bus to nowhere

As Baker was following Roy Truly up to the roof, Oswald was seen casually walking out of the building with a bottle of soda by at least one employee. Truly said that Oswald's hands were empty when Baker had him at gunpoint. Apparently, after the gun-point, employment verification, Oswald bought a soda from the machine, or picked up a soda he previously purchased, and casually strolled out of the building.

There was no reason for Oswald to go anywhere. He certainly knew he would be charged with the murder. The FBI claims he left his fingerprints on the rifle and other objects on the 6th floor, so it was just a matter of time before he would be caught. His wife told the Commission that he left his money and wedding ring at home that morning, implying that he knew that he may never go home again. He may as well wander around the area and enjoy the commotion, and perhaps he did exactly that. According to the Warren Report, Oswald first walked down the street and then got on a bus:

> ...at about 12:40 p.m., Oswald boarded a bus at a point on Elm Street seven short blocks east of the Depository Building. The bus was traveling west toward the very building from which Oswald had come. Its route lay through the Oak Cliff section in southwest Dallas, where it would pass seven blocks east of the rooming house in which Oswald was living, at 1026 North Beckley Avenue. On the bus was Mrs. Mary Bledsoe, one of Oswald's former landladies, who immediately recognized him. Oswald stayed on the bus approximately 3 or 4 minutes, during which time it proceeded only two blocks because of the traffic jam created by the motorcade and the assassination. Oswald then left the bus.

In case you didn't understand that paragraph, Oswald walked 7 blocks *away* from the murder site and got on a bus that was barely moving because of the traffic jam. He spent 3 or 4 minutes riding two short blocks *towards* the murder site, and then got off the bus. A few more of those rides and he would be back where he started, except that he could walk faster than the bus was moving.

The bus Oswald decided to ride was not the bus he normally rode to get home, so why would he get on that particular bus? Did he get on the wrong bus by mistake? Or

was he enjoying the chaos? His bus ride was as idiotic (i.e., suspicious) as giving oxygen to Kennedy's dead body.

Roger Craig

Roger Craig, one of the Deputy Sheriffs of Dallas County, was standing in Dealy Plaza when the shots were fired. He remained outside afterwards to talk to witnesses. Roger estimates that about 15 minutes after the shooting he was standing near the area where Kennedy was killed, and he heard a person whistle. At this time Oswald may have been walking around the same area.

> Mr. Belin: You heard someone whistle?
>
> Mr. Craig: Yes. So I turned and —uh— saw a man start to run down the hill on the north side of Elm Street, running down toward Elm Street.
>
>   ...
>
> Mr. Craig: I saw a light-colored station wagon, driving real slow, coming west on Elm Street from Houston. Uh— actually, it was nearly in line with him. And the driver was leaning to his right looking up the hill at the man running down.
>
>   And the station wagon stopped almost directly across from me. And—uh—the man continued down the hill and got in the station wagon. And I attempted to cross the street. I wanted to talk to both of them. But the —uh— traffic was so heavy I couldn't get across the street. And —uh— they were gone before I could—

He did not finish his last sentence, perhaps because he was interrupted. Craig later points out that this event stuck in his mind for a long time. He says he clearly saw the man who was running, but did not get a good look at the driver. He mentioned the station wagon had a built-in luggage rack on the top. He said that when he heard a suspect had been arrested he called Captain Fritz's office (of the Dallas police) and gave a description of the man he saw running. He asked if the suspect resembles this man. The person who answered the phone told him to come over and look for himself. (At this time the reporters had not yet jammed into the police station to see Oswald, so it was quiet at the police station.) Craig said that when he saw the suspect he told Captain Fritz that it was the man he saw running to the station wagon. The Warren Report describes the situation like this:

> Captain Fritz then asked him about the —uh— he said, "What about this station wagon?"
>
> And the suspect interrupted him and said, "That station wagon belongs to Mrs. Paine" —I believe is what he said. "Don't try to tie her into this. She had nothing to do with it."

And —uh— Captain Fritz then told him, as close as I can remember, that, "All we're trying to do is find out what happened, and this man saw you leave from the scene."

And the suspect again interrupted Captain Fritz and said, "I told you people I did." And —uh— yeah— then, he said —then he continued and he said, "Everybody will know who I am now."

And he was leaning over the desk. At this time, he had risen partially out of the chair and leaning over the desk, looking directly at Captain Fritz.

Most of the witnesses were asked a lot of questions, including lots of irrelevant questions, such as where they grew up, where they went to school, and how many children they had. Roger Craig was getting the same sort of treatment until he mentioned the remark about Ruth Paine.

I never went to Interrogation School, so I don't know the proper procedure when a deputy sheriff mentions something a murder suspect blurts out. I would have done something stupid, such as ask Craig for more details. For example, has he seen the Paine's station wagon? If so, did he believe it was the same as the one he saw Oswald get into? Did he know either of the Paines, or know anything about them?

It is a good thing I was not on the Warren Commission because apparently the proper procedure is to try to confuse the deputy sheriff, change the subject, divert his attention, and suggest that he is in error:

> *Mr. Belin:*   *Have you discussed with Sheriff Decker the fact that when Oswald was picked up they found a bus transfer in his pocket?*
>
> *Mr. Craig:*   *No; I knew —uh nothing about a bus transfer.*

The bus transfer may explain why Oswald rode the bus for what appears to be no sensible reason. Perhaps he was told to ride the bus in order to pick up a bus transfer because the FBI was planning to use the bus transfer as evidence that he rode the bus out of the area rather than got a ride with a member of the conspiracy.

Craig's testimony ended with a final attempt to make him change his mind:

> *Mr. Belin:*   *Do you feel that you might have been influenced by the fact that you knew he was the suspect —subconsciously, or do you —*
>
> *Mr. Craig:*   *Well, it's —it's possible, but I still feel strongly that it was the same person.*
>
> *Mr. Belin:*   *Okay. That's it. Thank you.*

Call the next witness! Roger Craig refuses to cooperate! Get out of here, Craig! Now!

Lee Oswald's brother was asked a lot of detailed questions. In fact, there is a point in the interview when Mr. Jenner asks whether Lee Oswald was ever left handed. Jenner asked more questions about this issue than Belin asked Craig about Ruth Paine. Why would Jenner spend a lot of time discussing whether Oswald was ever left handed while Belin terminates a discussion of Paine? Did Jenner suspect the real sniper was left handed? Or was he hoping that Oswald had been left handed during his youth so that this farce did not look quite so absurd? (It would be awkward for a right-handed person to make the shots that Oswald supposedly made.)

The Warren Commission interviewed Ruth Paine to an incredible extent in order to get all sorts of details about Oswald. Her testimony is about 26 times the volume of Roger Craig's (in terms of bytes in a computer file). The Warren Commission spent more time talking with her than any other person. The Commission obviously considered her to be the most important person in this trial. She was more than "a nice lady" to the Commission; she was the *key witness*.

If Roger Craig is correct about the events that occurred, Oswald was getting a ride in Paine's station wagon (a man was driving; she was home with Marina Oswald at the time). However, the Warren Commission came to the conclusion that Craig's testimony belongs in the trash. As the Warren Report explained it:

> *The Commission could not accept important elements of Craig's testimony.*

As you see, the Commission would accept only the *unimportant* elements of his testimony. What a coincidence that the Ruth Paine connection was never discussed by the Warren commission.

"Roger Craig? Duh… who is Roger Craig?"

Captain Fritz insisted to the Warren Commission that he did not know anybody named Roger Craig, even after the commission reminded Fritz that Craig is a deputy sheriff and he had met Craig in person. When the commission told Fritz some of Craig's remarks, Fritz insisted that none of the conversations or events that Craig described could possibly be true.

Craig was the most dangerous person to the US government in this killing, so the people involved with the scam tried to counteract his testimony.

It is OK for Oswald to ride in a car

The FBI wants us to believe that Oswald rode a bus, but what difference would it make if somebody gave him a ride in a car? Consider bank robbers to understand this issue. Often one or two will go into the bank to do the robbery while somebody else waits outside in a car. The FBI does _not_ try to prove that the bank robbers walked home or rode a bus. Rather, they try to figure out who the driver was.

It is possible for Oswald to have arranged for somebody to pick him up in a car. Oswald did not have a driver's license or a car, so he had to ride a bus, take a taxi, or ask somebody to drive him. If the Warren Commission was serious about this crime, they would have asked who Ruth Paine was. They would have investigated the possibility that she was a friend who was helping him, or that somebody borrowed her car. However, if the Paines were on the payroll of the FBI or CIA, the Warren Commission would not want anybody to look into their background because that might expose the conspiracy.

Rather than treat the Paines as prime _suspects_, the Paines were the government's most important _witnesses_ against Oswald. The government did not want anybody looking closely at their most important witnesses, so Craig's testimony had to be terminated, and everybody involved in the killing had to discredit Craig.

Mr Holland saw a station wagon, also

Mr. Holland was a supervisor for the railroad. Unlike the other witnesses, he brought his attorney, Mr. Morrison, to the interview. Why would a _witness_ to the killing bring a lawyer? The Warren Commission only wanted to ask him what he saw that day, not charge him with a crime. Something is wrong here.

Holland was on duty the day of the motorcade, and some policemen asked him to identify the railroad employees who were working that day on the tracks so the police could determine who did not belong near the tracks. Some of the unauthorized people, such as James Altgens, were told to leave. However, a lot of people came up to the tracks at the last moment. By the time Kennedy came into view Holland estimated that there were 14 to 18 people on the tracks, some of whom he did not recognize as employees.

Holland told the commission there were "definitely" four shots, and he had "no doubt" about seeing a puff of smoke come from the trees near him. Mr Stern of the Warren Commission did not approve of this and tried a couple of times to correct him about the number of shots:

Mr. Stern: _Now, that statement makes clear that you heard four shots, thought you heard four shots, at that time?_

Mr. Holland: _Yes._

Mr. Stern: _All right._

Mr. Holland: _But, two of them was rather close together, though._

Mr. Stern: _So close do you think that might have been one shot?_

Mr. Holland: _No, it was four._

Mr. Stern: _You are clear there were four?_

If you recall, Spector reminded Tomlinson of a special visit he had with the FBI when Tomlinson would not give the correct answers; Stern also reminded Holland of a special visit:

Mr. Stern: _Mr. Holland, do you recall making a statement to an agent of the FBI several days after?_

<Holland confirmed that he remembered>

Well, the FBI report that I have said that you heard either three or four shots fired together, and I gather the impression of the agent was that you were uncertain whether it was three or four.

Unfortunately for Stern, Holland stubbornly refused to agree to three shots. He also insisted the shots sounded different, implying more than one gun. No doubt Stern was thinking to himself, _"Damn these witnesses who insist on being honest! Don't they understand that we are doing this for the good of the USA and the entire world? We are heroes who are saving the world from Kennedy, and they fight us!"_

Holland told the commission that after the shots were fired he ran over to the picket fence to look for the sniper:

Mr. Holland: _By the time I got there there were 12 or 15 policemen and plainclothesmen, and we looked for empty shells around there for quite a while…_

Why were so many cops looking behind the fence if Oswald was firing the shots from the Depository building? Were they the _honest_ cops who heard the shots come from that area and were looking for the sniper? Or were they the _dishonest_ cops were who trying to create such confusion that the sniper(s) could get away? Were those cops looking for bullet shells in order to _identify_ the killer? Or were they looking for shells in order to _hide evidence_ that a sniper was at the picket fence?

A large number of police and other people (e.g., Mr. Holland) were searching the area by the picket fence while Lt. Baker was running up the stairs of the Depository building with Roy Truly. In other words, most of the cops and people were searching the _wrong_ location! How could so many people believe the shots came from the picket fence if Oswald fired the shots from the Depository building?

Stern eventually gives up asking questions and asks Mr. Morrison if he has any to ask:

Mr. Stern: _All right. Mr. Morrison, are there any questions you would like to ask Mr. Holland to clarify any points that we discussed?_

Finally Holland's lawyer gets the opportunity to speak, so perhaps we will find out why he was brought to the meeting:

> Morrison: Mr. Holland, is there anything you might add to this?

That was all the lawyer had to say! Why did Holland bring a lawyer to this meeting to ask such a stupid question? If you think that perhaps later in the interview the lawyer asked more intelligent questions you would be incorrect. We do not find out until the very end of the interview why Holland brought the lawyer. In Holland's final remark to the commission he mentioned that he wanted his lawyer only because _"I was real nervous when I went over to that sheriff's office that afternoon."_ Morrison was in the role of a mother who was comforting her frightened child. While this explains why Morrison was asked to come along, Holland never explained what happened at the sheriff's office that made him so nervous that he wanted a lawyer at the Warren Commission.

After Morrison asked that silly question it must have felt to Holland as if he was now talking to a friend rather than the Commission. He relaxed a bit and began to discuss a subject he never talked about before. Specifically, he mentioned that he saw a station wagon that was parked next to the fence. He said it seemed as if somebody had been standing near the station wagon for a long time because there were hundreds of footprints in the mud in a small area near it.

Mr. Stern, who probably thought the interview was finished, immediately took over when Holland made that remark. Morrison resumed his role of a nearly silent observer.

Holland told the commission that he saw mud on the bumper of the station wagon in two places, as if the person had stood up on the bumper to see over the fence towards the motorcade. He also said he doesn't think he told the police about the station wagon before; this was the first time he told anybody about it. Why didn't he mention this at the time of the killing? Why was he bringing up the issue now? Was the incidence of no importance to him? No; rather, the station wagon created intense emotional turmoil:

> Mr. Stern: And you thought about it later in the day?
>
> Mr. Holland: I thought about it that night.
>
> Mr. Stern: I see.
>
> Mr. Holland: In fact, I went to bed——it was about a week there I couldn't sleep much, brother, and I thought about it that night, and I have thought about it a lot of times since then.

Roger Craig was also disturbed by the behavior of a station wagon. Perhaps Holland saw Ruth Paine's station wagon in the parking lot, and the suspicious aspect of it was that somebody had been pacing back and forth in the mud

and looking over the fence, as if he was anxiously waiting for something, while everybody else was watching the motorcade. But why would Holland be so nervous about this station wagon that he needed his lawyer? My guess is that his previous encounters with the police were uncomfortable because the police tried to convince him that he was incorrect about seeing a puff of smoke near the trees, hearing four shots, and for insisting the shots sounded different. I suppose Holland was expecting to be put under the same pressure at the Warren Commission. Holland never mentioned the station wagon to the police at the time of the killing because the police never let him finish his conversation; rather, as soon as he mentioned the puff of smoke and the four gunshots, the police pressured him into changing his story.

Neighborhood spies

Roger Craig helps us understand the Ruth Paine connection. She was an American woman, but she was living in an area where many recent Russian immigrants had decided to settle. She spent a lot of her time visiting with the Russian immigrants in her area. She had even learned the Russian language. She claims that she was interested in getting to know the Oswalds and all of the other Russians because of curiosity. However, it is more likely that she learned the Russian language and became friends with the Russian immigrants only to send reports about those evil commies to the CIA. Paranoia of commies was more extreme in 1960 than paranoia of Arabs is today, so a lot of Americans in that era were trying to protect us from the evil commies. Possibly thousands of Americans learned to speak Russian, but only to spy on Russians, not become their friends. Nowadays the paranoia is of Arabs, but not many Americans have learned their language…yet. The CIA is trying to correct this; there have already been news reports of them encouraging Americans to learn Arabic.[†]

Ruth Paine drove to New Orleans twice; once to drop off and once to pick up Marina Oswald and her possessions. Was she really such good friends with the Oswalds that she would drive such a long distance to help them move into her house?[‡] She admitted that the Oswalds were not paying rent, or doing anything in return. Furthermore, neither of the Oswalds were desirable house guests; rather, both of them were sloppy and neurotic, and they fought with each other

---

[†] I suppose in ten years, if America still exists, there will be paranoia of Chinese. I suggest we develop a paranoia of the British, or the residents of New Jersey, so we don't have to learn a new language.

[‡] For the younger readers, she had a 1955 station wagon, and automobiles in 1955 were not as reliable, quiet, smooth, or pleasant as they are today, so long trips were more annoying.

on a routine basis. Paine was spending a lot of her time and money on a couple of losers, but getting nothing in return. She also claimed to dislike Lee Oswald, in which case, why would she spend so much of her time and effort helping the Oswalds? The only sensible explanation is that the CIA was paying her to do it.

Neither of the Paines appear to be true friends with the Oswalds; rather, they appear to be providing information about them to the CIA. The reason the Warren Commission spent a lot of time talking with the Paines was because they, especially Ruth, had been studying the Oswalds; Ruth had become an Oswald expert.

I made a remark at the beginning of this chapter that the CIA discovered that Oswald had contacted the Soviet Embassy in Mexico. How would the CIA know that? In Michael Paine's testimony we find that Oswald used Ruth's typewriter to write a letter to the Soviet Embassy in Washington, and the Paines read a draft of the letter that Oswald left on the table. However, I doubt that Oswald left such a letter on the table; rather, the Paines probably routinely searched his room and possessions. Oswald may have written other letters that the Paines secretly read, and the Paines probably told the CIA about lots of other things that Oswald said and did.

I also asked how the FBI located Oswald so quickly when Oswald was trying to hide from them. My guess is that Ruth Paine told them where he was.

Paine told the Commission that Oswald didn't like General Walker. She would have mentioned that remark in her reports to the CIA. The CIA would have then wondered if Oswald was the person who tried to kill General Walker. Oswald complained to his wife that his meetings with the FBI were unpleasant; perhaps the FBI was trying to use the Walker incident to blackmail Oswald.

The testimony of the Paines gives me the impression that they were living an odd, artificial life; specifically, many (maybe all) of their friendships were merely to gather information. However, Lee Oswald never realized that Ruth was a CIA spy. Rather, he naively believed she was his friend. The remark that Oswald blurted out to Roger Craig (*"Don't try to tie her into this. She had nothing to do with it."*) might now make sense to you. Oswald considered Ruth Paine to be a generous, loving woman. Oswald didn't want to see her dragged into the killing.

Do we really need more neighborhood spies?

The FBI wants to recruit us to spy on Arabs, just as they paid citizens during the 1960's to spy on communists. This policy would put more people like Ruth Paine on the government payroll. How will the nation improve from this policy? We will spend a lot of tax money on it, but what do we get in return? The Paines and other spies did not help

America or the world during the 1950's or 1960's; what makes anybody believe these spies will do us some good today? The only spies we might benefit from are the ones who spy on the FBI and CIA.

Sergeant Patrick Dean

Patrick Dean, a sergeant in the Dallas police force, was so upset by his interview with the Warren Commission that he demanded a second interview. At the second interview he explained that one reason he wanted another interview was that Mr. Griffin, the person interviewing him during the first interview, told the court reporter to stop taking notes and leave the room:

> Well, after the court reporter left, Mr. Griffin started talking to me in a manner of gaining my confidence in that he would help me and that he felt I would probably need some help in the future.

Seems to me that Griffin was letting Dean know that if he cooperates, he will be rewarded. However, Dean was one of those hopelessly honest cops, of which the Dallas police department had perhaps three or four, so he refused to cooperate. Griffin then became more demanding:

> ...and then very dogmatically he said that, "Jack Ruby didn't tell you that he entered the basement via the Main Street ramp."

> ...Mr. Griffin, further said, "Jack Ruby did not tell you that he had thought or planned to kill Oswald two nights prior." And he said, "Your testimony was false, and these reports to your chief of police are false."

> ...he said, "Well now, Sergeant Dean, I respect you as a witness, I respect you in your profession, but I have offered my help and assistance, and I again will offer you my assistance, and that I don't feel you will be subjecting yourself to loss of your job," or some words to that effect, "If you will go ahead and tell me the truth about it."

Obviously, Jack Ruby and Mr. Griffin were involved in this scam. Ruby was known to be dishonest, so the idea of him walking into a police station and shooting somebody who was surrounded by cops is absurd. The cops let Ruby into the police station during the brief moment when Oswald was being transferred out of the station. They also cleared a path for both him and a photographer who was standing in the appropriate location to capture the shooting on film. Then they took Ruby to jail, where he eventually died of cancer (Ruby supposedly complained he was given cancer causing chemicals while in jail.)

Roger Craig after the killing

According to Internet rumors, by 1970 Craig was in the process of writing a book about the killing (his manuscript is available on the Internet, although with all the lies about the Kennedy killing I have to wonder if he wrote it, and if so, if anybody edited it). In this manuscript he claims his testimony to the Warren commission was changed in 14 places to better fit the FBI's version of the incident. For example, Craig claims that he told the Commission that he clearly saw the driver of the station wagon, but his testimony was edited to say that did *not* clearly see the driver. If his accusations are true, other testimony may have been edited, also.

Craig's manuscript also mentions that sometimes a few men would sometimes follow both him and his wife in an attempt to intimidate them. He also mentions there were a few attempts to murder him, and that government officials interfered with his employment opportunities.

Near the beginning of this chapter I mentioned that Oswald told his wife that he wanted to hide from the FBI because his meetings were unpleasant, and I asked how many meetings they were having. In his manuscript Craig mentions that a cop told him that Oswald was paid a monthly fee by the FBI to be an informer. If that rumor is true, Oswald and the FBI may have had frequent meetings. In a sense, Oswald was a part time government employee, probably due to his desperation for money. (As I remarked earlier, in a free enterprise economy the useless workers tend to end up on the government payroll.)

On March 6, 1975 Geraldo Rivera showed a copy of Zapruder's film on his television show, *Good Night America*. The government was trying to keep Zapruder's film a secret, but somehow Rivera got a copy and showed it to the world. The film increased interest in the Kennedy killing, and it provided evidence that the killing was a scam. Roger Craig's life was a mess by this time. For example, his wife left him, and he could not find much of a job. With Zapruder's film creating an interest in the killing, Craig might be able to sell his book. However, about two months later, May 15, Roger Craig decides to shoot himself. Coincidence? Or was the FBI worried that Craig might soon publish his book?

By the way, the hiding of Zapruder's film is a sign of guilt, just as is the hiding of the video from the Pentagon security cameras. Furthermore, Life magazine bought the original of Zapruder's film for $25,000, which was a lot of money in 1963.**†** You might expect the editors to use the film to sell their magazine, such as by printing individual frames. Instead they kept the film hidden (or destroyed it). For a publisher to

pay a high price for a unique film of a crime and then hide it from the world is the same as admitting they are involved in the scam. However, none of the stockholders of the company complained that the management was wasting $25,000, nor did anybody accuse the editors of Life magazine with being an accessory to Kennedy's murder.

Why do McAdams, Posner, etc, support the FBI?

John McAdams, a professor at Marquette University, is maintaining an Internet site to convince us that Oswald killed Kennedy; Gerald Posner, a professional author, wrote the book *"Case Closed"* to convince us that Oswald killed Kennedy; and several other people are spending their free time supporting the Warren Report. Why are those people doing this? Do they truly believe Oswald killed Kennedy? Do they really believe it made sense for the doctors to give oxygen to a dead man with a large hole in his head?

Many Americans boast about our legal system, but our legal system is so crummy that people can easily get away with incredible scams. Consider:

- Military officials originally said they did not have video of Flight 77 hitting the Pentagon, and later they released 5 frames of video. However, they did not lose their jobs for *lying*; nor were they arrested for *obstructing justice*.

- Some citizens insist they saw Flight 77 hit the Pentagon, but even if somebody could prove they were lying they would not be considered as accessories to murder.

- University professors say idiotic things about Kennedy, 9-11, and other scams. There does not seem to be any concern among professors that their remarks will get them in trouble. They have permanent positions regardless of what they say. Why does nobody care about these professors?

- Many news reporters lied about Kennedy, 9-11, and other crimes. None of them seem to worry about being considered criminals. And editors who purchase photos of scams in an attempt to hide them from us are never arrested.

- The FBI does not show any interest in identifying the suspicious stock market investors who seemed to know the 9-11 attack was going to take place.

- Some Dallas doctors and police assisted in the assassination of Kennedy, but none of them need to worry about being considered criminals.

- Our government is full of alcoholics because alcohol is not a "drug" and alcoholism does not disqualify us from high level positions.

---

† Zapruder initially resisted telling the Warren Commission the fee he received, but eventually admitted to that amount. He said he gave it all to the Firemen's and Policemen's Fund.

Now consider what will cause an American to be arrested or lose his job:

- When Bill Clinton lied to us about what he and Monica did, millions of Americans considered him to be committing a crime so serious that we must spend tens of millions of dollars investigating, and then we must remove him from office.

- Some military men and women have been discharged for having sex in unapproved manners.

- Millions of people considered Bill Clinton unfit for the presidency when they heard he smoked marijuana.

- The police in my city sometimes ride horses to get to a beach where some people are naked, and then they arrest a few for _public_ nudity, even though the beach is so isolated the cops ride horses to get to it.

- A woman who breast feeds her baby in public will be arrested or harassed, regardless of how well she hides her body.

- People who view "child pornography" on their computer have been arrested, even though sexual photos with children are so rare that I wonder if the FBI is using child pornography as a convenient excuse to arrest people.

The pattern I see is that if a crime does not involve sex or marijuana, it is not a crime.

Abraham Zapruder

If the sniper with Oswald had killed Kennedy instead of hitting Connally, the snipers near the trees would have put their guns away. In such a case Zapruder's film would have provided proof that Kennedy was killed by a sniper from Oswald's direction. His film would have been broadcast millions of time on television. However, since the sniper at the trees killed Kennedy, Zapruder's film had to be hidden.

Zapruder worked in the building across the street from Oswald. He could have taken a few steps out of his building and stood at the corner of Elm and Houston streets to film the motorcade. This was an area where the motorcade would be traveling slowly. Instead he walked down Elm street, past almost all the people. He could have stood along the sidewalk, which would have provided a view similar to that of Altgens (Figure 12-1), but instead he decided to climb on top of a concrete structure that was 1¼ meters (4 feet) above the grass and near the picket fence. The worst aspect of this location was that the motorcade was finished at this point and would be speeding up. By coincidence, this location gave him the best view of the killing.

After the killing he told the commission that policemen were running to the fence behind him, verifying Holland's testimony of police running behind the fence to look for the sniper. Zapruder was very close to the puff of smoke that Holland described seeing, but Zapruder didn't notice any gun shots near him. Rather, his testimony makes him appear to be a politician who doesn't know what the correct answer is so he mumbles a lot of gibberish, partially agrees to everything, and then changes his mind when he worries that he may have given an incorrect answer. The end result is that he doesn't commit to anything, so it is impossible to determine what he believes. For example:

Mr. Liebeler: Did you have any impression as to the direction from which these shots came?

Mr. Zapruder: No, I also thought it came from back of me. Of course, you can't tell when something is in line it could come from anywhere, but being I was here and he was hit on this line and he was hit right in the head—I saw it right around here, so it looked like it came from here and it could come from there.

Mr. Liebeler: All right, as you stood here on the abutment and looked down into Elm Street, you saw the President hit on the right side of the head and you thought perhaps the shots had come from behind you?

Mr. Zapruder: Well, yes.

Mr. Liebeler: From the direction behind you?

Mr. Zapruder: Yes, actually—I couldn't say what I thought at the moment, where they came from—after the impact of the tragedy was really what I saw and I started and I said—yelling, "They've killed him"—I assumed that they came from there, because as the police started running back of me, it looked like it came from the back of me.

Mr. Liebeler: But you didn't form any opinion at that time as to what direction the shots did come from actually?

Mr. Zapruder: No.

Zapruder said a "girl" from his office (today she would be described as a "woman") was standing behind him. He does not tell the commission what she was doing, but some descriptions of Zapruder from independent reports of the killing claim that she was holding him steady as he took photos. Why would he need somebody to hold him? Was he partially crippled? If so, why did he climb onto a concrete structure instead of sit on the grassy slope?

If Zapruder knew snipers would be firing high powered rifles directly behind him, he may have been concerned that he would be startled by the shots, in which case he would want somebody to hold him to help him remain steady. The camera shook a bit after the shot that hit Kennedy's head, but Zapruder claimed it was because he was startled by the visual sight of the brains flying. Zapruder did not mention the sound of the gunshot.

After the killing Zapruder walked back to his office. He claimed that along the way he yelled: *"They killed him, they killed him!"* He went into his office and remained there until the police came to talk to him.

Zapruder's description to the Warren Commission of the bullet hitting Kennedy was emotional:

> *Mr. Zapruder: I heard a second shot and then I saw his head opened up and the blood and everything came out and I started--I can hardly talk about it [the witness crying].*

An easy way to stop yourself from laughing is to force yourself to cry; it gives you an excuse to hide your head and justify strange noises that resemble laughter.

Zapruder claims he gave the $25,000 to charity, but how do we know he is telling the truth?.[†]

Zapruder was involved in manufacturing women's dresses, and he said he was in New York (I assume New York City) at the time the Warren Commission made an appointment for him to be interviewed. It might be interesting to see who Zapruder was friends with in New York City. Perhaps some of his friends decided they could get away with the 9-11 scam after noticing how easy it was to get away with the Kennedy killing.

Oswald's arrest

Johnny Brewer, the manager of a shoe shop next to a movie theater, said he heard police sirens. He noticed a sloppy man walk into his store. The man stared at nothing in particular, and when the police cars passed by, the man walked out. Brewer wondered if the man was hiding from the police, so he walked outside to see where the man went. He asked Julia Postal, the cashier of the theater, if a weird man just bought a ticket. She said a suspicious man seemed to be hiding when the police cars drove by, but he didn't buy a ticket. She turned around to look at this suspicious man, but he was gone. About this time her boss walked out of the theater and drove away. His car was parked in front of the theater, and Postal told the commission that he wanted to follow the police cars to see what the police were doing. What are the chances that he would jump in his car and follow cops that have their sirens blasting? It is more likely

that he just let Oswald into the theater and wanted to get out of the area before the cops arrived. Warren Burroughs, the man who took the tickets from customers, said he didn't see anybody sneak into the theater, but he may be involved also.

A possibly meaningless bit of trivia is that Julia Postal was shocked to hear that Officer Tippit was killed because Tippit used to work part-time at the theater.

What was Tippit's connection?

Dallas policeman Tippit was supposedly killed by Oswald 40 to 60 minutes after Kennedy was killed. While Oswald certainly may have killed him, it is also possible that Tippit was killed for being one of the pesky, honest cops who refused to join scams.

America's "free press" is a disgrace

Zapruder told the Warren commission that *Life* magazine bought the original of his 8mm film from him, and that the police received only copies. Obviously the FBI doesn't care whether they get originals or copies of photos of major crimes. What if *Life* magazine had purchased Kennedy's *dead body* and gave the FBI a photocopy of the body? How absurd would the situation have to be before you agree with me that the USA is suffering from a seriously corrupt media and government?

Jean Hill went to the motorcade with her friend Mary Moorman. One part of her testimony is about the behavior of a newspaper reporter:

> *Mrs. Hill:*   There was a man holding Mary's arm and she was crying and he had hold of her camera trying to take it with him.
>
> *Mr. Specter:*   Who was that?
>
> *Mrs. Hill:*   Featherstone of the Times Herald and—
>
> *Mr. Specter:*   Dallas Times Herald?
>
> *Mrs. Hill:*   That's right. I ran up there and told him we had to leave.

Moorman took a Polaroid photo just after the first bullet hit Kennedy, and Featherstone wanted it. Featherstone managed to drag both women to a small room, and then he stood by the door to stop them from leaving. Television and newspaper cameramen and reporters were brought into the room to interview them and take pictures. [‡]

The women became increasingly annoyed with the abuse. Jean Hill demanded that she be allowed to leave. A man soon entered the room and offered Moorman $10,000 for her photo. The women considered the photo lousy (it

---

[†] As you might have noticed, I am not willing to believe anything these suspicious people say.

[‡] For the younger readers who consider it exciting to have your photo taken, in 1963 color cameras required bright flash bulbs for indoor photos, which was irritating. The video cameras of that era also required bright lights.

was lousy!) but when they looked for the photo they discovered it was gone. Featherstone had taken it during the commotion. When Hill demanded he return it he reassured her that _"we'll get it back."_

The reporters who were coming into the room asked Hill and Moorman about the killing. Hill would repeat the story about the man she saw running away after the shots were fired, and that shots were coming from near the fence. Featherstone did not approve of her story. Hill described his reaction:

> He said, _"You know you were wrong about seeing a man running."_ He said, _"You didn't."_
>
> ...and I said, _"But I did,"_ and he said, _"No; don't say that any more on the air."_

Featherstone told her that the shots came from the Depository. How would he know where the shots came from?

Eventually Featherstone allowed Hill and Moorman to leave. As they walked out of the room they immediately encountered the police. Did the police arrest Featherstone for theft? Did the police arrest Featherstone for kidnaping and abuse? Of course not. Rather, the police took Hill and Moorman to the station for more abusive interviews.

Why did Featherstone want the photo so badly? Why would a publisher offer $10,000 for a low quality photo? The first answer that pops into your mind is that Featherstone wanted to publish the photo in his newspaper. However, _Life_ magazine paid a lot of money for Zapruder's film but then kept it hidden. It is more likely that Featherstone was concerned that her photo might show evidence that the sniper was in front of Kennedy.

Moorman's photo was soon published, but it did not show anything that would suggest the killing was a scam. Perhaps when Featherstone had a chance to look closely at the photo he realized it was of no importance, so he allowed it to be published. Or perhaps the FBI altered the photo to ensure it was of no importance.

Moorman was eventually paid $600 for the photo, or was the money to keep her quiet about the theft and abuse? It reminds me of the 9-11 victims, who were also offered lots of money in return for keeping their mouths shut.

The most interesting aspect of this event is Featherstone's attempt to correct a witness to a crime. A reporter's job is to _gather information_, not _tell us what to say_. Furthermore, if a Dallas news reporter is so corrupt that he will steal photos, abuse people, and pressure witnesses into changing their testimony, wouldn't he be likely to steal other items, abuse other people, and correct other news reports?

How suspicious would the media reporters have to be before the common American realized that the killing was a scam and that the American media is disgusting? What if, instead of verbally telling Jean Hill that the shots came from

the Depository, Featherstone had given her a printed copy of the correct events and told her to study them at home? What if he also told her that somebody will visit her in a week to quiz her on the events to ensure she understood the material? What if he also arranged classes for the witnesses at a local college?

Jean Hill mentioned that about 10 days after the killing a group of TV reporters came to her house for an interview. She was upset by the interview; she said the interview _"left me very doubtful and confused."_ She also said she never saw the interview on TV, and she doesn't know if it was ever put on TV. Therefore, it is possible that the TV crew was a group of FBI agents who were merely trying to confuse her about the events, or maybe it was a group of television reporters who were involved in the scam and trying to confuse her.

Are CIA agents disguised as news reporters?

Perhaps some CIA agents are working as reporters both to hide their connection to the CIA and to give them access to the news so that they can manipulate it. Since the CIA has a virtually unlimited budget, the CIA can easily afford to pay newspaper and television companies to allow their agents to work as reporters; all the CIA needs is some "patriotic" editors who want to help America fight the evil commies (or, nowadays, the Evil Terrorists). Perhaps Featherstone was a CIA agent. Incidently, Featherstone does not show up in the list of witnesses of the Warren Report. Why ignore a witness who knew where the shots came from?

Will Americans take an active role in their nation?

If we want a better nation, we must demand higher standards for news reporters. In a free enterprise economy the _consumers_ determine which newspapers and magazines survive. Therefore, unless the American people cancel subscriptions to these dishonest magazines and switch to the more respectable publications, nothing will improve.

The widespread attitude in America is that we "ordinary" citizens are helpless victims of rich people, the "military establishment," the government, or some other mysterious entity, but we are helpless only because most citizens refuse to take an active role in maintaining a healthy nation. The citizens must stop supporting the media organizations that lie and deceive. For example, the magazine _Scientific American_ published an article in October, 2001 to convince us that World Trade Center towers collapsed because of fire. The author ignored Building 7, as does everybody else who claims fire caused the towers to collapse. By purchasing _that_ magazine rather than a publication that is more honest you are providing jobs for the people who are dishonest, and you are hurting the honest reporters.

The American people are not helpless; rather, most of them simply don't do anything to make a better nation.

What Happens Now?

Why is the FBI hiding information?

From a news report by the *Richmond Times* about Jose Velasquez, the supervisor of a gas station:

> *Velasquez says the gas station's security cameras are close enough to the Pentagon to have recorded the moment of impact. "I've never seen what the pictures looked like," he said. "The FBI was here within minutes and took the film."*

That implies the FBI was *waiting* for the crash at the Pentagon, and as soon as it happened they drove around the area to confiscate videos from security cameras so that nobody could see what actually hit the building.

A report from the *Washington Times* claims that a security camera at a nearby hotel recorded Flight 77 as it hit the Pentagon, but the FBI did not get to the hotel quickly enough:

> *Hotel employees sat watching the film in shock and horror several times before the FBI confiscated the video as part of its investigation.*

Bill Gertz and Rowan Scarborough, the reporters who wrote that article, were under the impression that the FBI confiscated the video as part of their "investigation." The FBI has good reason to demand information about a crime, but was the FBI *gathering* information or *hiding* it?

The FBI did not confiscate all videos of the airplanes crashing into the towers, so why did they confiscate all videos of the airplane hitting the Pentagon? More amazing, why do so few people care that the FBI did this? Why don't news reporters demand answers? Why are people so willing to accept what would normally be considered *highly suspicious behavior*? Why didn't the *Washington Times* locate and interview those hotel employees and ask them what they saw in that video?

Why is Information vanishing from the Internet?

A lot of Internet sites that had information or photos about the September 11th attack have vanished. Sometimes the sites are removed because the authors became tired of maintaining them and/or paying the fees. However, some sites disappeared without explanation. The strangest aspect of this is that there is an organization that has been archiving Internet data for several years, and there is a void in their archived data concerning the September 11th attack. When I tried to access some of the archived data of an Air Force site, the following error message appeared:

> Blocked Site Error.
>
> Per the request of the site owner, http://www.airforcetimes.com/ is no longer available in the Wayback Machine.

That error message implies that the Air Force had posted some documents and/or photos at their web site and the Wayback Machine eventually archived it. Later the Air Force decided to remove these particular pages from their site, and they demanded the archived copies of the entire site be removed, also. What was on the pages that the Air Force wants to keep secret? If the material is so dangerous, why did they post in the first place? Why so much secrecy about this 9-11 attack? If the American government has nothing to hide, why are they hiding so much information?

I have since discovered that an Internet site (*whatreallyhappened.com*) is pointing out that archived data relating to the attack is also missing from major news organizations, United Airlines, and NASDAQ. This implies that somebody is trying to stop investigations of the suspicious investors (discussed on page 4).

The people at *whatreallyhappened* insist that Flight 77 hit the Pentagon, so their reasoning ability (and/or honesty) has to be questioned, so I checked the archives myself. Sure enough, the data is missing. Why are the news reporters ignoring this?

Is information about Dyncorp hidden, also?

After leaving the Army, Ben Johnston took a job as an aircraft maintenance technician with Dyncorp. He was sent to Bosnia to maintain American military aircraft. A year-and-a-half later he was fired from his job. He filed a lawsuit that accused Dyncorp personnel of corruption and buying sex slaves. Is Johnston a disgruntled employee who fabricated ridiculous accusations rather than admit that he was fired because of his own incompetence?

In April, 2002 a hearing was held by the House of Representatives to investigate the sex slave trade. Johnston testified that *"Dyncorp was involved in slave trading of young girls"* and *"Dyncorp personnel had young children living with them for sex."*

What became of the investigation of the sex slave trade? Did Congress decide that Dyncorp was involved with it? Or did they decide that there were no sex slaves, and that Johnston was insane? Were you aware that Congress was looking into this issue? If not, what were the news reporters providing you in April, 2002 that was more important? Why has this issue vanished from the news?

If Linus Pauling is harassed, what happens to us?

After America developed the atomic bomb in 1945, the military began testing them in the atmosphere, on the ground, and in the ocean. They also demanded the scientists develop bigger bombs, and the hydrogen bomb. Other nations wanted nuclear bombs, also.

In 1946 Linus Pauling joined the Emergency Committee of Atomic Scientists. This group had the attitude that the atomic bomb was so powerful that there was no need for nations to compete with each other to develop hydrogen bombs. While other famous scientists were in this group, such as Einstein, Pauling was perhaps the most active member. He traveled around the country to give speeches and circulate petitions. He also complained that testing nuclear weapons in the atmosphere was spreading radioactive waste, which in turn would cause birth defects and cancer. To further annoy the US government, he complained about President Truman's insistence that government employees take oaths of loyalty.

Many officials in the US government considered Pauling to be an enemy, and possibly a communist. The official government attitude was that it was safe to test nuclear bombs in the atmosphere, and that the world will become a better place when America has a lot more bombs.

Pauling continued to complain year after year about atmospheric testing, but rather than convince government officials of the danger, they became increasingly angry at him. In 1952 Pauling was invited to London to speak at a conference of scientists, and the US government took that opportunity to deny him a passport. In response, Pauling decided to invite some European scientists to America. The US government responded by refusing to allow Rosalind Franklin, a British scientist, into America. The US government was behaving like a child having a temper tantrum.†

---

† Franklin had taken some X-ray photographs that were important to Pauling's work. Two other scientists, Watson and Crick, were British citizens, so they could see Franklin's work. Her X-ray photographs put all of the pieces of the DNA puzzle into place, and Watson and Crick soon announced the structure of the DNA molecule. If Pauling had been allowed a passport, it is probable that Pauling would have been the first to figure it out.

At the same moment in time that Pauling was denied a passport, millions of Americans were boasting that America was a better nation than Russia because the Russian government refused to let its citizens travel to other nations. Most Americans were either oblivious to the hypocrisy of their statements, or they agreed with the US government that Pauling was a communist who deserved punishment.

In 1954 Pauling was awarded the Nobel Prize in chemistry. This created an embarrassing dilemma for the US government. The award ceremony was in Europe, but the US government was not permitting Pauling to travel to other nations. If they continued to deny him a passport, other nations might complain that the US Government was behaving exactly like the Russian government. The US government gave in and allowed him a passport. What would have happened if he hadn't been awarded the Nobel Prize until 1960, or 1971? Would he have been denied a passport all those years?

The American government had no interest in practicing what they preached. They preached "Free Speech" but they tried to silence critics. In an interview at UC Berkeley in 1996 Pauling recalled:

> *"I was threatened by the Internal Security Subcommittee of the Senate with a year in jail for contempt of Senate, when I was being harassed by the Internal Security Subcommittee."*

Pauling remained an enemy of America for many years after winning the Noble prize because he continued to complain about atmospheric weapons testing. In 1958 he obtained 2000 signatures from American scientists asking for atmospheric testing to stop. Scientists from foreign countries then asked to sign. Eventually Pauling presented 13,000 signatures to the United Nations. The American government eventually gave in. On July 25, 1963 the Limited Test Ban Treaty was signed by the United States, Britain and the Soviet Union.

In 1963 the Nobel Committee decided to award Pauling a Peace Prize. Rather than boast that Americans won another Nobel prize, an editor of *Life* magazine responded with an editorial entitled, *"A weird insult from Norway."*

Was Pauling the only person the American government harassed or threatened with jail? Was Pauling the only person that the editors of *Life* magazine tried to give a bad image to? If a famous scientist has his passport blocked for complaining about radioactive waste falling on us, what happens to ordinary people who complain about the 9-11 scam; sex slaves at Dyncorp; or corruption at the FBI? If a world-famous scientist is threatened with a year in jail after using his freedom of speech to disagree with the American government, what might happen if an ordinary person used his freedom of speech?

Was the explosion at Port Chicago nuclear?

You may now be ready to consider the possibility that the *incredibly* large explosion at a Navy port in San Francisco Bay at 10:20 PM on July 17, 1944 was actually the first test of a nuclear bomb. The US Navy claims that a ship at Port Chicago was being loaded with conventional bombs for the war when one of the bombs accidently ignited, which then set off all other bombs in the ship and on the dock.

The most suspicious aspect of the accident is that some scientists and engineers from Los Alamos Laboratories, who were struggling to develop a nuclear bomb, were at the site the next morning to investigate. They eventually produced 400 to 600 pages of documents about the accident. The scientists were frantically struggling to develop a nuclear bomb at the time, so telling them to investigate an irrelevant accident and then write *hundreds* of pages about it is equivalent to telling surgeons who are in the middle of surgery to stop what they are doing and go to the store to pick up coffee and donuts. Obviously, that "accident" was extremely important to the nuclear bomb project.

Witnesses had no concept of a nuclear bomb, so it never occurred to them that it might be nuclear, but their descriptions seem to describing a tiny nuclear bomb. For example, a pilot who was at 2700 meters (9000 feet) is reported to have seen pieces of white-hot metal "as big as a house" fly by. Other witnesses mention a brilliant flash of light. In addition to vaporizing the ship and destroying the port, it carved an oval crater at the bottom of the port that was 20 meters deep, and 90 by 210 meters at the top (66 ft deep, 300 by 700 ft at the top). Seismic sensors showed a magnitude of 3.5; can anybody offer evidence that conventional explosives in a floating ship can create such a powerful shock in the earth?

If you need more evidence that the explosion was nuclear, the Contra Costa County Office of Education has a web site about it, as well as links to other sites and books. Of course, since they are part of the US government, they have a note on their site to let us know that they believe the official explanation. In other words, they provide information about the nuclear possibility only for entertainment. So enjoy it, but don't believe it.

Imagine yourself in their era

It is difficult for somebody in our era to imagine the military testing a nuclear bomb on themselves, but in 1944 nobody knew what a nuclear bomb was. The physicists certainly had a good idea about the possible destruction, but the military may have been visualizing a very large bomb. The military placed the nuclear bomb underneath the ship, or at the bottom of it. The purpose of the test may have been to see if a nuclear bomb could sink a ship. The military may have been shocked (actually, excited) when it destroyed the entire port and carved a giant crater.

Did somebody give nuclear technology to Russia?

The Russians developed a nuclear bomb so quickly that the American government was certain that somebody had provided them with the technology. This is difficult to believe because Stalin's troops were still in control of Eastern Europe at the time. Furthermore, it was widely believed that Stalin was a violent man who could not be trusted. So who would provide him with nuclear technology? And why?

Ethel and Julius Rosenberg were given the death penalty for providing nuclear technology to Russia, but I cannot see how they had access to it or would know what it looked like. I would think that one of the nuclear physicists would have to be involved.

Oppenheimer was one of the physicists who had access to the important information. Soon after the bomb was developed the US military considered him a potential threat to America because of his opposition to hydrogen bombs and because he associated with people the military considered to be communists. However, why would he or any other physicist provide the technology to Russia when they would be given the death penalty if they were caught? How could providing the technology to Russia be worth risking their lives when the Russians were capable of figuring it out on their own?

Imagine for a moment that Oppenheimer put the first bomb together in July, 1944. Imagine he suggested that it be tested it in a remote location in the desert because of the radiation hazard and the size of the blast. What would Oppenheimer think if the military disregarded everything he said and insisted the bomb be tested on a real ship so that they can see how it operates in a real situation? What if Oppenheimer explained over and over that it would be beyond a mere "explosion," and what if the arrogant and stubborn military leaders responded with such remarks as, *"We will test the bomb at night, when only niggers are working."* †

From 1945 onward scientists pointed out to the military that a one-megaton bomb is equivalent to all the bombs dropped during the entire second world war, and that the only use for such a large bomb would be the annihilation of cities. The military did not merely ignore the scientists; rather, they demanded hydrogen bombs much larger than one-megaton. The US government also disregarded warnings about atmospheric testing of bombs; actually, they harassed scientists who complained about it. For all we know, Oppenheimer was harassed as well. Would the scientists be impressed with the US military?

---

† Of the 320 people killed in that blast, 202 were black. If the ship had been the only object destroyed in the blast, rather than the entire port, all of the casualties may have been black because black people were loading the ship at the time. There was still a segregation of the races in 1944.

To further make the USA look stupid, in 1945 Americans were boasting that the war was over and that the Americans had won. However, Stalin's troops were still in control of Eastern Europe. The war didn't end in 1945; rather, America simply decided that Germany and Japan were the "enemies" and that Britain and Russia were the "allies." I would say Stalin won that war, or at least benefitted greatly from it.

Incidently, General Patton complained in 1945 that Stalin was not our ally, and that war was not over. In response to those and other remarks, he was discharged from the military. American citizens have freedom of speech, but not top military leaders. A couple months later Patton died in a car accident.†

Are *you* impressed by the behavior of the American government? If not, what are the chances that the scientists were?

Perhaps some of the scientists experienced the type of sadness and concern that you would feel if you were to see a group of children with guns, *and* who were demanding *gigantic* guns, *and* who were harassing people who told them not to test the guns by shooting them in air because the bullets eventually fall down somewhere in the city.

Many of the scientists came to the USA from Europe, and some of them may have felt that they had just given a powerful bomb to a group of idiots. Perhaps one or more of them decided a nuclear adversary might keep America under control.

Why no progress with Anthrax?

Barbara Rosenberg is a molecular biologist at the State University of New York. She also has the title of "Chair of the Federation of American Scientists Working Group On Biological Weapons." She has been complaining since at least 5 February 2002 that only a few dozen microbiologists in the entire nation have both access to anthrax and the expertise to work with it. With so few possible suspects, she asks, *"Is the FBI Dragging Its Feet?"* She claims it should be easy for the FBI to figure out who did it.

If you agree with me that the 9-11 and Kennedy investigations were scams, you should consider the possibility that the anthrax investigation is also a scam. First, the FBI may not be trying to figure out who mailed those anthrax letters. Rather, the FBI may be trying to cover up the attack, just as they hide information about the 9-11 attack.

---

† The US Navy claims Patton was driving 48 kph (30 mph) when a truck driving 16 kph (10 mph) made a left turn in front of him. Why should we believe it was an accident when the US military lies so often?

Second, Rosenberg has taken an active role in helping us figure out who mailed those anthrax letters. However, for all we know, she is a member of the Axis Of Good, and her friends mailed those letters. The Axis of Good may be looking for a patsy to blame the anthrax on. Once that patsy has been arrested or killed, most Americans will consider the case closed.

The JFK and 9-11 Pied Pipers

If you agree with me that many professors, news reporters, doctors, policemen, and government officials lied about Kennedy and 9-11, how can we trust anybody on the anthrax issue? I think some of the people who have taken the role of helping us understand these issues are actually in the role of "Pied Pipers" who are trying to lead the citizens in the wrong direction.

Has the US government been taken over?

It is common for government officials to change their positions, be fired from their job, and retire. However, the changes that have been going on since September 11th seem beyond "normal." From the *Washington Post* on 11 April 2002:

> *President Bush has approved widespread changes at the top of the US military that will put in place a new generation of relatively nonconformist officers who are likely to be more supportive of the administration's goal of radically changing the armed forces, Pentagon officials said last night.*

That is an example of the vague statements that come out in the news every so often about management changes in our government. Note that the report describes the people being promoted as *"more supportive of the administration's goal."* This is the same as saying that people being promoted are more submissive; less able to think for themselves; more willing to do whatever they are told without asking why; and/or a member of the Axis of Good.

Furthermore, what is *"the administration's goal?"* The *Washington Post* wrote that the goal was *"radically changing the armed forces,"* but what are they "radically changing" it to? How can our government make such vague statements without news reporters asking for details? Why are so few people questioning what our government is doing?

Would the military promote a person who advocated releasing all video tapes of Flight 77 hitting the Pentagon? Would President Bush be willing to promote a person who demanded an investigation of the World Trade Center attack? Would the CIA promote a person who demanded an investigation of Dyncorp or the issue of sex slaves? Would the FBI be willing to promote a person who advocated an investigation of why the FBI hides information?

I suspect that members of the Axis of Good are being given high level government jobs. This gives them more control of our government. This also makes the *Coup* record label even more of a coincidence. In a sense, America was taken over on September 11th. Unlike typical revolutions, which involve fighting, America has been taken over with deception.

After the 9-11 attack Jerry Hauer became advisor for the nation's health secretary, Tommy Thompson. Did he get this job because he was "more supportive of the administration's goal"? One reporter referred to Hauer as a "New York City bioterrorism specialist." Is Hauer using his bioterrorism expertise to help the FBI solve the anthrax case? Why do so few Americans care who these people are and what they do?

Is it safe to contact the FBI?

If you have information about who is a member of the Axis of Good, or how the towers were blown up, and if you contact the FBI to tell them about it, will the FBI be grateful, or regard you as an enemy? Is the FBI trying to solve these crimes, or cover them up? Are you willing to trust your life to the FBI? John O'Neill was a Deputy Director of the FBI, and he is dead; how long do you think *you* would survive a fight with the Axis of Good?

As many as 14 biologists have died in strange ways since 9-11. For example, on 15 November 2001 Professor Don Wiley of Harvard University was in Memphis, Tennessee to attend a dinner of the St. Jude Children's Research Hospital. He left at midnight and drove off in his rental car by himself to his father's home in Memphis, where he was staying. Four hours later the police found his car abandoned on a bridge across the Mississippi River, which was the wrong direction to get to his father's house. The keys were in the ignition, there was nothing wrong with the car, and he never turned on his hazard lights. Why was he driving in that direction? And why would he stop on a bridge at midnight? Was he intoxicated? Perhaps, although nobody at the dinner admitted to drinking with him or noticing him showing signs of intoxication.

Harvard University and the St. Jude Children's Research Hospital offered a $10,000 reward to encourage citizens to help find him, but nobody came forward with information. About five weeks later his body was found along the river. How did he end up in the river?

While the strange deaths of these biologists may be coincidence, we would be foolish if we did not consider the possibility that they were connected to the Anthrax attacks. Perhaps those biologists had naively contacted the FBI (or Barbara Rosenberg) with information about who did it.

The Axis of Good is risking more than a murder charge. They are certain to go to tremendous extremes to protect themselves. Since many members are government officials (and some seem to be from other nations), they have access to a lot of money and advanced weapons. Does it make sense for you or me to start a fight with them? When corruption is as extreme as it is in the USA, it is best to avoid trouble until you have more support.

There is nobody to protect us

The FBI was designed specifically to deal with serious crimes, but they appear to be involved in one scam after the next. The military was also designed to protect America, but they seem to be involved in as many scams as the FBI. The same goes for the CIA, FEMA, and just about every other government agency. This means we have *no government agency to protect us*. This in turn means that you would be a fool to fight the Axis of Good; you would be a fool to put your life in the hands of President Bush, the FBI, or the US military.

More amazing to me, we cannot even get support from the American citizens; rather, most of them will insult us as being "conspiracy nuts." This situation reminds me of the child who ran away from Jeff Dahmer, went to the police for help, and the police handed him back to Dahmer. If you find yourself in trouble with the Axis of Good, and if you run to the American citizens for help, they will turn their back on you.

I think the World Trade Center attack was a scam, but I am *not* going to fight the Axis of Good. If you know any critical information about this attack, you might want a similar attitude. In other words, discuss what you know, but don't fight the Axis of Good. As long as the American voters create crummy, dishonest governments, and as long as most Americans regard us as conspiracy nuts, there is no sense worrying about this corruption. A nation cannot be helped when the majority of citizens refuse to admit it needs help.

The situation in America right now reminds me of the stories of the corruption in the city governments of Chicago and New York City many decades ago; i.e., everybody knew those city governments were corrupt, but nobody did anything about it. As individual citizens, none of us can do anything about organized crime. One of the purposes of the FBI was to deal with these organized criminal groups, but the FBI appears to be one of them.

Who is really to blame?

Congresswoman McKinney of Georgia suspects the Bush administration is lying about the 9-11 attack, and she was involved in the investigation about the Dyncorp sex slaves. In response to her requests for more investigations, Kathleen Parker of the *Orlando Sentinel* insulted her as *"possibly a delusional paranoiac."* Jonah Goldberg of the *National Review* wrote that McKinney is *more repugnant than Yasser Arafat's three-week-old underwear.* These journalists do not provide news reports or encourage discussions; rather, they encourage their readers to insult McKinney.

Freedom of speech has no value if you cannot use it. The scientific progress that has been made during the past few thousand years came from scientists who *discussed* issues, not scientists who *insulted* one another. Many scientists proposed a theory that later turned out to be completely or partially incorrect, but if they had not considered all theories, they never would have figured out which theories were more accurate. Another way to describe this is, *unless you are willing to fail, you will never achieve progress.*

These same concepts apply to the 9-11 attack. The only way to understand what happened on September 11th is to discuss the issue. Many of our theories will turn out to be completely or partially incorrect, but unless we can freely discuss our thoughts, we will never be able to figure out which theories are most accurate. We cannot be afraid to discuss an issue simply because it may be incorrect.

The problem is the American people

Some people accuse the CIA of being behind, or taking advantage of, the 9-11 attack. There are also accusations that Britain, Israel, China, Iraq, France, Saudi Arabia, and/or other foreign nations are involved. However, regardless of how many foreign nations or US government agencies were involved, the ultimate responsibility lies with the American people. The American people were the ones who created the American government, the FBI, the university system, and the media that is deceiving us about this attack. Also, American citizens are working for those agencies and subscribing to these deceptive publications, not Al Qaeda terrorists or people in foreign nations.

You probably know at least one alcoholic. When you think of that person, do you feel anger towards the businesses that produce alcoholic beverages? Or do you feel sadness for that person? Do you feel that he is the source of his own problems?

Next consider cocaine users. When you think of a cocaine user, do you feel that he is the source of his own problems? Or do you find yourself becoming angry at those

South American drug "pushers" for "pushing" him into purchasing drugs at high prices and then using those drugs to excess?

Most Americans realize that an alcoholic is the source of his own problems, but the widespread attitude in America is that people who use heroin or cocaine are being controlled by foreigners who push drugs on us. As a result, US taxpayers waste millions of dollars each year in an attempt to stop the Mexican and South American drug pushers from forcing us to take drugs. Rarely does an American tell a drug user to be responsible for himself.

I don't feel anger towards farmers who grow opium poppies, nor do I feel anger towards the people who committed this 9-11 scam. Rather, I feel sad for America. A nation that has an incompetent government is vulnerable to abuse from both its own citizens and from foreign nations.

The American people are allowing these scams to occur, just as they allow themselves to abuse drugs. Blaming foreign nations or the FBI for this attack is not dealing with the problem. The problem is that the American people are doing a terrible job of selecting government officials and managing their nation.

It would certainly be interesting to see who is in the Axis of Good, which nations they work for, and how they accomplished the scam, but even if all of them were arrested we would still have the same incompetent government; the same ugly, disorganized cities; the same lousy television news; the same deteriorating economy; and the same lousy train system. The only way to make a better nation is for the American people to become better citizens and better voters.

We need higher standards for government officials

During the 1990's Republicans subjected us to many years of lectures in which we were told that President Clinton was unfit for the presidency, mainly because he lied about his sexual activities and he had smoked marijuana. The Republicans were furious in 1996 when Clinton beat the Republican candidate once again.

I was certain that the Republicans were so upset after losing twice to Clinton that they would make an effort to find somebody for the 2000 elections who was truly better than what the Democrats would offer. However, their superior alternative to a marijuana smoker who lies about his sex life was a man who was born into wealth; a man who was an alcoholic for many years; a man who was rumored to have had cocaine problems; a man with no useful skills. George

Bush appears to be a puppet. His vice president seemed on the verge of dying from a heart attack. How is the Bush Administration an improvement over the Clinton Administration?

In the 2000 election, the Democrats offered Al Gore. While Al Gore may not have drug problems, he seems neurotic beyond what I would call "normal."

How can a nation take care of itself when the American voters believe Gore and Bush are the two best candidates this nation can find?

Where do all the bad kids go?

When I was a child there was an older child living a few houses away who would occasionally torture animals and hurt other kids in the neighborhood. His family moved to another city before he finished high school so I never saw him as an adult. I often wondered where such violent people find jobs. If torturing animals and other kids is entertainment to them, how could they fit in with "normal" people?

Some mentally ill people are capable of controlling themselves enough during the day to hold jobs in private businesses without any of us realizing that in their leisure time they are killing and torturing people. John Wayne Gacy (he raped, tortured, and killed a lot of people) is an example. But what happens to the people whose personalities are so undesirable and/or so violent that private businesses do not want them?

From what I have seen, our government and universities are like sponges, soaking up the unemployable citizens. This results in a lousy government and school system, plus these people create a tax burden on us and cause tuition to rise.

Every nation's military has always provided mentally defective people with jobs, even if they have serious alcohol or other drug problems, and even if they have a history of arrests and jail sentences. Parents with badly behaved children often push their kids into the military in the hope that the military will make them behave better. These parents use the military as a treatment center for the mentally ill. However, if any of those mentally ill people get promoted, they may promote other mentally ill people, as well as fire people such as General Patton. The end result is a military dominated by lunatics.

The secrecy of the CIA makes it difficult to determine the mental stability of its employees, but I suspect mental illness is widespread in that agency, also.

Will any nation deal with mental illness?

The process of creating a human seems so simple; a sperm and egg join together and then a little baby develops. In reality, creating a new life requires a lot of extremely complex chemical reactions to take place, and mistakes are common with those reactions. A mistake can result in a human mind or body that does not function properly. Take a serious look at yourself and the people around you and notice all the defects we all have. While many defects are trivial, such as a non-symmetrical face or a blemish on the skin, some are serious, such as siamese twins and Downs syndrome. Creating a human is a difficult, sensitive process.

Furthermore, brain damage can occur after birth. It may be a coincidence, but when Westley Allan Dodd was a child he fell off a fence and hit the ground so hard that he went unconscious. (Dodd raped, tortured, and killed a lot of children). Boxers suffer brain damage from the pounding they take; why wouldn't children also risk brain damage when their heads are hit hard? For all we know, a child will suffer *more* brain damage than a boxer because the child's brain is in the process of developing.

John Wayne Gacy was hit in the head by a swing when he was eleven years old, and it caused a blood clot that doctors didn't notice until he was sixteen. During those five years he experienced many blackouts. The blackouts stopped when doctors gave him medication to dissolve the clot. For all we know, he suffered brain damage during those five years.

People with mental defects have a difficult time enjoying life. The people with the most severe defects often end up living in the streets, eating out of garbage cans, and committing crimes. People with less severe defects seem to end up in the military and CIA, where violence is an accepted *part of the job*. Ted Bundy may have fit in among the people who planned the 9-11 attack. Gary Heidnik kept as many as three women at a time alive as sex slaves in a pit under the floor of his home, so he might have loved working at Dyncorp.

We should face the unpleasant fact that life is a tricky process, and that defects will always occur in all animals, plants, and humans. We must set higher standards of mental health for our government employees. Parents with badly behaved children should not push them into the military, FBI, or CIA; rather, we need to keep the mentally ill under control.

Adolf Hitler supposedly spent some time living in a park, and sleeping on a bench. However, not many German voters considered his inability to take care of himself to be a sign that he was unfit to be a government leader. Nor were voters concerned that his tantrums were a sign of trouble.

No nation yet shows any concern about whether their government leaders have alcohol or other drug problems, nor do voters care about the mental health of government leaders. Actually, rather than be concerned about the issue, most Americans try to pretend that *nobody is mentally defective*. The defective people are referred to as "autistic," or "disadvantaged," or "developmentally challenged." This is equivalent to a used car salesman insisting that a car is not "defective," rather, it is a "mechanically challenged" car, or an "autistic" car.

Americans frequently blame their problems on the "poverty" they suffered during their childhood, despite the fact that even the poorest of Americans are extremely wealthy in comparison to people in other nations and eras. Americans also love to blame their problems on the lack of a mother or father during their childhood due to divorce or death. However, it takes only a few minutes to look through the American population and realize that many of us experienced identical childhoods. Linus Pauling's father, for example, died when Linus was only 9 years old, and his mother had to struggle to support herself and her children. If Pauling had become a serial killer, he could have used the excuse that it was due to his poverty and the lack of a father.

We must face the unpleasant fact that many people are defective at birth, and it makes no difference what type of childhood those defective people have. George Bush, for example, was born into a wealthy family that had both a mother and father, but he ended up – from what I can determine – as an alcoholic with no useful skills who is getting a free ride in life because of the family he was born into.

We should also try to understand how to keep children in good mental health. Instead of making more bombs we should do research into nutrition and the effect sports has on a child's brain. For all we know, allowing children to play sports in which their heads are hit or shaken is more dangerous than allowing them to use cocaine.

Our leaders should be happy and healthy

How can we do nothing with the CIA after they got caught conducting LSD experiments on American citizens? Their experiments were only slightly more scientific than the electric shocks that Jerry Brudos gave to Linda Salee's body after he killed her. (He was trying to make her body dance, but he discovered that _"Instead it just burned her."_) How can we give billions of dollars to these people, allow them to develop whatever weapons they please, and never check to see what they are doing with these weapons? Why is there so much concern about Bill Clinton's sexual activities while thousands of mentally defective people are spending billions of tax dollars on weapons and plotting fake terrorist attacks?

A better society would allow only happy, healthy citizens in control of it, and the unhappy, angry, and defective people would be monitored and suppressed. America is the exact opposite. The healthy people are enjoying life and working at normal jobs, while the mentally defective people are taking management positions in government and working as government contractors. Nobody is watching these nutty officials or contractors. They can spend their time drinking, buying sex slaves, and planning wars without anybody noticing or caring.

For years I have heard people complain about abuse by the FBI and other government agencies, and I assumed that those people were just criminals who were upset because they were arrested for their crimes. Mike Ruppert, who was fired from his job as a narcotics investigator for the Los Angeles Police, appears to be a disgruntled employee when he claims that he was fired because he discovered in 1977 that the CIA was dealing drugs, and the book _The Franklin Coverup_ by former Senator John DeCamp appears to be delusional. However, our government was involved in 9-11, so shouldn't we at least consider those other accusations?

What was the Motive for the 9-11 Attack?

It's difficult to find a sensible motive for the 9-11 attack. The attack seems to be _hurting_ America, not helping us. One theory is that a few rich families or corporations did it for money, but why would our military attack its own headquarters and spend tens of billions of dollars just so some rich people could make a few more million dollars? Other people assume the motive was to get oil, but what oil have we gotten?

For all we know, the CIA and other agencies are dominated by people who have mental disorders. Perhaps they truly believe that they will make America a better nation with scams that appear to be taken from the TV show _"Mission Impossible"_. To be more blunt, perhaps our government is full of lunatics who are taking us on a wild ride in an attempt to help us.

Also, some government officials may be easily deceived, bribed, and blackmailed into doing things that hurt America. Other officials may go along with the scams simply because they feel helpless to stop them, or because they worry about having a mysterious accident or suicide if they resist.

**Figure 13-1** _Richard Ramirez (the serial killer) drew this in prison. Do any of our government leaders have similar attitudes?_

9-11 was like
the 1776 Revolution

All nations are created from violence, lies, and treachery, including the United States of America in 1776. Violence is also used to bring about improvements to a nation. For example, violence helped workers achieve safe conditions in factories during the 1800's. One of the unfortunate characteristic of humans is that we resist changes in our nations and our lives. Violence and threats of violence are one technique to make us seriously consider alternatives.

The 9-11 scam is no more "wrong" than any other act of violence. Or, to rephrase that, if the World Trade Center scam was wrong, then every other act of violence is wrong, including the creation of America. This is true regardless of whether the scam was conducted by Americans, Osama, or some foreign group.

Unfortunately, not many people can look at the 9-11 attack without getting emotionally carried away. For example, there are reports of children who have been devastated by the loss of a mother or father. Many adults also claim to be devastated due to the loss of a friend or spouse. However, if the thousands of people who died in that attack had died from an automobile accident or cancer, nobody would be devastated. Instead, people would be telling each other and their children to quit crying and get on with life.

Millions of Americans reacted to the attack by advocating a slaughter of Arabs. They were willing and eager to spend billions of dollars to kill Arabs. Compare this to their reaction when people die in car accidents. Only a few people react to car accidents by advocating we design better cities and better public transportation; only a few people are eager to spend money to make better cities. Actually, when most people see a car accident up the road, they slow down to look, as if it is family entertainment.

All nations can easily find funding for war, but no nation can easily find funding for city planning or public transportation. This is why America has an enormous collection of advanced weapons, but our cities are a haphazard jumble of ugly buildings and lousy public transportation. The CIA gladly spends billions of their secret budget on weapons, but they will not spend any money on the study of better public transportation systems or better designs for cities. The CIA prefers to spend their time and money on destruction and death.

Humans love to fight with each other, just as animals do; there is no other way to explain our priorities and our endless acts of violence.

Who would support the 9-11 scam?

If the result of the 9-11 scam had been a better nation and a better world, I would gladly support it, and so would most people. When an act of violence improves life, we regard the violence and the perpetrators the same as we regard surgery and doctors; specifically, we dislike the pain and destruction, and we are relieved when it is finally over, but we are thankful to the people for doing it. However when violence does not improve our lives, or when it creates more problems than it solves, we condemn the violence and want to kill the people who conducted it.

Has America or the world improved since September 11th? Some people might say it has. For example, some people who develop weapons are profiting from the scam. The CIA and FBI also seem to have benefitted because they now have fewer restrictions and more money. I suppose Dyncorp has benefitted, also, because the accusations of sex slaves and corruption has not made it in the news. However, life has not improved for "normal" people. The American economy has become worse for most of us; morale is slightly worse; and our cities are still the same ugly, haphazard jumble of buildings and roads. Life in Afghanistan has yet to improve, also. Americans are also wasting an incredible amount of money and their personal time on security. America is becoming a nation of fear and war-time security procedures, not a happier nation.

Revolutions are attempts to make better nations. While revolutions are chaotic and violent, and while they all create new problems as a side effect, my point is that the *purpose* of a revolution is to improve a nation. Compare that to this fake attack by Osama; what was the purpose for it? To justify killing Arabs? To justify larger military budgets? To get rid of the World Trade Center? To get access to Caspian oil? To have an excuse to attack Iraq?

If the Axis of Good has noble goals, why do they keep their goals and themselves a secret? The American Revolution in 1776 did not have a secret purpose; rather, its purpose was discussed in newspapers and books. If the people conducting this 9-11 scam have nothing to be ashamed of, why don't they explain who they are and what they are trying to do? Why are these people behaving like David Berkowitz rather than like Thomas Jefferson?

I say the reason is because the American government is full of people like David Berkowitz; the American government is a sponge that has soaked up a lot of the unemployable, mentally ill people. I bet that if Thomas Jefferson was alive today he would advocate rebelling against the US government.

Why did the Air Force allow the attack?

How could everybody in the U.S. Military and air traffic controller system ignore all four hijacked airplanes? Perhaps because of the exercises that were taking place that morning. In November 2002, a few months after the first edition of this book was published, Christopher Bollyn wrote about an exercise conducted by the National reconnaissance Office in which an airplane would crash into a building near the Pentagon on the morning of September 11th.

Several other exercises were taking place near New York City. These exercises could easily be used to deceive the air traffic controllers and the military into thinking that the highjacked airplanes were part of an exercise.

Maj. Gen. Larry Arnold, commander of the Continental U.S. NORAD Region, told ABC news that when he was informed about the hijacked aircraft about 8:40 a.m., *"The first thing that went through my mind was, 'Is this part of the exercise? Is this some kind of screw-up?'"* A small group of people could have deceived thousands by scheduling those particular exercises on that particular morning.

The Northwoods Document

A document written in 1962 describes scenarios in which the U.S. military could justify attacking Cuba. This document is referred to as the Northwoods document. In the section **Pretext to Justify US Military Intervention in Cuba** are many scenarios, four of which are:

3. A "Remember the Maine" incident could be arranged in several forms:

    a) We could blow up a US ship in Guantanamo Bay and blame Cuba.

    b) We could blow up a drone (unmanned) vessel anywhere in the Cuban waters. We could arrange to cause such incident in the vicinity of Havana or Santiago as a spectacular result of Cuban attack from the air or sea, or both.

4. We could develop a Communist Cuban terror campaign in the Miami area, other Florida cities and even in Washington. The terror campaign could be pointed at Cuban refugees seeking haven in the United States. We could sink a boatload of Cubans enroute to Florida (real or simulated).

6. Use of MIG type aircraft by US pilots could provide additional provocation. Harassment of civil air, attacks on surface shipping and destruction of US military drone aircraft by MIG type planes would be useful as complementary actions. An F-86 properly painted would convince air passengers that they saw a Cuban MIG, especially if the pilot of the transport were to announce such a fact.

8. It is possible to create an incident which will demonstrate convincingly that a Cuban aircraft has attacked and shot down a chartered civil airliner enroute from the United States to Jamaica, Guatemala, Panama or Venezuela. The destination would be chosen only to cause the flight plan route to cross Cuba. The passengers could be a group of college students off on a holiday or any grouping of persons with a common interest to support chartering a non-scheduled flight.

The Northwoods document shows that the U.S. military was looking for a way to deceive the world into justifying a war with Cuba. Is it outlandish to suspect our government of conducting the 9-11 attack in an attempt to justify wars in the Mideast?

To complicate the 9-11 attack, some of the people involved in the deception may have decided to secretly take advantage of it. For example, the demolition of the World Trade Center may not have been part of the "official" plan.

Should we plan America's funeral now?

Many Americans believe the best way to fight "the Axis of Evil" is through warfare. I think the best policy is to make America into a truly impressive nation, thereby inspiring other nations to become more like us. Unfortunately, instead of impressing other nations, we are allowing our nation to deteriorate, and we are giving the world reasons to despise us.

When citizens ignore crime and corruption, it is likely to encourage more crime and corruption. There are two reasons for this. One is that the people committing the crime may decide to do another, and another, and then one more. The second reason is that other groups of people, including people in foreign nations, may decide that since America is hopeless and helpless, they may as well conduct some crimes also.

Will the American people do something to correct the situation? Or will they allow the USA to deteriorate?

Thanks for your sacrifices, guys!

As I review the lies and deception of the Kennedy killing and the 9-11 attack I find myself wondering,

> *"Is this the Free Press that the Americans killed all those Nazis, Vietnamese, Japanese, and Iraqis for? Is this the government that John McCain suffered in a Vietnamese prison for? Is this the university system that Bob Dole lost the use of his arm for?"*

If so, thanks for your sacrifices, John and Bob, and all you other vets!

Figures

Photos (italic)   Diagrams (normal)